Dreamweaver

Complete Course

Joyce J. Evans

Wiley Publishing, Inc.

Dreamweaver® MX Complete Course

Published by:

Wiley Publishing, Inc.

909 Third Avenue

New York, NY 10022

www.wiley.com/compbooks

Published simultaneously in Canada

For general information on our other products and services or to obtain technical support please contact our Customer Care Department within the U.S. at 800-762-2974, outside the U.S. at 317-572-3993 or fax 317-572-4002.

Library of Congress Cataloging-in-Publication Data:

Library of Congress Control Number: 2002110244

ISBN: 0-7645-3686-9

Manufactured in the United States of America

10 9 8 7 6 5 4 3 2 1

1K/QT/RQ/QS/IN

» Credits

Publisher: Barry Pruett

Project Editor: Kezia Endsley

Acquisitions Editor: Michael Roney

Editorial Manager: Rev Mengle

Technical Editors: Tyler Regas
Mary Rich

Interior Designers: Edwin Kwo
Daniela Richardson

Cover Designer: Anthony Bunyan

Layout: Beth Brooks
Marie Kristine Parial-Leonardo
Heather Pope

Production Coordinator: Regina Snyder

Proofreading: Christine Pingleton

Quality Control Technicians: Andy Hollandbeck
Susan Moritz
Linda Quigley
Charles Spencer

Indexer: Richard T. Evans

Special Help: Tim Borek
Angela C. Buraglia
Donna Casey
Cricket Franklin
Japi Honoo
Gerry Jacobson
Al Sparber
Maureen Spears
Jacquelin Vanderwood

» Dedication

To my loving and wonderful family. I couldn't have done it without you.

» Acknowledgments

I'd like to thank Japi Honoo for the design of the index page. I'd also like to thank Donna Casey (Lynda.com trainer) for writing the two database chapters and offering advice and counsel throughout this book, especially with problems encountered throughout the beta cycle of Dreamweaver. Also thanks go to Jacquelin Vanderwood for the illustrations used in the Frames chapter.

It takes an entire crew of people to get a book into your hands. I'd like to thank my acquisitions editor, Mike Roney, for giving me the opportunity to write this book. I'd also like to thank my project editor, Kezia Endsley, as well as the in-house folks at Wiley, including Rev Mengle, Cricket Franklin, Maureen Spears, and Regina Snyder.

Much appreciation goes to Macromedia and their top-shelf team of engineers and support staff for producing such a great program as Dreamweaver. Thanks also go to the hard-working guys and gals who write the extensions for Dreamweaver that extend its capabilities so greatly.

» Author Bio

Joyce J. Evans is a dynamic communications professional, with a lifetime of experience in instructional design and human interaction. With over 10 years of experience in educational training, speaking, tutorial development, and Web design and usability, she faces every challenge with a genuine concern for the user. Joyce writes articles and tutorials for several online graphics magazines including *Web Review* and *Graphic Design* and is a trainer/speaker. Her current projects include *Macromedia Studio MX Bible* (Wiley), *Fireworks Magic* — contributed two chapters (0735711402), *Dreamweaver Magic* — contributed two chapters (0735711798), and *Paint Shop Pro Savvy X* (0782141129).

Joyce founded, designed, and maintains the Idea Design Web site (http://www.je-ideadesign.com), a Web design studio. She also has a personal site (http://www.JoyceJEvans.com).

» Table of Contents

Confidence Builder

In this lesson, you construct an entire Web page very quickly. You get some hands-on experience that gives you a feel for the Dreamweaver interface and some of its capabilities. By constructing a simple Web design, you can discover how powerful and easy it is to develop a Web site using Dreamweaver. You add images, text, and links to your first Web page.

One of the issues touched upon in this book is accessibility for the disabled. You add text links and alternative text to your pages to comply with Section 508 of the accessibility laws enabling disabled users to access your site.

TOOLS YOU'LL USE
Property inspector, Page Properties dialog box, Insert menu, and Main menu

MATERIALS NEEDED
From the accompanying CD-ROM, you'll need the ConfidenceBuilder folder.

TIME REQUIRED
90 minutes

Tutorial
» Setting Up Your First Web Page

There are many ways to lay out a Web page in Dreamweaver. You can choose from several different design views, you can use tables for positioning, or you can position using CSS (Cascading Style Sheets). You learn each of these techniques in this book, but in this lesson you make a simple Web page to familiarize yourself with the Dreamweaver interface.

Insert Menu   Title Bar   Menu Bar   Toolbar   Docked Panels

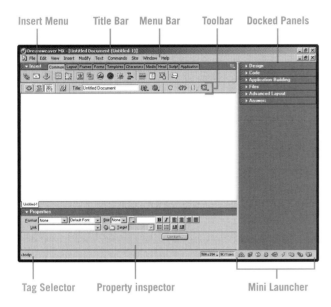

Tag Selector   Property inspector   Mini Launcher

<NOTE>
Windows saves the document with the default extension of .HTM, and Macintosh saves with the default extension of .HTML. There is no difference in the actual HTML file.

<NOTE>
You look at the other options in the Properties dialog box in a tutorial later in this book.

1. **Copy the ConfidenceBuilder folder from this book's companion CD-ROM onto your hard drive.**
   All the images you need for this lesson are included in this folder.

2. **Open Dreamweaver.**
   A new document is opened by default.

3. **In the toolbar in the Title field, enter the text** My first Web page**.**
   To enter the text, click in the Title field to place your cursor and then type the title name.

4. **Choose File→Save As from the Menu bar.**
   Save the file into the ConfidenceBuilder folder and name it index.htm.

Every Web site has either an index.htm or a default.htm file. Often, it's your preference of which to use, but your ISP host or administrator may specify that you have to use one or the other.

5. **Choose Modify→Page Properties from the Menu bar.**

6. **Click the color box next to the Background field.**
   Your cursor turns into an eyedropper. Hold the cursor over the second green swatch from the left on the top row and click it.

   The hexadecimal number for this color is #006600, and it is automatically added to the Background color field in the Properties dialog box.

7. **Click OK.**
   You just made the background color of the Web page dark green.

Tutorial
» Inserting Images

Inserting images into Dreamweaver is extremely easy. You can't actually make the images in Dreamweaver, so you need to produce them from an image editor, such as Fireworks, or obtain them from the client. For this tutorial, the images have been placed in the ConfidenceBuilder folder for you.

1. **In the Insert menu, on the Common tag, click the Image icon.**
   The image inserts in the location of your cursor. The cursor placement is in the upper-left corner by default.

2. **Navigate to the Images folder inside the ConfidenceBuilder folder, select the logo.gif file, and then click Open.**
   Doing this places the image in your document.

3. **In the Property inspector, locate the Alt field, click in it to place the cursor there, and type** RV Destinations.

<NOTE>
The Alt field is important for users who browse with images turned off. It's also important for users who rely on accessibility readers. These readers use the text that you enter into the Alt field.

4. **Click to the right of the logo image to deselect it and then press the Enter/Return key to add a paragraph space.**
   Be sure that the cursor is in the space below the logo image.

5. **Click the Image icon in the Insert menu.**

6. **Navigate to the Images folder in the ConfidenceBuilder folder, select the navbar.gif file, and then click Open.**
   Add the alternate text of **Navigation Bar** into the Alt field. You now have two images inserted into the Web page, one on top of the other.

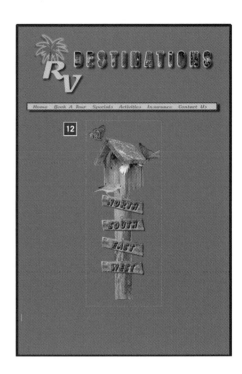

7. **Click the logo image and then in the Property inspector click the Align Center icon.**

8. **Click the Nav bar and center it in the document by clicking the Align Center icon.**

9. **Click to the right of the Nav bar to deselect it and press the Enter/Return key.**

10. **Choose Insert→Interactive Images→Fireworks HTML from the Menu bar.**
    The Insert Interactive Images dialog box opens.

11. **Click the Browse button and navigate to the ConfidenceBuilder folder and open the Navigation folder.**

12. **Select navigation.htm and click Open.**
    The birdhouse navigation image appears.

< N O T E >

These images and HTML code were exported from a Fireworks document. The document is actually a small table containing all the images and code needed to reconstruct the navigational element.

Tutorial
» Making an Image Map and Adding Text

In this tutorial, you add hotspots to the Nav bar image you inserted. You then add hyperlinks to each area of the Nav bar. A list of text links is added for readers who can't see your images.

1. **Select the Nav bar image.**

2. **In the Property inspector locate the Rectangular Hotspot tool and click it.**

3. **Drag a rectangle shape around the word Home.**
   The rectangle shape appears blue. It is a representation only of the hotspot, which is a clickable area, and not visible in a browser.

4. **In the Link field of the Property inspector, type** index.htm.
   When users click this link, they are returned to the home page.

5. **Add the alternative text of** Home **in the Alt field of the Property inspector.**

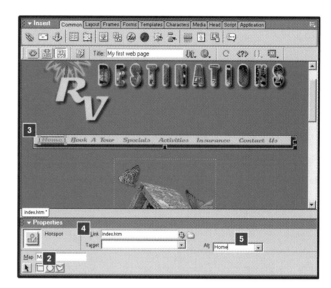

6. **Repeat Steps 2-5 for the links Book a Tour, Specials, Activities, and Insurance.**
   Use links of **booking.htm**, **specials.htm**, **activities.htm**, and **insurance.htm**. For the alternative text, just type the name of each link into the Alt field.

7. **Add a hotspot for Contact us, but in the Link area type** mailto: tours@rvdestinations.com **with alternative text of** Contact us.

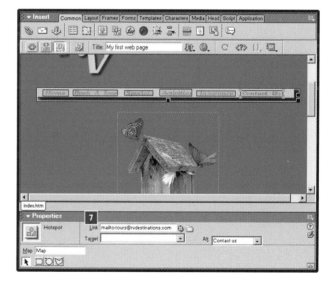

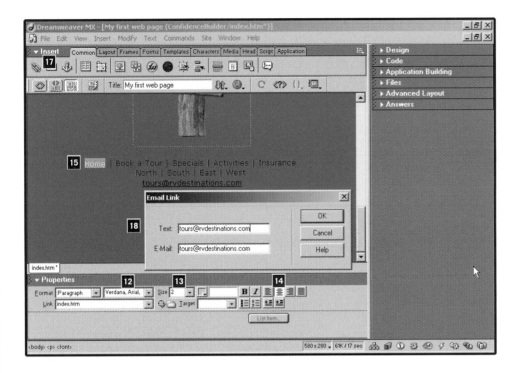

8. **Click your cursor to the right of the birdhouse navigation image and press the Enter/Return key to place the cursor below the navigation.**
   You are adding text to your document. The text you are going to add is actually used for navigation. So far all of the navigation used in this Web page relies on images. You need to provide an alternative way to navigate your site when users cannot view your images.

9. **Type the following text:** Home | Book a Tour | Specials | Activities | Insurance.

10. **Press Shift-Enter to add a <br> tag (one space) then type** North | South | East | West.

11. **Place the cursor in front of Home and then click and drag over both lines of text to select them.**

12. **In the Property inspector, click the down pointing arrow next to the Font field, and choose Verdana→Arial→Helvetica→sans-serif.**

13. **In the Size field, click the down arrow and choose 2.**

14. **Select the Align Center icon in the Property inspector.**

15. **Click and drag over the word Home, and in the Property inspector type the link text of** index.htm.

16. **Repeat for all the other links, adding links and alternative text as you did in Step 6.**
    For the word North, use a link of **north.htm** and alternative text of **Northern tours**. For South, use a link of **south.htm** and **Southern tours**. For East, use **east.htm** and **Eastern tours**, and for West, use **west.htm** and **Western tours**.

17. **Press Shift-Enter after the word West, and in the Insert menu click the Email Link icon.**

18. **In the Text and the link fields of the Email Link dialog box type** tours@rvdestinations.com **and click OK.**

< N O T E >
You typed the link into the text area so that users who don't have their e-mail clients set to work with their browsers can copy and paste your e-mail address into their e-mail programs.

19. **Choose File→Save from the Menu bar and save your document.**

Part I:
Course Setup

In this part of the book you get a glance at what Dreamweaver MX is good for and its strong features. You also learn a few of the basic HTML terms and tags. From there you get a description of how this course works and how it benefits you, followed by brief descriptions of each session. A few computer specifics are discussed, such as requirements needed to run Dreamweaver and some differences in the Windows and Macintosh versions of Dreamweaver.

Dreamweaver Basics

Dreamweaver is a program for producing and managing Web sites. At its core is HTML (HyperText Markup Language), a language containing a series of tags that define the structure of a Web page.

Dreamweaver is a deceptively easy tool, but it's also an industrial-strength application, making it a favorite among Web design professionals. With Dreamweaver you can develop one page or a huge site. You can also open pages from co-workers or even produced in other editors, just to edit and clean up the code.

Dreamweaver is a great visual design tool in which you can add JavaScript, forms, tables, and more without ever writing or viewing a piece of code. As your skills develop, you may want more access to the code. It has this built-in functionality and can be as easy or as complex as you desire.

Dreamweaver utilizes Web technologies and HTML standards and also provides backward compatibility for older browsers. It was designed for the professional Web developer so it can accommodate a designer's workflow. There are basically two kinds of Web developers — coders and designers. Designers typically want to design in a visual environment so Dreamweaver provides Design view or the

WYSIWYG (or almost) environment. For the coders, Dreamweaver provides Code view. Then there is Design and Code view for those who want it all.

ROUND-TRIP HTML

Round-Trip HTML, which leaves your custom code and/or changes intact, is an exciting feature of Dreamweaver and one that has attracted the serious Web developers. I learned to code HTML by hand in Notepad prior to Dreamweaver. I tried a few so-called WYSIWYG editors, but they all had such bloated code and would often change my custom code. Then Dreamweaver came along, which promised not to touch my code and allowed me to change its code as well. I was hooked from version 1. Dreamweaver is just so cool and hard to beat.

When the HTML standard was developed, no one had any idea how fast the Web would grow. The HTML code standards were very basic. But browsers began to support more than the standard HTML, allowing designers and developers to experiment with more non-standard HTML options. This experimentation helped develop the HTML standards that we enjoy today. The World Wide Web Consortium (W3C) develops the standardized supported HTML code.

Because you could experiment with non-standardized HTML code, editors such as Claris, FrontPage and NetFusion were limiting. You couldn't change their proprietary code without breaking it and these programs would rewrite your code. So when Dreamweaver entered the picture, developers were leery to say the least. When Dreamweaver proved that it did in fact allow you to change its code *and* write your own, it was accepted by coders and designers alike.

BASIC HTML

You can actually get by designing in Dreamweaver without knowing any HTML code at all, but you are better off learning at least the basics. I taught my children to hand-code before I'd allow them to use Dreamweaver. Why? Because now they can troubleshoot their own documents and determine what's wrong when something doesn't work. HTML isn't nearly as intimidating as it looks. It's very easy to learn the basics. You are introduced to a bit of code here and there throughout this book. Before you know it, you'll be recognizing HTML code and understanding it, naturally.

Required Tags

In order for a browser to know a file contains HTML, the document has to declare itself with an `<html>` opening tag and end with a closing tag of `</html>`. Every HTML document requires an opening and closing `<head>`, `<body>`, and `<title>` tag. Dreamweaver generates all these tags automatically whenever you open or add a new document. The complete code Dreamweaver generates when you choose File→New looks like this:

```
1 <html>
2 <head>
3 <title>Untitled Document
  </title>
4 <meta http-equiv="Content-Type"
  content="text/html; charset=iso-8859-1">
5 </head>
6 <body bgcolor="#FFFFFF" text="#000000">
7 </body>
8 </html>
```

» `<html>` is the opening HTML tag that declares to the browser that this page contains HTML.

» `<head>` is the area that contains the page title, and also information that is invisible to the browser. Scripts and styles are placed in the head section as well as Meta tags. You add Meta tags and descriptions in Session 2.

» `<title>` is where the title of your page goes. This is what users view in the browser in the top title bar. Some search engines also use the title content when searching keywords. The title is enclosed in the `<head>` tag.

» `<meta>` tags include keywords that someone may use in a search engine to find your site. You can also add a Meta description, which describes your site.

» `</head>` is the closing `<head>` tag, denoted by its forward slash. Almost all tags in HTML have a closing tag, but there are a few exceptions.

» `<body>` contains the content of your Web page that is viewed in a browser.

» `</body>` is the closing `<body>` tag.

» `</html>` is the closing `<html>` tag.

Some Other Basic Tags

There are a handful of other tags you use every time you build a Web page, whether you see the code or not. You briefly take a look at some of them. Don't worry if you don't remember them, you see and use these tags throughout this course.

Paragraph tags are extremely common; they appear as `<p>` and close with `</p>`. This tag places an empty line of white space around each block of text contained within the tag container. The container consists of the opening and closing paragraph tags.

Anchor tags are used for linking from one page to another or to another spot within a page. A typical anchor tag looks like this:

```
<a href="linknamehere.htm"> Click on this text </a>
```

When the users click the text they are taken to the page referenced in the anchor tag.

Image tags surround every image you insert into your document. Dreamweaver automatically adds the height and width dimensions of the image into the tag and the Alt text if you've entered it into the Property inspector. An image tag appears like this:

```
<img src="images/logo.gif"
width="300" height="100"
alt="Palmetto Design Group">
```

There are no ending tags for the image tag.

The common tags used to denote a table are:

```
<table></table>
<tr></tr> row
<td></td> cell
```

Tags for JavaScript and styles and other scripts are commonly placed in the head of a document, but can be found in the body as well. Some of those tags are:

```
<style></style>
<script language="JavaScript"></script>
```

NAMING CONVENTIONS

There are a few characters in HTML are reserved for HTML code and can't be used in filenames, as outlined in Table P1.1.

HTML LEARNING RESOURCES

There are a lot of locations on the Internet to learn about HTML and about design in general. Listed here are a few to get you going. There are also additional links and resources listed in Appendix A.

World Wide Web Consortium
```
http://www.w3.org/MarkUp/
```

Webmonkey
http://www.hotwired.lycos.com/webmonkey/teachingtool/index.html
Web Reference
www.webreference.com
Builder.com
www.builder.com

NEW FEATURES

There are a lot of new features in Dreamweaver MX. Some of the highlights for the visual designer and the coder are mentioned here. One of the most interesting new changes is the fact that there is no longer a separate UltraDev application. Its functions have all been incorporated into the Dreamweaver application.

Design-Oriented Developer

For those of us who prefer to work visually, Macromedia has included some great features to accommodate our needs:

» Improved workspace layout, featuring an integrated windows user interface that has fully dockable panels and panel groups as well as tabbed document windows. There is also an option to use the Dreamweaver 4 workspace with the floating panels if you are more comfortable with that.

» Predefined sample page layouts or Web components that include professional layouts to give developers a head start on designs.

» Something else that's new is the Snippets panel, which you can use to write pieces of HTML, JavaScript, CFML, ASP, JSP, and more, and save the code as a snippet to be used again.

» Improved cascading style sheets (CSS) support, featuring design-time style sheets, the ability to distinguish between locally defined styles and external style sheets, as well as many new CSS 2 constructs.

» Enhanced Dreamweaver templates that enable developers to set up rules for how contributors input data. This helps avoid design integrity risks.

» Site Setup Wizard enables you to configure site information for a dynamic site or for FTP purposes.

» Pop-up menus can now be added automatically in Dreamweaver. These menus are like the ones that formerly could only be made automatically in Fireworks.

Table P1.1: HTML Reserved Characters

Characters	Function
: (colon)	Used for some command scripts.
! (exclamation point)	Used for comments.
/ or \ (slashes)	Forward slash is used in a file pathname to indicate files in a nested folder. The backward slash is not permissible on Windows servers.
"" (double quotes)	Used to denote a value of tags and attributes. For example, `<body BGCOLOR="#FFFFFF">` indicates that the attribute is background color and its value is white.
. (dots)	Dots (or periods) are used for the filename extensions.

Coders and Developers

Coders and developers can work in a code-oriented workspace layout, which they may be more comfortable using. It has the following features:

» Coders and developers can use HomeSite or Macromedia ColdFusion and set the workspace to look similiar (Windows only).

» Pop-up menu hints contain lists of tag attributes, a list of object methods, and a property list of hints.

» The Snippets panel stores snippets of HTML or JavaScript code as well as CFML, ASP, ASP.NET, JSP or PHP that you can reuse, insert, or wrap around a selection.

» There are also Server Code Libraries for ColdFusion, ASP, ASP.NET, JSP and PHP.

» The Quick Tag Editor allows you to edit properties of HTML, CFML, and ASP.NET tags as well as import new ones. There is also fantastic ColdFusion support built in.

» Full support of DataSets, DataGrids and DataLists, ASP.NET Web Forms, and custom Macromedia ASP.NET tags.

Project Overview

Dreamweaver MX Complete Course is designed to walk you through all the design stages from planning a Web site to connecting to a database. Each session builds upon the others while you develop the Palmetto Design Group Web site. This company is a fictitious design firm that also specializes in custom corporate training courses. You may discover that the needs of this Web site may be very similar to your own personal goals if you are a new Web designer/developer.

Dreamweaver Complete Course is broken into manageable sessions that are also topic related so that you can use this book as a reference when you need to refresh your memory. The instructions are succinct and to the point. It is taught in a way that beginners can understand but it is also laced with intermediate skills right from the start. The focus is on productivity as well as training. For instance, most Dreamweaver books teach you how to insert text and images, and then show you how to use tables to control your layout. It makes more sense from a workflow perspective to insert the tables and learn how to control them prior to adding content and images. It's this sort of logic that is used in this training course.

Dreamweaver is a very complex program and offers many ways to achieve the same results. For example, adding links to images and text can be accomplished in several ways. Instead of being presented with a boring list of different options, you will try each technique at different times so you get a feel for using each one, and then you can choose which method fits the way you work best.

As the course progresses it does get considerably more complex. By the time you complete this course you will have first-hand experience developing a business Web site that's interactive and contains dynamic content. This version of Dreamweaver is very complex. It has the capability to do much more than can be covered in one book. Dreamweaver supports several server models such as ASP, ColdFusion, PHP, and ASP.NET. We will use only ASP in this course. If, after learning how to develop a Web site, you want to dig deeper into the nitty gritty of every tool and function of Dreamweaver, I recommend that you also obtain a good Dreamweaver reference book such as *The Macromedia Dreamweaver MX Bible* from Wiley Technology Publishing.

STEPPING THROUGH THE PROJECT STAGES

Session 1 — Laying the Foundation explains the key questions to ask when planning a site. You are introduced to the Dreamweaver authoring environment, learn how to define a site, and use the Site and Assets panels to manage your site's files.

Session 2 — Building the Sites Framework begins to build the structure of your Web site. You delve into setting the page properties such as background and text color. You also learn how to use Design notes to communicate with co-workers or as a reminder to yourself. In this session you also add the <head> content of Meta tags and descriptions to your Web page.

Session 3 — Working with Tables shows you how to insert and test your table structure in different browsers. You learn how to develop fixed-width tables as well as a fluid table design that changes with the size of the user's browser.

Session 4 — Working with Images teaches you how to add images such as photos, buttons, and logos to your document. You also learn how to align them and use images as a background.

Session 5 — Adding Text shows you that adding text is quite easy in Dreamweaver. You learn some of your options and how to change fonts and their attributes. You also add some Flash text.

Session 6 — Adding Navigational Links helps you become comfortable using the many techniques of adding links. You also learn how to make rollover images and use the Behaviors panel.

Session 7 — Using Cascading Style Sheets (CSS) teaches you how to control your text using style sheets. You learn how to embed a style sheet and how to use an external one. You also learn how to use CSS for page layout and to control background images.

Session 8 — Using Templates and Libraries helps you automate your workflow. You learn how to set up a template and add editable and repeating regions as well as learn how to attach, edit, and update pages using templates. You make a library item and use it as well.

Session 9 — Adding Dimension with Layers adds a lot of control over how the users can interact with your Web site. You can make animations using layers and, as you'll see in a later session, you can also make dynamic menus.

Session 10 — Dynamic HTML (DHTML) teaches you how to make a basic animation, edit it, and how to install and use extensions.

Session 11 — Making a Pop-Up Menu teaches you how to use the new pop-up menu behavior in Dreamweaver. Not only do you learn the basics, but you also see how to edit the menu and perform complex positioning.

Session 12 — Adding Forms and Behaviors teaches you how to add and use various styles of forms and attach behaviors to do things such as validate the form after it's been submitted.

Session 13 — Building a Frame-Based Site shows you how to set up a frames site and how to work with and save a frameset. The site you are building does not use frames so this is a bonus session to teach you the fundamentals of using frames.

Session 14 — Performing Site Checks shows you how to run various reports and how to make repairs.

Session 15 — Round-Trip Between Dreamweaver and Fireworks teaches you how to edit images from within Dreamweaver and directly in Fireworks and how to return to Dreamweaver again. In the process you learn how to use many of Fireworks editing tools, including exporting, slicing, and optimizing.

Session 16 — Getting Your Web Site Online walks you through the procedures to get your files to a remote server as well as get a domain name if you choose to get one. Several free servers are recommended if you want to practice on one before purchasing space on an ad-free server.

Session 17 — Setting Up a Database Connection teaches you the steps to take to connect your Web site to an ASP database. The methods are taught for Windows users but tips are given for Mac users as well.

Session 18 — Building a Web Application teaches you the basics of manipulating a data source (the database) to provide dynamic Web content.

Appendix A — Resources provides a lot of wonderful resources for you to check out. It includes demo software offers and mini reviews of products I've personally used and found helpful in Web site design.

Appendix B — What's on the CD-ROM tells you how to access the program files and bonus software on the CD included inside the back cover of this book.

General Work Tips and Computer Instructions

In Session 1 you set up a local root folder that contains all the files used in your Web site. Dreamweaver has built-in site-management features that requires you to keep all your site's assets in one root folder. Of course you can have other folders within the root folder. You also set up a "remote root folder" in Part VI of this book when you learn how to connect your Web site to a database.

COPYING FILES FROM THE CD

As mentioned, all the images you need to complete this course are included on this book's companion CD-ROM. A starter site is included for you, which contains files for an intranet. You add files and folders and functionality as the Web site design progresses. A copy of the completed and working site is included for your reference as well.

Copy the files from the CD to your hard drive from within Dreamweaver. After you define the site that is the focus of this course, you can simply access the CD files from the Site panel by selecting the files you want and dragging them to the appropriate folder in your site. This procedure is advantageous to Windows users, who don't have to unlock the files.

If you want to copy files from the CD to your hard drive *prior* to defining a site, go ahead, and then — after completing Session 1 — when a session instructs you to copy files from the CD to your hard drive, follow these steps:

1. In the Site Panel, navigate to the CD files and select what you want.

2. Drag the files to your site's root folder and drop them into the appropriate folder.

By copying this way, Windows users don't have to unlock the files.

If Windows users want to copy files to the hard drive *after* defining a site, follow these steps:

1. Open the Site panel.

2. Ctrl-click each file with a lock icon (or Shift-click to select multiple files).

3. From the File menu in the Site panel, choose Turn off Read Only.

USING THE SESSION FINAL FILES

At the end of each session is a folder named Session#final, whereby the # sign represents the number of the session in question. In that folder are the files that have changed or have been added during that session. This course builds one session upon the other so if you do decide to skip a chapter, you need to copy the session's final folder to your hard drive, unlock the files, and then drop them (or copy and paste) into your CompleteCourse root folder, overwriting the files. You need to do this in chapter sequence, however.

For example, let's say you did sessions 1, 2, and 3 and then decided to skip sessions 4 and 5. You picked up again in session 6. You'd need to copy the session4final and the session5final files to your hard drive, unlock them, and then paste them (beginning with session 4) into your CompleteCourse folder. You could then pick up in session 6 with all the current files.

SYSTEM REQUIREMENTS

System requirements for Microsoft Windows are as follows:

» An Intel Pentium processor or equivalent, 300 MHz or faster, running Windows 98, Windows 2000, Windows Me, Windows NT (with Service Pack 3), or Windows XP

- » Version 4.0 or later of Netscape Navigator or Microsoft Internet Explorer

- » 96MB of RAM (random-access memory) plus 110MB of available disk space

- » A 256-color monitor capable of 800x600 pixel resolution or better (millions of colors and 1,024x768 pixel resolution recommended)

- » A CD-ROM drive

System requirements for Apple Macintosh are as follows:

- » A Power Macintosh G3 or later, Mac OS 9.1, Mac OS 9.2.1, or Mac OS X 10.1 or later

- » Mac OS Runtime for Java (MRJ) 2.2 or above (included on the Dreamweaver MX CD)

- » Version 4.0 or later of Netscape Navigator or Microsoft Internet Explorer

- » 96MB of random-access memory (RAM) (128MB is recommended)

- » 275MB available disk space

- » A 256-color monitor capable of 800x600 pixel resolution (millions of colors and 1,024x768 pixel resolution recommended)

- » A CD-ROM drive

Those are the minimum requirements that Macromedia lists. But here are real-world recommendations/limitations:

- » Any legacy Mac (using a Motorola 601, 603, 604 or variant CPU) needs to be at least 200MHz and have at least 128MB of RAM.

- » Any G3-based PowerMac should have at least 192MB of RAM.

- » Any G4-based PowerMac should have at least 256MB of RAM.

- » MacOS X–based systems should have either the system limit or a minimum of 512MB of RAM. Most PowerBooks can only take 384MB of RAM.

- » There are no Macintosh-compatible monitors that have a maximum color depth of 256 colors.

MAC AND PC DIFFERENCES

For the most part, Dreamweaver looks and works the same for the Windows and the Macintosh operating systems. There are a few differences noted here. Mac users will be pleased to know that Dreamweaver for the Mac was written for the Mac and not for Windows and ported over. Some general notes:

» The counterpart of Windows Control (Ctrl) key is the Macintosh Command key (⌘, the Apple propeller key).

» The counterpart of Windows Alt key is the Macintosh Option (Opt) key (it's also marked as ALT on all newer Mac-compatible keyboards).

» When opening files, the Windows selection button is named Select whereas the Mac button is named Open.

» In Windows, windows close by clicking the close box in the upper-right corner. The close box on a Mac is in the upper-left corner.

» The Mac version doesn't have the integrated workspace option. Mac users must use the floating panel layout.

Part II:
Getting Started

In this part, you build a complete Web site:

Laying the Foundation

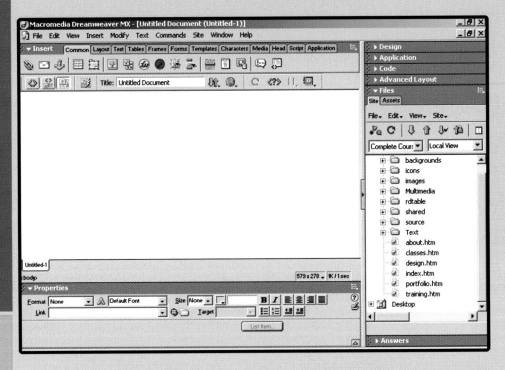

Laying the Groundwork

Getting comfortable with your design tool such as Dreamweaver increases your productivity and shortens the learning curve. This session helps you explore the major menu and panel areas in the Dreamweaver workspace and shows you how to customize it for the way you work best. You won't look at every panel and every tool in this session — that would be really boring. Besides, the manual that ships with Dreamweaver and the help files are more than efficient for tool recognition. What you will do is explore the major areas you'll use all the time plus a couple of the panels that you'll use while developing a Web site. So instead of boring you to death with the details of every panel and tool, this session delves into the various panels as the need arises throughout the development of the Palmetto Design Group Web site.

You set up a local root folder in which to develop your site. Later in the book you will set up a remote folder and learn how to upload your Web site to a server.

TOOLS YOU'LL USE
A little bit of everything as you get familiar with the Dreamweaver workspace

MATERIALS NEEDED
CompleteCourse folder

TIME REQUIRED
90 minutes

Discussion

Laying the Foundation

In this tutorial you see some of the things you need to think about and decide when planning a Web site. There are questions only the client can answer, and some that can be determined only by testing. The planning stage is vital to a Web site's success. You can find additional questions to consider on a questionnaire I developed at www.je-ideadesign.com/question.htm.

Consider, for example, the following questions when planning your site:

1. What is your objective?

Putting a Web site onto the Internet for the sake of establishing a presence isn't a good reason for a Web site; you need to gain an understanding of the site's purpose. Is the site going to sell something, train, entertain, or perhaps disperse information? You need to determine the site's primary objectives.

2. Who is your audience?

Palmetto Design Group determined that its audience would most likely be businesses who want a Web site developed and corporations who need the Web development team trained in the use of Web tools. The audience would probably be using both Netscape and Internet Explorer browsers and perhaps even Opera. They also determined that users would access the Web site by both modem and high-speed connections.

3. Who is your competition?

For the Palmetto Design Group Web site the competition is worldwide, but any local competition should also be checked out. See what the Web sites look like, what works, what doesn't, what their clients like or dislike about the competition's site.

Once you have answered these questions, consider the following initial steps to planning the new Web site:

1. Make a mock up to determine the visual look and feel.

You might develop a site that causes the users to stare in awe, but then they might discover the content has nothing to do with the look of the site. Or the site could be so poorly designed that great content gets lost. You need to get the correct look and content to evoke the intended emotional response of the users.

The mock up may contain actual graphics, placeholders, or just outlines of where different components will be placed. The mock up will assist you and the client in determining the user experience. Is it logical; is there consistency throughout the site; can the users find what they are looking for?

2. Evaluate navigational options.

According to recent studies, top and left side navigation are the most widely used. That is not to say that other navigation isn't right for your site. The main thing to consider is that the users can find their way around your site without frustration. Users must understand where they are in relation to everything else. Links should be identifiable by text or at least text that appears as the mouse passes over the link.

3. Determine the available assets.

Is the client providing images, text, logo, and so on? If not, are you responsible for developing it? If the client is providing you with assets, when are they due?

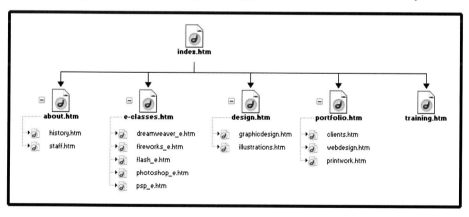

4. Set up the site structure.

From your planning session with the client and answers to the questions you've asked, you can develop a preliminary mock up of the Web site. You now know what your links will be and the pages needed to contain the necessary information.

Tutorial
» Setting Up and Viewing the Workspace

Your work environment is an important one. You set it up in this tutorial as well as get a feel for where all the tools are in your workspace.

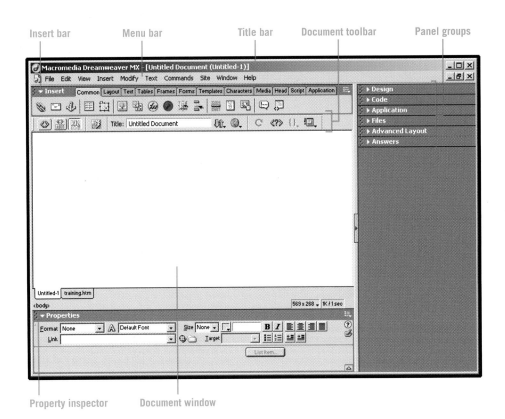

Insert bar   Menu bar   Title bar   Document toolbar   Panel groups

Property inspector   Document window

1. **Open the Dreamweaver application.**
   In Windows, click the Start button and then choose Programs➔Macromedia Dreamweaver MX.
   Mac users, double-click the hard drive icon and then the Macromedia Dreamweaver MX folder, and then double-click the Dreamweaver MX program icon. A new untitled document opens by default.
   If this is your first time running Dreamweaver MX, a dialog box opens.

2. **Windows users click the Dreamweaver MX workspace in the dialog box.**
   This book assumes you are using the Dreamweaver MX workspace.

   <NOTE>
   The integrated workspace using MDI (Multiple Document Interface) isn't supported on the Mac so the windows and panels are floating.

Gripper

Expander arrow

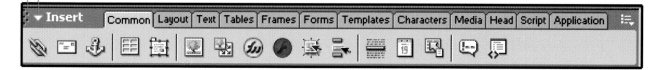

3. **Look at the Title bar.**

   The program name and document name are displayed in the Title bar. Untitled Document (Untitled-1) is the default name until you name and save it.

4. **Look at the Menu bar.**

   The Menu bar contains menus with various commands. Many of the menu items can be accessed using shortcut keys or by using various panels.

5. **Look at the Insert Bar.**

   The Common tab, selected by default, shows the most commonly used functions. There are ten buttons with categories to insert objects into your document. You can close the Insert Bar by clicking on the expander arrow.

6. **Look at the Document toolbar.**

   The Document toolbar has buttons and pop-up menus with options for different views of the Document window, as listed in Table 1.1.

Table 1.1: The Functions Accessed from the Document Toolbar

Name	Function
Design View	Provides a visual working environment.
Code View	Provides a view of just code for those who want to hand-code or edit any other type of code such as JavaScript or ColdFusion.
Code and Design View	Provides a split working environment with the code on top and your visual work area below.
View Live Data	Shows how dyamic content can affect the layout of a page.
Title	Where you type the title of your page.
File Management	Displays file management options.
Preview/Debug in Browser	Gives you the choice of browser to use for a preview.
Refresh Design View	Forces the browser to reread the page to view any changes you made.
Reference	Activates the Reference panel.
Code Navigation	Allows you to navigate through the source code.
View Options	Activates the Options menu.

Tag selector

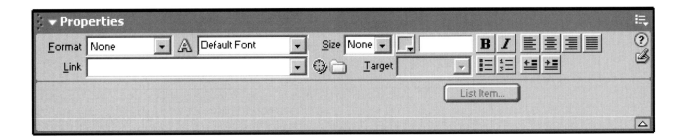

7. Look at the Status bar.

The status bar is at the bottom of the Document window and contains information about your document.

» Tag selector. The Tag selector shows the hierarchy of tags that surround the current selection in your document.

» Window Size pop-up menu. If your document window is maximized the window sizes will be grayed out. Click the Restore Down icon (in the Title bar), and then choose the window size you'd like from the Window Size pop-up menu.

» Document size and estimated download time for the page are shown in the status bar.

8. Look at the Property inspector.

The Property inspector is context-sensitive. The options displayed depend on which element you have selected. To see all of the properties of a selected element, click the expander arrow in the lower-right corner.

9. Look at the Panel groups. To access the various panels, click the expander arrows, and then click the specific panel tab you want.

If a panel isn't open by default you can open it by choosing Window→Panel name. You can also customize the panel area for the way you work, as shown in the next tutorial.

Changing Workspaces

If you have previously chosen to work in the Dreamweaver 4 workspace, choose Edit→Preferences. Click General and then click the Change Workspace button. Click the Dreamweaver MX workspace option (also select the HomeSite/Coder-Style option if you use HomeSite or ColdFusion Studio and want a familiar workspace). You can always change it back when you finish this book if you find you prefer to work in the Dreamweaver 4 workspace. You have to restart Dreamweaver to change the workspace.

Tutorial

» Customizing the Workspace

Everyone works differently, and Dreamweaver is such a complex program you might be using advanced portions such as ColdFusion, PHP, and other programming languages. The panels you need easy access to depend on your workflow. This tutorial shows you how to rearrange your workspace.

1. **To expand (or collapse) the Files panel group, click the expander arrow in the Files panel group.**
   Tabs for the Site panel and the Assets panel appear.

2. **Click and drag the Files panel's gripper (little gray dots on the left) to the document.**
   You have just undocked the panel group. You can use this floating panel group as it is or rearrange in a custom configuration. If you have a large monitor you might want to place some of the most used panels on the right and left edges.

3. **Click the Site tab.**
   You have to be slightly tricky to separate the panels from within a panel group. Select the tab of the panel you want to remove or move from a panel group first.

4. **Click the Files option menu and click Group Site with→New Panel Group.**
   This removes the Site panel (or the selected panel) from its current group. You can move it independently or you can choose to place it in another panel group. Notice that the Files panel group name changes to Assets once you move the Site panel out as a new panel.

5. **If desired, put these two panels back together again by:**
   » Clicking the Site panel options menu
   » Clicking Group Site With Assets
   » Clicking the Option menu again
   » Clicking Rename Panel Group and naming it Files again

6. **Click and drag on the gripper bar to drag back to the docked panel area.**
   When you see a white grid-like line, release the mouse button to dock the panel group again.

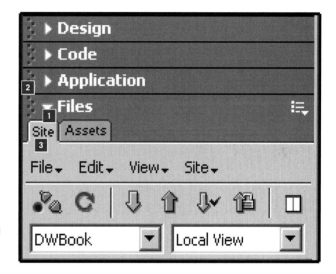

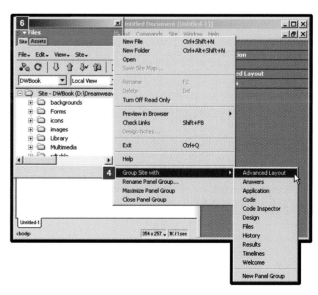

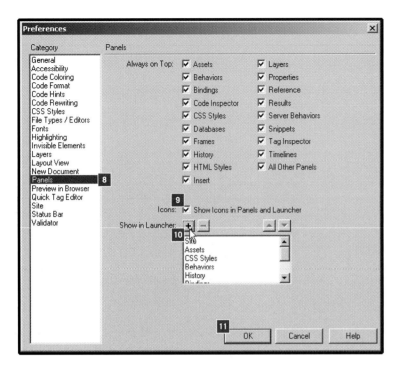

7. **Click the grabber of the Properties inspector and drag it below your document area if you want.**
   Some people using smaller monitors may prefer to move the Property inspector off of the document window to give more design space.

8. **Choose Edit→Preferences and select Panels from the Category area.**

9. **Click on Show Icons if you want the Launcher bar to appear in the Status bar.**
   The Launcher bar contains the shortcuts to the functions you choose.

10. **In the Show in Launcher area, add or delete the items you'd like on your Launcher bar.**
    For example, I use layers often, so I choose Layers and click the plus (+) sign. You can delete an icon by selecting a current one from the list and clicking the minus (-) sign.

11. **Click OK.**
    The new Layers icon is added to the Launcher bar.

12. **Choose Edit→Keyboard Shortcuts to edit or add your own keyboard shortcuts.**
    You can use the Macromedia standard shortcuts or one of the predefined sets such as BBEdit, HomeSite, or Dreamweaver 3 if you are more comfortable with those. You can also customize any of these sets by changing or adding your own shortcuts.

<NOTE>
The default Dreamweaver MX workspace is being restored after this tutorial for use in the rest of the book. Not everyone has a large monitor or chooses to work with the example used here.

Tutorial
» Defining a Site

In Dreamweaver, defining your site is extremely important, so don't even be tempted to skip this part. Believe me, you are not utilizing the full power of Dreamweaver if you don't define each site that you make. Defining every site you work with allows Dreamweaver to track your assets and links and provide you with a lot of other functions as well.

1. **Copy the CompleteCourse folder from this book's CD-ROM onto your hard drive.**

2. **Choose Site→New Site from the Menu bar.**
   The Site Definition dialog box opens to the Advanced tab, and the Category of Local Info is highlighted and selected.

3. **In the Site Name field, highlight the default name and type** CompleteCourse.
   You don't have to be concerned about long names here; this name in no way affects any of your files.

4. **Click the yellow folder icon in the Local Root Folder area, navigate to where you have the CompleteCourse folder saved, select it, and click Select.**
   The local folder is your working directory for all your Web site's files. You need to make a local folder for every Web site you design.

5. **Click Refresh Local File List Automatically if it is unchecked.**
   This option shows you any changes made to your site structure and files in the Site and Assets panels.

6. **Click the yellow folder icon in the Default Images Folder area and browse to the Images folder inside the CompleteCourse folder. Select the Images folder and click Select/Open.**

7. **If you already have a hosting service and want to add the HTTP address, go ahead and add it now.**
   You need this information later in the book if you want to utilize Dreamweaver's FTP capabilities for uploading your site files to an Internet server. Many free services are available. See Appendix A for free and reasonably priced servers.

8. **Leave Enable Cache checked if you want quick access to your links and site assets.**
   This is up to you. I always leave the Enable Cache option checked, but if you are low on computer RAM (memory), you might want to uncheck this option.

9. **Click OK to finish defining your site.**
   I'm sure you noticed a lot of other categories in the Site Definition dialog box. You use most of them as you progress through the Palmetto Design Group Web site design.

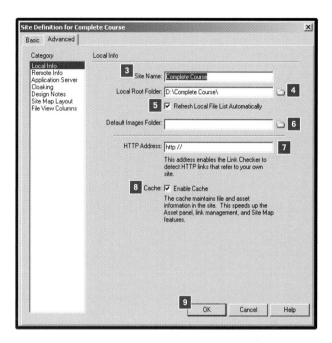

<NOTE>
You can also use the Basic tab, which contains a wizard, to set up your Site definition.

<NOTE>
If you encounter a situation where you didn't set up a local folder ahead of time like you did for this tutorial, you can add the new folder after you click the Browse for folder icon in the Site Definition dialog box, by browsing to the partition or area you'd like to set your site up in. I am using drive D with a folder named CompleteCourse. Just click the Create New Folder icon in the Choose Local Root Folder for Site CompleteCourse dialog box.

Tutorial
» Using the Site Panel

The Site panel is one that many beginners avoid or never use. You begin using it right away because it is a great timesaver and is not nearly as intimidating as it appears. The Site panel is in the Files panel group. The Site panel is where you can view a list of files, rename files, add files and folders, and refresh the view when changes have been made.

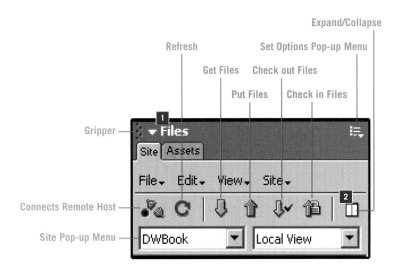

1. **Click the Files panel group expander arrow and click the Site tab if it isn't already active.**

   As you can see from the labels in the image, you can manage a lot of functions in this panel. You can check your files in and out in a shared work environment, define your sites, upload and download files, and much more.

2. **Click the Expand/Collapse icon.**

   Notice the additional icons in the expanded and split view. Use this portion of the Site panel when you get to the section of this book in which you connect your site to a database.

3. **Click the Expand/Collapse icon to return the Site panel to the normal size in the panel group area.**

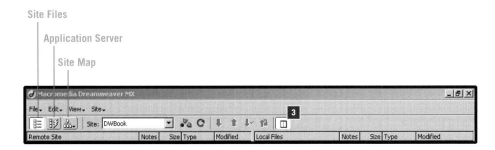

4. In the Site panel, right-click (Ctrl-click) the site name of Site: Complete Course.... and choose New File from the menu that appears.

A new untitled file is added and the name is highlighted.

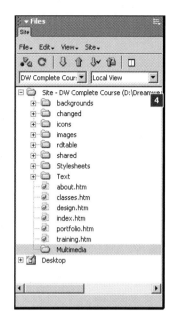

<NOTE>

Alternatively, click on any folder that you want to add a file or folder to and the new file or folder is added to the one you have selected.

5. Type index.htm.

The default file extension is .HTM for Windows and .HTML for Macintosh. There is no difference in the file.

6. Add the remaining files you'll need for this Web site, naming them as follows: about.htm, portfolio.htm, training.htm, design.htm, and classes.htm.

7. Right-click/Ctrl-click the site name and choose New Folder.

If you prefer not to right-click/Ctrl-click, you can also choose the File menu in the Site panel and click on New Folder. Either way, a new, untitled folder is added.

8. Type Multimedia.

You can add as many files and folders as you'd like. You will add more as you progress through the project.

<NOTE>

You can rename any file or folder by choosing File menu in the Site panel and selecting Rename, and then typing in the new name. You can also right-click for the contextual menu and choose Rename. On a Mac, choose Site→Rename or Control-click for the contextual menu and choose Rename. Type the new name.

Tutorial
» Using the Assets Panel

The Assets panel is your control center for all the media you will use in your Web site. It includes the images, sound files, Flash movies, custom scripts, and more.

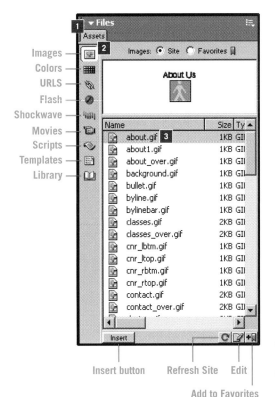

Images
Colors
URLS
Flash
Shockwave
Movies
Scripts
Templates
Library

Insert button   Refresh Site   Edit

Add to Favorites

1. **Click the Files panel group expander arrow and click the Assets tab, if it isn't already active.**
   The Assets tab opens with a list of available files.

2. **Click the top icon (Images) on the left side of the panel.**
   If you have a site defined (Site panel) that has images in its root or local directory, you see the filenames in this panel. You also see an icon representation in the top portion of the panel.

3. **Select one of the images.**

4. **Click on the Edit button.**
   The appropriate application — Fireworks for images, Flash for a Flash movie — launches.

5. **Select logo.jpg and then click the Favorites icon in the lower-right corner to add one of the assets to a list of assets you use frequently.**
   A warning dialog box opens stating that the assets have been added to the Favorites list. You can check the Don't Show Message Again option so this dialog box won't open each time you add an asset to the Favorites list. To view the Favorites list, choose Favorites at the top of the Assets panel.

<NOTE>
By adding something to the Favorites list, you are simply making a shortcut to it so you can access the asset faster. The asset isn't removed from its original location. This is extremely helpful when you are developing a large site with a lot of assets to scroll through.

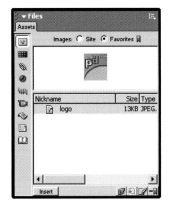

6. **Select an image, and then click the Insert button to add it to your Dreamweaver layout.**
   This is just for practice, so delete the image after you insert it.

» Session Review

In this session you fired up Dreamweaver and made it your friend while visiting its diverse workspace. You then got down to the business of preparing a Web site by setting up a local root folder and using the Site and Assets panels to manage your content.

1. Can you change your chosen workspace? (See "Tutorial: Setting Up and Viewing the Workspace.")

2. How do you dock a panel? (See "Tutorial: Customizing the Workspace.")

3. How do you move a panel group? (See "Tutorial: Customizing the Workspace.")

4. How do you add files or folders to your site? (See "Tutorial: Using the Site Panel.")

5. Is defining your site optional? (See "Tutorial: Defining a Site.")

6. Name several types of assets accessed through the Assets panel. (See "Tutorial: Using the Assets Panel.")

In this session you took a look at some of the planning stages you need to go through prior to designing a Web site. You then familiarized yourself with the Dreamweaver workspace. You learned how you can customize the panel groups to your liking as well as using the Site and the Assets panels. You then prepared to begin your Web site by defining the Complete Course root folder.

» Additional Projects

This project enables you to expand your new skills learned in this session. Challenge yourself to plan a new Web site, perhaps one with a different theme than the one you are currently building. Then determine the look and feel and the type of navigation you want to use.

A new client has approached you to design a site for its new bed and breakfast business. It is a quaint home with four luxurious rooms set in the mountains of Colorado. Much of their business comes from the winter skiers. Your challenge is to make the first mock-up showing the client how the site will encourage potential customers to explore the various areas of content and how the navigation will be easy to understand.

Session 2

Building the Sites Framework

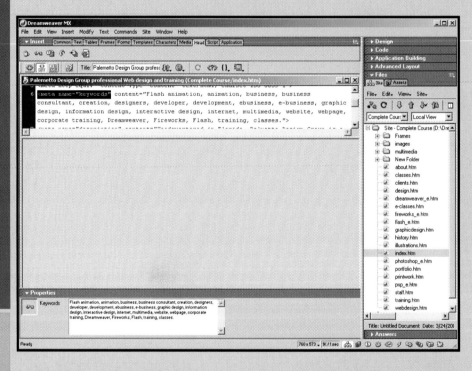

Page Property Basics

In this session, you set your home page for the Palmetto Design Group Web site and learn how to insert Design notes to yourself and others. You then begin to set the page properties such as the title, background color, text color, and margins. These are all elements that are present in the entire Web page. Dreamweaver automatically generates the code for the page properties for you.

Another part of the `<head>` code is the Meta tags, which contain the keywords and description for each page. Many search engines use the content in the Meta tags. They send out spiders and robots, which gather the information from the Meta tags to help index and categorize your Web pages.

A Web page contains two very specific areas, the head and the body. The body contains the code, which enables the user to view your Web page. Although the head contains elements invisible to the viewer, the information that you enter in this area takes a visitor to your site.

Elements — such as the page title, the background color and/or image, text and link colors, as well as margins — apply to an entire page rather than an individual object. Dreamweaver automatically adds the HTML code for these elements to the head section when you use the Page Properties dialog box, which you will do in just a bit.

You need to make some important decisions before you even begin building your Web site. Planning saves you numerous hours of work and countless headaches. You need to decide not only the navigation and layout of the site, but also elements such as the background color (which fills the entire browser) or image.

TOOLS YOU'LL USE
Site window, Property inspector, Code, Design and Code and Design
views, Page Properties dialog box, Insert menu, and Preferences

MATERIALS NEEDED
Session 1 files from the CD-ROM added to your CompleteCourse root
folder if you didn't complete the previous tutorial

TIME REQUIRED
90 minutes

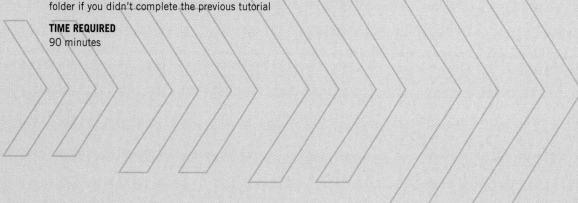

Tutorial
» The Home Page and Design Notes

The home page is the starting point and the road map to the rest of your site. You need to specify the home page in Dreamweaver for some of its functions, such as the site map, to work properly. Design Notes help you and your co-workers remember important information and notes.

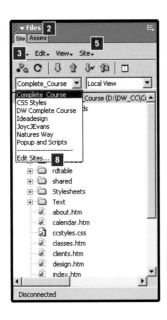

1. **Open Dreamweaver.**

2. **Click the Files panel group extender.**

3. **Click the Site tab.**

4. **Click index.htm to select it.**

5. **Click the arrow for the Site menu and click Set as Home Page.**
   The index.htm page is now set as the home page.

6. **Double-click the filename index.htm to open it.**

7. **Click the down arrow of the Site Definition box.**

8. **Click the Edit option.**
   The Edit Sites dialog box opens; be sure you highlight the Complete Course site.

9. **Click the Edit button.**

10. **Click Design Notes.**

    Be sure there is a check mark in the Maintain Design Notes
    and the Upload Design Notes for Sharing check boxes.

11. **Click OK, and then click Done in the Edit Site dialog box.**

12. **Click index.htm in the Site window to select it.**

    You need to select the page you want in order to add a note.

13. **Choose File→Design Notes from the Menu bar.**

    The Design Notes dialog box will open with the Basic Info tab
    selected.

14. **Click the arrow for the drop-down menu for the Status Field and
    select revision1.**

    This list contains different stages of the page development
    cycle.

15. **Type your note.**

16. **Click the Insert Date icon to insert today's date.**

17. **Click the Show When File Is Opened check box and click OK.**

    After you click OK, in the Site panel you will notice, to the
    right of the filename, a yellow note icon if the site panel is
    expanded.

18. **Double-click the note icon in the Site window to open the note.**

<**N O T E**>

If you select the Show When File Is Opened option, the note opens
every time you open index.htm. Just click OK to close the note. If
you'd rather not have the note open with the file, uncheck this
option.

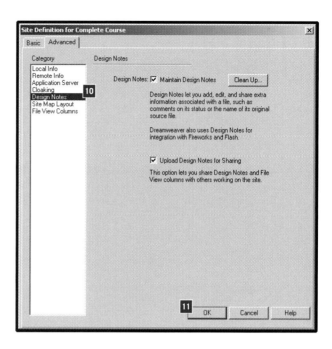

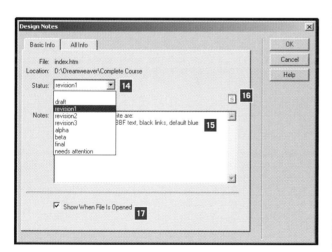

Tutorial
» Opening and Saving a Document

In this tutorial you open a new document, make a new folder, and save the new file in the new folder. It's very easy to open and save documents in Dreamweaver.

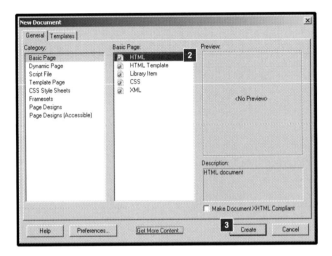

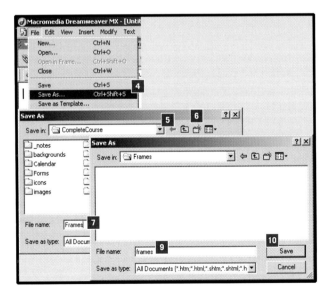

1. **Click File→New in the Menu bar.**

2. **Click HTML in the Basic Page box.**
   Notice how many different file formats you can open from the New Document dialog box.

3. **Click the Create button.**
   You now have a blank HTML page. You need to save the page before you add content. You will use this page later in this course.

4. **Click File→Save As.**

5. **Click the Save In list arrow. Choose the drive in which you saved the CompleteCourse folder, and then double-click CompleteCourse to open it.**

6. **Click the Create New Folder icon/button.**
   Dreamweaver adds a folder inside the Complete Course folder.

7. **Type Frames in the File Name/Name field.**
   If a filename already exists in the File Name field, highlight it and type a new name. We are also using a capital letter for folder names in this course.

8. **Click Open.**

9. **Type frames (lowercase f) in the File Name/Name field.**

<NOTE>
Some platforms such as Unix are case-sensitive. Using all lower-case characters for filenames is a good convention to use to ensure that all your files can be loaded in all platforms.

10. **Click Save.**
    The file named frames.htm is now saved in the Frames folder.

<NOTE>
Once you save a file, you can save any changes by simply clicking File→Save.

11. **Click the index.htm tab on the bottom of the document window.**

Tutorial
» Choosing a Design View

Dreamweaver allows you to work the way you are most comfortable. If you write code, you may fine the Code view helpful. You can design in a total visual environment by using the Design view. You can also have the best of both the Code and Design views.

1. **Click the Show Code View icon in the Toolbar.**
   You can now see just the code in the document window. To help find code when you need it, you change a code view preference.

2. **Click View in the Menu toolbar and pass your cursor over Code View Options. Click Word Wrap.**

3. **Click View in the Menu toolbar and pass your cursor over Code View Options. Click Line Numbers.**

4. **Click the Show Design View icon in the Toolbar again.**
   The document window shows only the working area.

5. **Click the Show Code and Design View icon.**
   Notice how you have both code and the visual design in the same area. You can adjust how much code you see by dragging the code display up or down. You will use this view for this course.

6. **Click the Window Size pop-up menu and choose the 760x420 option.**
   If the options are grayed out, click the Restore Down button for the document page. If you need to view the page at a certain resolution to make sure it works within those constraints, you cannot have the document window maximized.

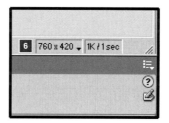

Tutorial
» Setting Browser Preferences

As you design your Web page, you should continually review your design in different browsers to assure that your page displays the way you want it to. To do so, you need to have a recent version of Netscape and Internet Explorer. In this course, you set the browser preferences often as you learn the quirks of each browser.

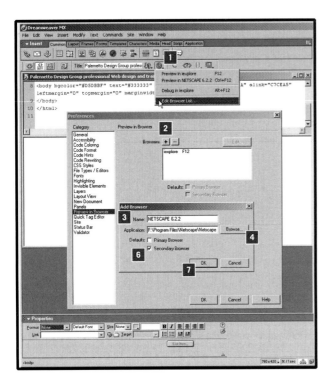

1. **Click the Preview/Debug in Browser icon in the Toolbar and click Edit Browser List.**
   The Preview in Browser category of the Preferences dialog box will be selected. Your default browser will most likely be shown in the browser window area.

2. **Click the plus sign next to the word "Browsers."**

3. **Type a name for the browser you are adding in the Add Browser dialog box.**
   Consider naming your browsers with actual browser names. The example uses Netscape 6.2.2.

4. **Click the Browse button next to the Application field and find the browser you want to add.**

5. **Locate the browser application's executable file. Select it and click Open.**
   If you don't have file extensions visible, you can usually find the executable file in the applications root folder with an icon next to it. Following the example, you use an icon with an N in it for Netscape.

6. **Click Secondary Browser to select it, or check Primary if you are adding a primary browser.**
   If you see a check mark, the option is selected. This example uses Internet Explorer as the primary browser because it has the largest user base. If you have Web statistics for your site, and your users more frequently use another browser, consider selecting it as the primary.

7. **Click OK.**

8. **Repeat steps 1 through 7 to add other browsers.**
   It's a good idea to have Internet Explorer and perhaps Netscape 4 and 5 versions. You may also want to test in an Opera browser.

9. **Preview in a browser by choosing one of these options:**
   » Press icon in the Toolbar.
   » Press F12 to access the primary browser.
   » Press Ctrl-F12/⌘-F12 for the secondary browser.
   » Choose File→Preview in the browser; from the pop-up menu select the browser.

<N O T E>
The Dreamweaver application disk has the most recent versions of Netscape and Internet Explorer. You can install multiple versions of Netscape easily, but if you do, they overwrite each other. To have multiple versions of Internet Explorer, you must install dual operating systems, each with a different version of Internet Explorer.

<N O T E>
In Windows, whenever you preview a file, a temporary file is generated. This can cause your system to slow down depending on your resources. To prevent this, set your disk cleanup utility to automatically delete temp files. See Windows help for more information on your particular operating system.

Tutorial
» Setting Accessibility Preferences

Making your site accessible to as many people as possible is not only the right thing to do but is also the law for many types of organizations. Dreamweaver has a built-in system that helps you add the appropriate tags and labels to various elements.

1. **Click Edit→Preferences→Accessibilty category.**

2. **Check all the options except for Make Dreamweaver use Large Fonts.**

3. **Click OK.**

Now whenever you insert one of the checked elements, a dialog box opens to enter data into. Each dialog box is discussed as it appears in your workflow.

< N O T E >
The Accessibility standards are set by the World Wide Consortium (W3C). For an extensive study of the standards you can go to their Web site at www.w3c.org. It's pretty heavy reading but very informative. You just use a few of the very basic accessibility standards. Also for more information on Accessibility issues refer to the Using Dreamweaver manual chapter on Accessibility and the Help files.

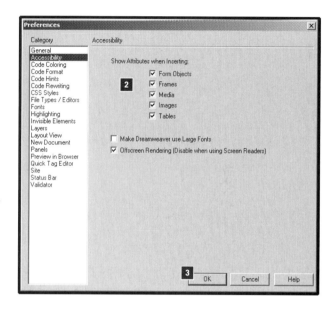

Choosing Colors

The background image, text, and links all have a small color box. When you select a color, such as the background, which is white by default, you see the hexadecimal code to the right of the color box. In the case of the background, the number is #FFFFFF.

You can change the color by clicking the square color box. This opens the color picker, where you can select a color either from a color palette, or from anywhere on your desktop. You can pick colors from an open document, which is a great way to coordinate your color scheme.

If you want different colors available in the palette, use the Options pop-up menu (top-right corner). You can select Color Cubes (default), Continuous Tone (these two are Web safe), Windows OS, Mac OS, and Grayscale.

You can make any palette Web safe by choosing Snap to Web Safe from the Options pop-up menu. Be aware that this option shifts your selected color to the nearest Web safe color, which can result in a different color than selected. If you select a color and notice that it does not appear as you intended it, or if you want to use a non-Web safe color, make sure that you uncheck the Snap to Web safe option.

Tutorial
» Setting Page Properties

A Web page contains two very specific areas, the head and the body. The head contains invisible elements and the body contains the code that makes your Web Page visible to the viewer. What you do first is set the attributes of the body tag (`<body>`).

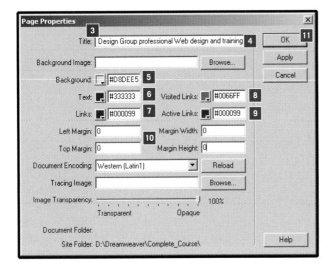

1. **Click inside the document window of index.htm to set the cursor.**

2. **Choose Modify→Page Properties (⌘/Ctrl-J).**
   If you find the Page Properties option grayed out, you may not have your cursor in the document window.

3. **Click in the Title field.**

4. **Type in the page title,** Palmetto Design Group professional Web design and training.
   Some search engines use the title to rank your site higher in a search. Try to use some of your most important keywords in the title. The title appears at the top of a browser window; it is not the filename.

5. **Type the hex code #D8DEE5 in the Background field.**
   If you have a difficult time selecting a color scheme, you can select from one of the sets that ships with Dreamweaver, by choosing from the Menu bar, Commands→Set Color Scheme. This is a nice way to experiment with different options.

6. **Type the hex code #333333 (near black) in the Text field for the text color.**

7. **Type the hex code #000099 in the Links field.**
   The link text appears in this color on the page in the browser. To determine the link color, a color sample was taken from the gold icon.

8. **Type the hex code #0066FF in the Visited Links field.**
   The link text appears in this color to indicate that a user has already visited the link.

9. **Type the hex code #000099 in the Active Links field.**
   The link text appears in this color when a user clicks the mouse on it.

10. **Type 0 in all four Margin fields.**
    This aligns all your elements to the edge. You may find that you have more control over your margins if you design your own margins by using tables.

11. **Click OK when you are done.**
    These are all the properties you set for now.

\<N O T E\>
If you forget to change the title name, Dreamweaver does not prompt you to do so, and it calls your page "Untitled Document."

\<N O T E\>
Color-blind people may have a hard time reading low contrast text.

\<N O T E\>
Internet Explorer reads the Left Margin and the Top Margin entries but Netscape reads the Margin Width and the Margin Height entries. To be compatible with both of the major browsers, enter your values into all four fields.

Tutorial
» Adding Meta Tags

If you want users to find your Web site, you must list the site with the various engines and insert keywords and descriptions into your Web page. These keywords and descriptions help the search engine categorize your Web site. This tutorial shows you how to enter Meta tags with specific attributes, making your Web page more user-friendly to search engines.

1. **Click the Head tab in the Insert menu.**
   The head content is invisible to users; they can't see what you enter, but what you enter can determine whether search engines find your site.

2. **Click the Keywords icon.**

3. **Type these keywords into the keyword dialog box:** Flash animation, animation, business, business consultant, creation, designers, developer, development, ebusiness, e-business, graphic design, information design, interactive design, internet, multimedia, website, webpage, corporate training, Dreamweaver, Fireworks, Flash, training, classes.

   Or, type any keywords you'd like to use.
   Type the words according to their importance; what you think users may enter into a search engine that will bring them to your site. Separate each keyword by a comma.

4. **Click OK.**

5. **Click the Description icon.**
   The Description dialog box opens.

6. **Type in this description:** Headquartered in Florida, Palmetto Design Group is a leading Web solution developer specializing in Ebusiness, Web Design and Corporate training **(also included in the design note).**
   Use as many keywords as possible. This is the description that appears in many search engine listings.

7. **Click OK.**

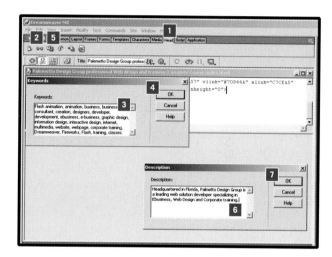

< N O T E >
If you want to use these keywords, you can find them in the Design Notes file attached to the index.htm page. You open the note by clicking the Expand/Collapse icon in the Site panel and double-clicking the note icon. Now you can copy and paste.

< W A R N I N G >
Do not use a certain word multiple times, this is considered *spamming* the search engine. Many search engines do not index your site if you do this. Another trick keyword spammers try, which is considered poor taste within the industry, involves adding keywords to the top of the document, but making the text the same color as the background. Spiders or robots think the document contains more relevant keywords in it, but users can't see the superfluous words. The search sites caught on to this trick and if they find text the same color as the background, they do not list your site.

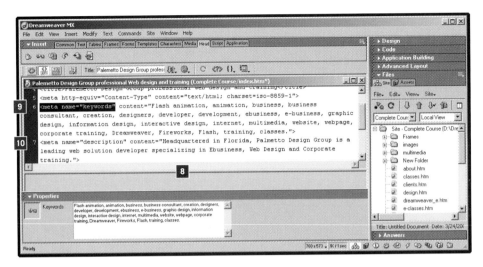

8. **Expand the code part of the window by dragging down a bit so you can see the** ⟨head⟩ **content.**

9. **Highlight just the part that says** ⟨meta name="keywords". Notice the Property inspector. You can see the keywords there. This is where you make any modifications. You can also directly edit the code if you are comfortable doing so.

<N O T E >

Do not click the keyword or description icons again to modify keywords or descriptions. This only adds another set of keywords and descriptions to the ⟨head⟩ of the document. If you were to add another set, search engines might consider this spamming and not list your site.

10. **Highlight the part of the code that says** ⟨meta name= "description". The description also appears in the Property inspector where you can easily modify it.

11. **Click File→Save (or Save As) to save your work.** A copy of everything up through this session is included in the Session2final folder of the CD-ROM. If you ever want to use any of the end of session files, simply copy and place them in the CompleteCourse folder. This overwrites any index files currently in that folder.

Keyword Usage

About 90% of Web hits are generated from a major search site. Knowing this, it is very important to choose your keywords wisely. The frequency of the keywords in a particular document can also influence your search rankings. Try to use some of your important keywords in the title of your page as well as in the document itself. Some engines even check the ⟨alt⟩ tag text so use it

wisely as well. For more information on coding your Meta tag information, visit some of these sites:

Search Engine Watch - www.searchenginewatch.com

Web Developer - www.webdeveloper.com/html/ html_metatag_res.html

» Session Review

Time to test yourself to see how much of this session you can remember. If you don't know the answer, you can refer back to each tutorial to find the correct answer.

1. How do you access a design note? (See "Tutorial: The Home Page and Design Notes.")

2. What is the difference in Code view, Design view, and Code and Design view? (See "Tutorial: Choosing a Design View.")

3. List two ways you can preview a Dreamweaver document in a browser. (See "Tutorial: Editing Browser Preferences.")

4. How do you set margins? (See "Tutorial: Setting the Page Properties.")

5. What part of the document code stores the Meta tags? (See "Tutorial: Adding Meta Tags.")

» Additional Projects

Although you haven't added anything graphical in this session, notice that Dreamweaver has added the Frames folder in the Site panel. The Property inspector also shows the keywords you added, and highlights them in the code section. The background appears green, because you changed the Page properties.

Session 3

Working with Tables

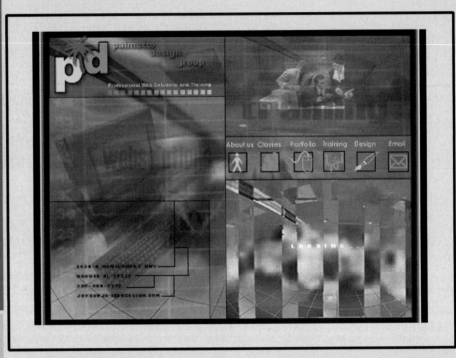

Using Tables for Layout

In this session, you learn the ins and outs of building tables. A table in Dreamweaver is a container with rows, columns, and cells. Tables were originally made to hold data, but Web designers discovered they were great containers to aid in the placement of images. You can also place tables inside of tables.

Tables come in two varieties: a fixed table, which is a specific size no matter what size a browser window is; and the autostretch table (also called fluid or stretchy table). The autostretch table expands to fill the browser window. The best table of all is a hybrid; it uses both fixed and autostretch. By designating certain columns to be a fixed width and one column to autostretch, you can control how the fixed areas appear in all browsers. The column that is set to autostretch fills whatever space is left in a browser window after the fixed columns are in place.

There is a hierarchy in tables — cell values have the highest priority. If a value of a row, column, or even a table contradicts the cell's value, the cell value overrides the others.

Tables are the backbone of your layout, offering you a lot of control. Later in this course you learn how to do some positioning of tables using cascading style sheets. But, standard tables are still the most widely used method of table layout. There are a lot of frustrating little details, such as selecting cells that collapse, that you encounter while building tables in Dreamweaver. In this session you learn how to overcome these small obstacles. You also learn some quirks about different browsers and what to do to make your tables look the same in Netscape and Internet Explorer.

TOOLS YOU'LL USE
Property inspector, Commands menu, Standard view, Layout view, Table tools

MATERIALS NEEDED
If you didn't do Session 2 tutorials, you need the index.htm file and notes folder saved from Session 2 (a copy is in the Session 2 final folder on the CD-ROM).

You use the file in the Xtras folder in the Session 3 folder on the CD-ROM, but you don't have to copy it to your hard drive.

You use the Database Chapter on the CD-ROM. Copy this to your hard drive, but not inside the Complete Course folder. Define a new site (refer to Chapter 2) and name it **PDGdynamic**.

TIME REQUIRED
120 minutes

Tutorial
» Learning Table Basics Using Standard View

In this tutorial you learn how to insert a table and add some quick formatting to see the difference in cell padding and cell spacing. Then you learn how to make modifications to the table. This table is used later in this session for a calendar.

1. **Open the Site panel.**

2. **Click on File→New Folder and name it Calendar.**

3. **Right/Control-click the Calendar folder name and click New File.**

4. **Name the file calendar.htm and double-click to open it.**
   You make the calendar on its own page.

5. **Click the Layout tab in the Insert menu; be sure the Standard view is selected.**
   The Standard view option is white when selected. If the options are grayed out, click in the document window first.

6. **Click the Insert Table icon and enter these values into the Insert Table dialog box:**

   | Rows: **6** | Width: **400** pixels | Cell Padding: **0** |
   | Columns: **6** | Border: **1** | Cell Spacing: **0** |

   If pixels aren't showing in the Width area, click the down arrow to access them. The choices are percent or pixels. Pixels are used to set an exact size for a table.

<**NOTE**>
The Cell Padding and Cell Spacing options in the Insert Table dialog box are blank by default. But blank does not mean zero. Most browsers have a default cell padding of 1 pixel and a 2-pixel cell spacing. To get zero you have to type it in.

7. **Click OK.**
   The Accessibility Options for Tables box alerts you to set values. Since the table is used for layout purposes only, all you need to do is enter a Summary and leave the other entries blank.

8. **Type** Page Layout Table **in the Summary Field and click OK.**

<**NOTE**>
You are adding a lot of layout tables in this chapter. So, repeat this action everytime the Accessibility Option for Table box opens.

9. **Click Commands→Format Table.**
   The Format Table dialog box opens. You learn how to color the rows yourself later in this session, but for now you can use this quick table format tool to do it for you.

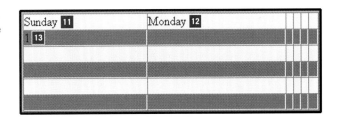

10. **Select AltRows:Blue&Yellow from the list of options and click OK.**
Every other row is now colored blue. You can now see what the difference of cell padding and cell spacing is; the color helps you see it.

11. **Click to place your cursor inside the top-left cell and type the word** Sunday.
Notice how the remaining cells collapse.

12. **Press Tab to get to the next cell and then type the word** Monday.

13. **Click to place your cursor inside the first cell in the second row and type the number** 1.
This content is being entered only so you can better see the effects of cell padding and cell spacing.

14. **Click the outside edge of the table to select it.**
When the table is selected, a dark black line appears around the outside edges.

15. **Change the CellPad to** 10 **in the Property inspector.**
After you type **10**, click in the document or press the Return/Enter key to apply the change. Notice the 10-pixel padding around the words and the number.

16. **Click Edit→Undo Set Attribute.**

17. **Change the CellSpace to** 10 **in the Property inspector and press Enter/Return.**
The white borders are the background showing through. A cell space does not take on the color you add to your table. Also take note that the text is up against the edges of the cell because there is no cell padding in this example.

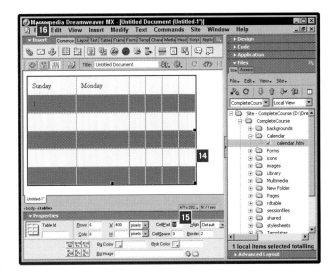

18. **Type** 10 **for the CellPad in the Property inspector.**
The white space is now added and the text is off the cell edges.

19. **Highlight the CellSpace number of 10 and delete it, then press Enter/Return.**
You use this table for the next tutorial, so save it now.

20. **Click inside of any cell of the table to activate the cell properties in the Property inspector.**
The properties for rows and columns are the same except that the Cell area changes to Row or Column, depending on what is selected.

< N O T E >

If you have an image in the cell and you want to see its properties, select the image and tap the right arrow key once. This places your cursor in the cell and the properties appear in the Property inspector.

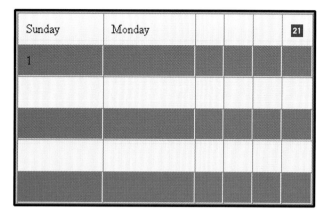

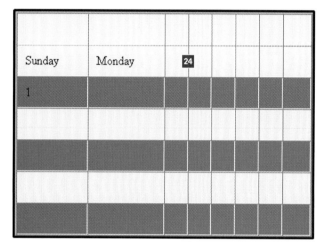

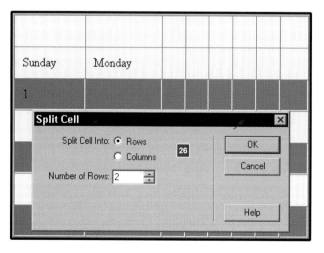

21. **Place your cursor inside the top-right cell of the first row.**
    You can see in the corresponding image, marked with a 21, where you should click.

22. **Right-click/Control-click and from the contextual menu, hold the cursor over Table and choose Insert Rows or Columns.**
    The Insert Rows or Columns dialog box opens.

< N O T E >
You could also choose Insert Column but there are no options — the column is inserted to the right of the selected column. You can also access the table options via the Modify→Table menu.

23. **Click the Columns radio button if it isn't already selected. Change the Number of Columns to 2, click After Current Column if it isn't selected, and click OK.**
    Two additional columns have been added; there are now eight instead of six. There is one more column than needed for a calendar, but that is taken care of in just a little while.

24. **Click inside any cell of the top row and right-click/Control-click then from the contextual menu, hover over Table and choose Insert Row.**
    With the Insert Row command, a row is added above the row that the cursor is in. By adding the row, the row colors no longer alternate (two yellow lines together). In the next tutorial you fix and change the colors.

25. **Click inside any cell and right-click/Control-click, then from the contextual menu hold the cursor over Table and choose Split Cell.**
    The Split Cell dialog box opens. You have the choice of splitting the cell into rows or columns. If you choose columns, there is a column/s added to the selected cell. If you choose rows, there is a row/s added to the cell.

26. **Choose Rows, enter the number 2, and click OK.**
    Notice that the selected cell now has two rows in it. Leave this file open; in the next tutorial you learn several ways to make selections in tables. You may want to save at this point (choose File→Save).

Tutorial
» Selecting Table Elements

It is sometimes difficult to select exactly what you want in a table, especially if a cell or column has no content and it collapses. There are ways to make the proper selection even when this happens. There are several selection options available.

1. **Hold your cursor over the upper-left corner of the table to select it. When you see the double crossed arrows, click to select the table.**

2. **Hold the cursor to the left of the first row. When you see the horizontal arrow, click to select the row.**
   You can select a column in a similiar manner. Place the cursor above the column and click when you see the dark arrow.

   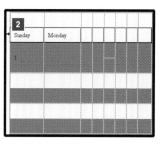

3. **Select the ⟨table⟩ tag in the Tag Selector to select a table or the ⟨tr⟩ tag to select a row or the ⟨td⟩ tag to select a column.**
   This is the most precise and easiest way to make a difficult selection. However, you choose whichever selection option works best for you.

Select a Table

Easier options for selecting a table:

» Click outside of the table and drag the cursor over the edge of the table.

» Click anywhere inside the table and then select the ⟨table⟩ tag from the Status bar.

» Choose Modify➔Table➔Select Table.

» Right-click/Control-click the table and, from the contextual menu, hover over Table and click Select Table.

» Press Ctrl-A/⌘-A two times.

Select a Row

Notice all the cells in the first row have a black border around them, indicating the entire row is selected. These are additional ways to select a row:

» Click in any cell within the row you want to select. From the Status bar, click the ⟨tr⟩ (Table Row) tag.

» Ctrl-click/⌘-click to the left of a row. Once you see the horizontal arrow, click. Repeat to select multiple rows, even non-continuous rows.

» Click inside the first cell of a row and drag across to select the entire row.

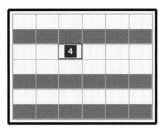

4. **Place your cursor in a cell and press Ctrl-A/⌘-A.**

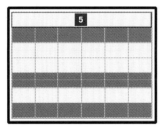

5. **Select the entire top row. Right-click/control-click and from the menu hold the cursor over Table and choose Merge Cells.**
The entire row is now just one large cell that spans the entire table. You can span just two cells if you want. You can span cells across rows, columns, or both.

Select a Column

Other ways to select columns include:

» Ctrl-click/⌘-click the top of a column. Once you see the vertical arrow, click and repeat to select multiple columns, even discontinuous columns.

» Click inside the first cell of a column and drag down to select the entire column.

Select a Cell

Other ways to select a cell or cells include:

» Click in any cell within the row you want to select. From the Status bar, click the <td> (Table Data) tag.

» Ctrl-click each cell you want to select, even discontinuous cells.

» Click inside the cell and drag across and/or down to select multiple continuous cells.

Tutorial
» Changing Colors in a Table

It's very easy to add or change colors in Dreamweaver. You need to make selections, of course, and then the color options are all found in the Property inspector.

1. **Place the cursor inside the top row you merged into one cell in the previous tutorial.**

2. **In the Property inspector, highlight the color** #FFFFCC **in the Bg color field (background) and type** #FFCC00 **for a deep gold color.**

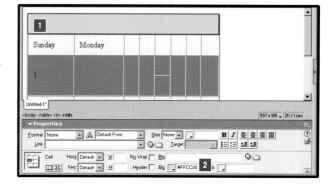

3. **Place the cursor inside the first left cell in the second row. Press the left mouse button and drag across and down to select all the remaining cells.**

4. **Type the Hexadecimal number of** #ACB7C5 **into the Bg color field.**
   Your table now has a gold bar across the top and the remaining cells are a light blue color.

5. **Select the table. In the Property inspector, type** #003399 **into the Brdr Color (Border) field.**
   Your borders are now dark blue instead of the default gray.

6. **Preview your work in different browsers.**
   You can press F12 for your primary browser or you can also select a browser from the Preview/Debug in Browser icon.

   In Internet Explorer the borders are dark blue, in Netscape 4.7 and 6.2.2 the borders aren't colored. This is why it's important to always check your work in various browsers. This way you can see how it is going to be rendered on a viewer's screen. The next tutorial shows you my preferred method to make a table with borders.

7. **Save the file as** mycalendar **(File→Save As).**

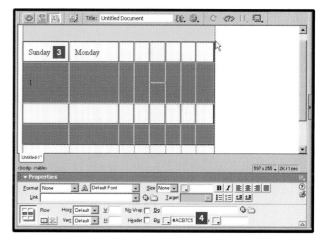

Tutorial
» Adding Custom Borders

In this tutorial you apply color formatting manually, not with the Format Table command. Doing it this way offers much more control over what is colored. You make a new table for a calendar for the Palmetto Design Group Web page. Once this is completed, you can choose which method you prefer — the automatic borders or a custom border with no dimension.

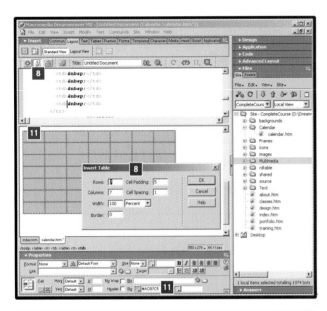

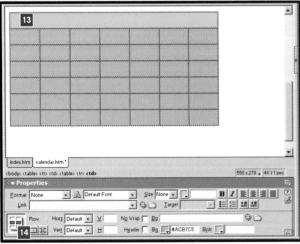

1. **Double-click the calendar.htm file in the Site panel to open it.**

2. **Select the entire table and delete it. You'll make a new one next.**
   You can delete this table because you already saved it.

3. **Click the Insert Table icon in the Common tab of the Insert menu and enter these values:**

Rows: **1**	Width: **400**	Cell Padding: **0**
Columns: **1**	Border: **0**	Cell Spacing: **0**

4. **Click OK.**

5. **Type** Layout Table **in the summary box and click OK.**

6. **Type #003399 into the Bg Color field in the Property inspector while the table is still selected, then press Return/Enter.**

7. **Click inside the table that is now in your document.**

8. **Click the Insert Table icon and enter these values:**

Rows: **7**	Width: **100** percent	Cell Padding: **5**
Columns: **7**	Border: **0**	Cell Spacing: **1**

9. **Click OK.**

10. **Type** Layout Table **in the summary box and click OK.**
    By placing a table within a table, you nest the second table.

11. **Click and drag your cursor to select all the cells. Type** #ACB7C5 **in the Bg field, then press Enter/Return.**
    You now have a one-pixel flat border of the dark blue color that renders properly in all the browsers.

12. **Preview your work in different browsers.**
    The border is now one pixel and flat without the extra dimension that the Border option adds.

13. **Place your cursor in the top left cell and drag horizontally to select the row.**

14. **Click the Merge Cells icon in the top row of the Property inspector.**

15. **Place the cursor in the merged cell and in the Bg field in the Property inspector, type** #FFFFCC **then press Enter/Return.**

16. **Preview your work in different browsers.**

17. **Save this file for use as a calendar.**

Tutorial
» Using Fixed Tables to Build the Home Page

You are designing this Web site to be viewed from a screen resolution of 800x600. If you are using a resolution higher than this, these Web pages may appear small to you. You want to design to the most common screen resolution, which is 800x600, without the users having to scroll to see the content on the home page.

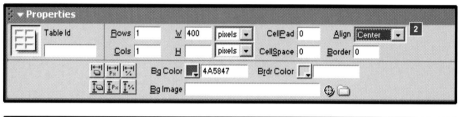

1. **Open the index.htm page, click OK to close the design note, and then click the Insert Table icon, accept whatever is in the Insert Table dialog box, and click OK.**
Just click OK for the Accessibilty dialog box.

2. **With the table still selected, choose the Center option in the Align field in the Property inspector.**
The code for this table is highlighted in the code part of your document window, assuming you are using Code and Design view. If you aren't, then choose it to see the code. Notice where the code says align="center". This is deprecated (being phased out) code and does not render properly on all browsers. The better tag to use is <div>. You see how to use it next.

3. **Delete your table.**

4. **Click the <body> tag in the Status bar, and then click the Align Center icon in the Property inspector.**
Now notice the code. It says <div align="center"> </div>. These are the opening and closing tags to center your table or content. The cursor placement is just before the closing </div> tag so whatever you insert now has the <div> tag wrapped around it.

5. **Click the Insert Table icon from the Insert menu and enter these values into the Insert Menu Table dialog box:**
Rows: **1** Width: **453** pixels Cell Padding: **0**
Columns: **4** Border: **0** Cell Spacing: **0**

6. **Click OK.**

7. **Enter** Layout Table **in the Summary area of the Accessibility dialog box and click OK.**
Now look at the code. Notice all the table tags are enclosed between the </div> tags. This table is on the small side but it's more of an entry page designed to load very quickly.

A Look at the Code

This is the complete code as seen when you center a table using Align in the Property inspector:

```
<table width="453" border="0"
align="center" cellpadding="0"
cellspacing="0">
```

This is the complete code as seen when you add the `<div>` tag to the `<body>` tag prior to inserting content:

```
<div align="center"></div>
```

This is how the code now looks after you have inserted a table:

```
<div align="center">
<table width="453
" border="0"
 cellspacing="0" cellpadding="0">
  <tr>
    <td> </td>
    <td> </td>
    <td> </td>
    <td> </td>
  </tr>
</table>
</div>
```

8. **Open the Assets panel.**

   If you don't see a list of the assets for this site, click the top Image icon.

9. **Click inside the left-most column of the table.**

10. **Click the yellow folder to the right of the Bg (background) field in the Property inspector. Navigate to the CompleteCourse/Images folder (which you saved to your hard drive). Select the l_bk.gif file and click Open.**

    You may see a series of black and gold stripes. Don't worry about it; you fix that soon.

   < N O T E >

   By using this very small image (18 pixels x 2 pixels) as a background image, it tiles to fill the column as it stretches when content is added to the rest of the table. Note that this background has been added to one column only, not to the entire table.

11. **Repeat step 8 for the last column on the right side of the table using the r_bk.gif image.**

    These little images make side borders.

12. **Place your cursor in the left column and select the spacer.gif image in the Assets panel and click Insert.**

13. **Press the spacebar when the Image Tag Accessibility Attributes dialog box opens and click OK.**

    You do this step every time you insert a spacer image.

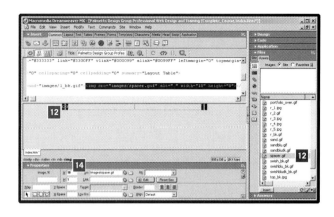

<N O T E>

If you lcavc the ALT text blank in the attributes window, Dreamweaver adds no ALT element in the IMAGE tag. By simply pressing the Enter/Return key you add a blank ALT tag that looks like this: alt=" ". By using the ALT tags your site passes the Accessibility reports that you run later in this chapter.

14. **In the Property inspector, set the W to** 18 **and leave the H at** 1.

<N O T E>

The spacer.gif image is a transparent placeholder. The reason we are using a spacer is because Netscape requires real content (versus a background image) in the cell in order to see background color or images. You could also use a non-breaking space. What I like about the spacer, though, is that you can set the height and width dimensions for spacing.

15. **Place your cursor in the left column cell, not the image, by pressing the right arrow key.**

16. **In the Property inspector type a value of** 18 **into the Horizontal W field and press Enter/Return.**

    By specifying a specific width for this column it forces the column to collapse to the image size.

17. **Repeat steps 10–13 for the right column.**

18. **Click the cursor into the second column.**

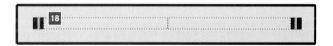

19. **Find the l_1.gif file in the Assets panel, click and drag it to the second column of the table, and drop it there.**

20. **Enter** Palmetto Design Group Logo **in the Alternative Text field of the dialog box and click OK.**

    The logo image is placed in the second column alongside the border.

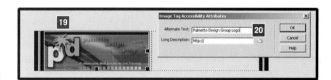

21. **Notice the image width in the Property inspector. It's 204px. Press the right arrow key to place the cursors in the same cell as the image.**

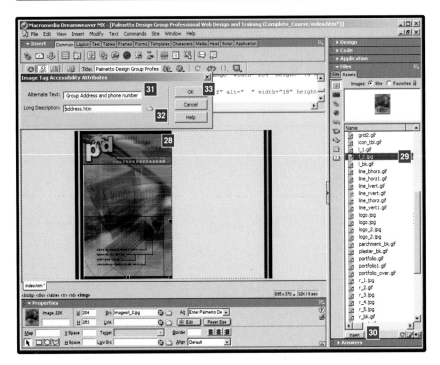

22. **Enter a Width of** 204 **in the Property inspector.**

< N O T E >

This collapses the column to the width of this image. If you didn't set the column width now and you added another image, it would collapse the column on the right since there is no content in it yet. It's difficult to select a collapsed column, but not impossible. You only need to set the column width one time so you don't need to do it again when you place images in the same column.

23. **Click File (in the Site panel) and click New file.**

24. **Name the new file address.htm.**

25. **Double-click address.htm to open it.**

26. **In the document window, type:**
    Palmetto Design Group (press Shift+Enter/Return)
    1634-A Montgomery Hwy #170 (press Shift+Enter/Return)
    Hoover, Al 35216 (press Enter/Return)
    205-884-7625

This file is used as a long description for accessibility. A long description is important when an image contains information that a text reader can't see.

27. **Save and close the address document.**

28. **Select the logo image again in the document window.**

29. **Click the l_2.jpg file in the Assets panel.**

30. **Click the Insert button.**

31. **Enter** Palmetto Design Group Address and phone number **for the Alternate text.**

32. **Click the yellow folder and navigate to the CompleteCourse folder on your hard drive and select the address.htm file.**

33. **Click OK.**
    The second image stacks right below the first image. It's because of this feature that you don't need additional rows to place your content into.

< N O T E >

Many of the applications that generate automatic tables for your images (Fireworks included) use separate rows for every image, making a table much more complex than necessary. The simpler the table, the faster it loads. Because this page is so graphic heavy (but still not bad at approximately 60KB), you want the table as simple as possible.

34. **Press the right arrow key to place the cursor in the cell.**
    Or, while the image is still selected, it is really easy to select the cell by clicking the <td> tag in the tag selector.

35. **Click the Vert. drop-down menu in the Property inspector and choose Top.**
    This option forces the images to align to the top of the table. You only have to set this one time for each column.

36. **Place your cursor in the top-right column.**

37. **Click the r_1.jpg image in the Assets panel and click the Insert button.**

38. **Type** Training Image **for the Alternative text and click OK.**

39. **While the image is still selected, notice the width of 212 in the Property inspector, and then press the arrow key on the keyboard to access the cell properties.**

40. **Type** 212 **in for the Horz W and choose Top from the Vert field dropdown, press Enter/Return.**
    The image is in place and the column is set to the exact size as the image. The remaining images all stack below this one.

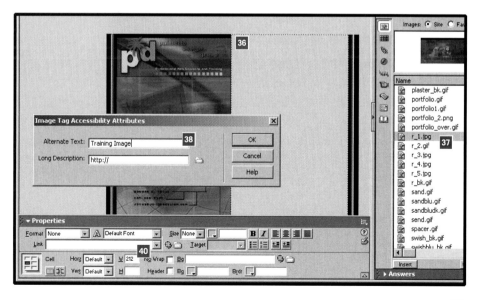

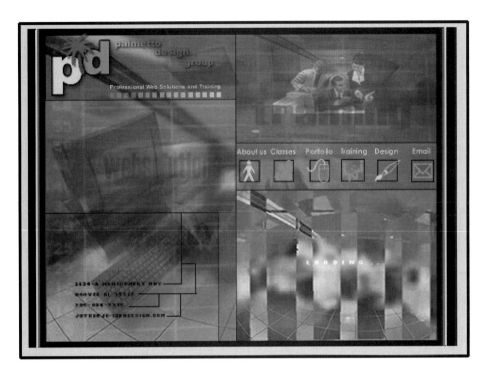

41. **Repeat steps 37–38 for the following images: r_2.gif (alt:** Navigation Icons), **r_3.jpg (alt:** press the spacebar), **r_4.jpg (alt:** Animation placeholder), **r_5.jpg (alt:** press the spacebar).

42. **Press the arrow key on the keyboard to access the cell properties. Type** 212 **in for the Horz W and choose Top from the Vert field dropdown, press Enter/Return.**

43. **Save your file.**

44. **Preview in a browser by choosing one of these options:**

    » **Press icon in the Toolbar.**

    » **Press F12 to access the primary browser.**

» **Press Ctrl-F12/⌘-F12 for the secondary browser.**

» **Choose File→Preview in Browser and from the pop-up menu select the browser you wish.**

If you have a screen resolution of more than 800x600, change it so you can view your work the way someone using 800x600 would see it. There are no issues with this layout in Internet Explorer 5.5, Netscape 4.7 or Netscape 6.2, other than using real content such as the spacer images to see the background images we used for the side borders.

45. **Close the file.**

Tutorial
» Using an Autostretch Table to Build the Interior Pages

Because you never know what size a user's browser is, it's a great idea to build your Web site to accommodate any size browser window. Because you are designing to the lowest common denominator, it looks better for users that have higher resolutions to have the screen show more of your design by stretching to fill the extra browser window space.

1. **In the Site panel, double-click the training.htm file.**

2. **Choose Modify→Page Properties (⌘/Ctrl-J) and enter these values:** Title: **Corporate training classes available**, Background: **#D3D9E1**, All four Margin areas: **0**
   Don't worry about the link colors. You actually change much of this information when you get to the session on CSS style sheets.

3. **Click OK.**

4. **Click the Head tab in the Insert menu and click the Keywords icon using these keywords:** Flash animation, animation, business, business consultant, creation, designers, developer, development, ebusiness, e-business, graphic design, information design, interactive design, internet, multimedia, Web site, Web page, corporate training, Dreamweaver, Fireworks, Flash, training, classes, **then click OK.**
   You need to add the keywords again because this is a new page. For your other files, this is done using a template, which you learn how to use later in this course.

5. **Click the Description icon from the Insert menu, Head tab and type this description into the dialog box:** Headquartered in Florida, Palmetto Design Group is a leading Web solution developer specializing in Ebusiness, Web Design, and corporate training, **then click OK.**

6. **Select your document and click the** ⟨body⟩ **tag in the Status bar, and then click the Align Center icon in the Property inspector.**

7. **Click the Common tab and then click the Insert Table icon and use these values:**

Rows: **1**	Width: **80** percent	Cell Padding: **1**
Columns: **1**	Border: **0**	Cell Spacing: **0**

8. **Click OK.**
   This is the main table that is used to add a border around the entire design. You nest other tables inside this one to keep it modular.

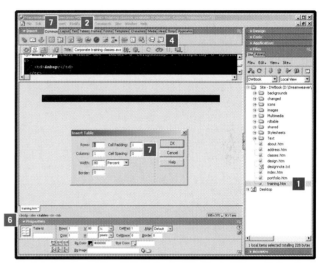

<NOTE>
The reason I use multiple tables is to keep a design modular; it makes it much easier to edit or alter this way. Each main area is contained in its own table.

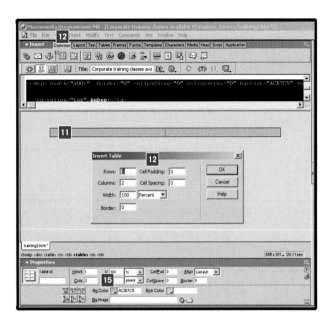

9. **Type** Layout Table **in the Summary box and click OK.**

10. **In the Property inspector, click the color box next to Bg Color and click on black.**

11. **Click inside the table you just placed.**

12. **Click the Insert Table icon and use these values:**
    Rows: **1**   Width: **100** percent   Cell Padding: **0**
    Columns: **2**   Border: **0**   Cell Spacing: **0**

13. **Click OK.**

14. **Type** Layout Table **in the Summary field and click OK.**
    This table is now nested inside the larger table. It is set at 100 percent, which means it totally fills the first table. But, because you used a cell padding of 1, the table fills with the new table except for the 1px cell padding.

15. **In the Property inspector enter** #ACB7C5 **for the Bg Color of the new table.**

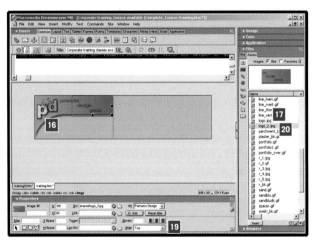

16. **Place your cursor in the left column.**

17. **Select logo.jpg from the Assets panel and click the Insert button.**

18. **Type** Palmetto Design Group Logo **for the Alternative text and click OK.**

19. **Click the down arrow for Align and click Left.**

20. **Click the logo2.jpg image in the Assets panel and click the Insert button.**

21. **Type** Palmetto Design Group **for the Alternative text and click OK.**

22. **Click the first logo image and note the width of 116; click the second image and note the width of 128.**

23. **Place the cursor in the cell and set the Width in the Property inspector to** 244 **and press Enter/Return.**

    The column collapses around the two images. But do you see a problem? Notice the light area between the images. This doesn't seem like it should happen, the images are exactly 244px and the column is 244px. The problem is the V Space and the H Space. See the sidebar *V Space and H Space* for a thorough explanation of why this happened.

24. **Click the first logo image and enter** 0 **for both the V Space and the H Space.**

    Now the images are contained nice and tight in their column.

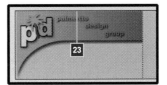

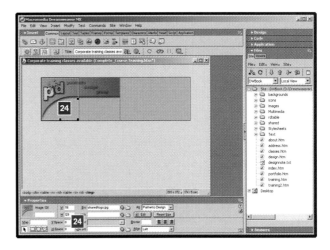

V Space and H Space

You may wonder why you need to specifically enter a value of 0 this time but not on the other image. Normally the default V Space and H Space is 0 but when you Left align an image it becomes a floating image with a baseline alignment (reason for the extra padding). You could avoid this issue by using two cells for the individual images but why add complexity to the table if it isn't absolutely necessary? As long as you understand that using Left or Right alignment has this effect you can remedy the problem.

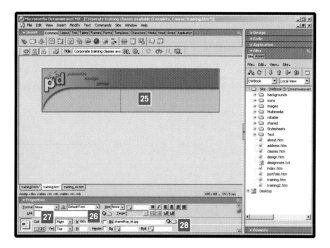

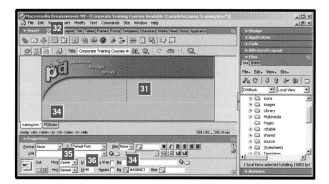

<NOTE>

Normally you don't need to set the height of a cell. But in this instance you are setting a minimum height. You can't set a maximum height even if you want to because content determines how high the cell is. Don't use paragraph returns for space because the non-breaking space is inconsistent in different browsers, plus the size is not concise. The size of a non-breaking space is dependent on the size of the text.

25. **Place the cursor in the right column.**

26. **Type** 100% **in the W field of the Property inspector.**
    You need to actually type the percent sign in the field. This column is now set to expand to 100% of the available space.

27. **Set the Horz field to Right and the Vert field to Top.**
    These settings push the content to the top of the cell and to the right.

28. **In the Property inspector, click the folder icon for Bg image and navigate to CompleteCourse/shared folder and choose the top_bk.jpg image. Click OK.**
    The small image tiles to fill the space. As this column expands, so does this background image.

29. **Check your page in as many browsers as you can.**

30. **Save the file.**

31. **Your cursor should still be in the right column. In the Tag Selector, click on the last** <td> **tag and press the right arrow key to get to the main table.**

32. **Click on the Insert Table icon in the Insert Bar and use these values:**
    Rows: **1**   Width: **100** percent   Cell Padding: **0**
    Columns: **1**   Border: **0**   Cell Spacing: **0**

33. **Click OK.**

34. **Click inside the new table and set the Bg color of the cell to** #ADB9C7 **in the Property inspector.**

35. **From the Horz drop-down menu click on Center.**

36. **Set the minimum height of the cell to** 50.

37. **Click in the top table.**
    Notice how the second table didn't collapse. You only have one table left to add to this layout. It holds the text navigation and company byline.

38. **Click inside the second table and click the last** `<td>` **tag in the Tag Selector and press the right arrow key.**

39. **Click the Insert Table icon and use these values:**

    Rows: **2**   Width: **100** percent   Cell Padding: **0**

    Columns: **1**   Border: **0**   Cell Spacing: **0**

40. **Click OK.**

41. **Click inside the first row of the new table and type** #99A8BA **for the Bg color.**

42. **Set the Height to** 25 **in the Property inspector.**

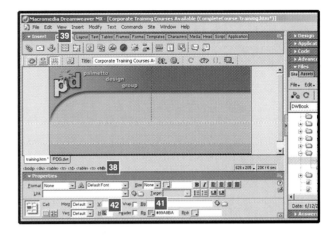

43. **Click in the bottom row and type** #556272 **for the Bg color.**

44. **Set the Height to** 15 **in the Property inspector.**

45. **You can now save your page.**

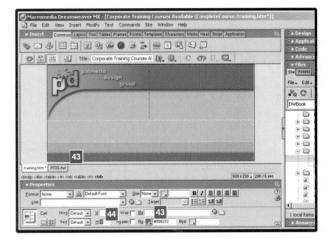

Tutorial
» Exploring the Layout View

If you have a very complex layout, the Layout view may be helpful. You can use a tracing image and draw your tables and cells visually. Don't confuse the Layout view with the Design view, Code view, or Code and Design view. The Layout view is accessed from the Insert menu, Layout tab. It's a table layout view only.

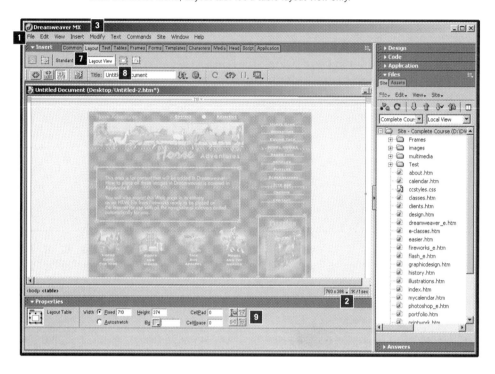

1. **From the Dreamweaver main menu, choose File→New and click Create.**
   You do not work on the Palmetto Design Group Web page for this tutorial. Because some of you may prefer to work this way, the main features of working in the Layout view are explained.

2. **Click the Window size arrow in the Status bar and choose 760x420.**

3. **Choose Modify→Page Properties.**

4. **Click the Browse button next to the Tracing Image field and navigate to the Xtras folder inside the Session3 folder on the CD-ROM. Choose the tracingimage.jpg file and click Open.**

5. **Move the Transparency slider to about 40% and click OK.**
   The image is now in your document.

6. **Click View→Tracing Image→Adjust Position. Use the keyboard arrow keys to center the image.** You can also enter specific coordinates to position the image.

7. **Click the Layout tab in the Insert menu and click the Layout View button.**
   A dialog box opens giving you tips on the two drawing tools available. Personally, I check the Don't show this window again option and click OK. Notice that in Layout view, the Insert Table and Draw Layer icons are both grayed out.

8. **Click the Draw Layout Table icon and place your cursor (now a crosshair) in the upper-left corner. Drag to cover the entire document.**

9. **Check the Property inspector to see the available options.**
   Notice that the properties are different in Layout view. You have the option of typing in a value for a fixed width or selecting Autostretch, which automatically makes your table stretchy.

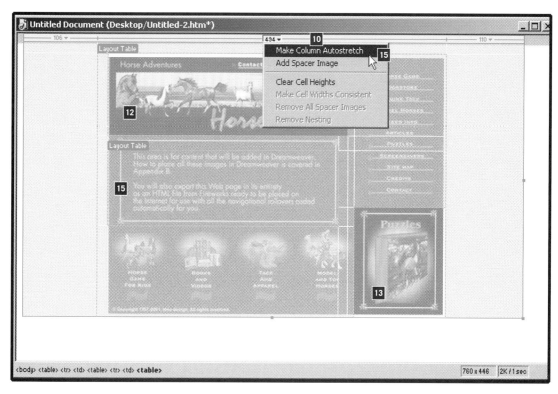

10. **Notice the bar at the top of the document with the number, arrow, and thin lines.**

<NOTE>

Although both Standard view and Layout view insulate you from the underlying code, the two options are quite different. It's easy to switch between views and use them both on the same layout.

11. **Click the Draw Layout Table icon and drag a table around the tracing image.**
    Notice the Layout Table tab on top. Next you draw a cell.

12. **Click the Draw Layout Cell icon and drag around the horse banner in the tracing image.**
    Notice that after you draw a cell there are lines marking where other cells would be generated automatically. They are white lines and may be difficult to see.

13. **Click the Draw Layout Cell icon and drag around the puzzles picture.**
    Notice that the white lines have automatically moved to generate new cell areas.

14. **Click the Draw Table Icon and drag a table in the cell around the horse banner. Can't do it? Okay, it was a trick step. You can't draw a table inside a cell in Layout view.**
    The second table you drew worked because you drew a table inside a table.

15. **Click the Draw Table Icon again (it's not a trick) and drag a table in the area below the banner.**
    Another Layout Table tab is visible so you can separate your tables from your cells. This design isn't really built for a stretchy table, but you can easily make any column autostretch by clicking the little arrow next to the fixed width number and clicking Make Column Autostretch.

16. **You can close this file without saving.**

Layout View Tips

You can't overlap cells. You can add background and cell coloring from the Property inspector. To select a cell, move the cursor over the edge, and when you see the red line, click it. To move a cell, click and drag after you've selected it.

» Session Review

It's time to review what you learned in this lesson. You covered a lot of ground, but it is important ground because table layout is the foundation for most Web sites today.

1. What is the difference between cell padding and cell spacing? (See "Tutorial: Learning Table Basics Using Standard View.")

2. List two ways to select a table. (See "Tutorial: Selecting Table Elements.")

3. List two ways to select a row or column. (See "Tutorial: Selecting Table Elements.")

4. Can you add color to an individual table cell? (See "Tutorial: Changing Colors in a Table.")

5. What is the trick you used to make a real one-pixel table border? (See "Tutorial: Adding Custom Borders.")

6. What determines a fixed table? (See "Tutorial: Using Fixed Tables to Build the Home Page.")

7. Why don't we use the `center="align"` option? (See "Tutorial: Using Fixed Tables to Build the Home Page.")

8. Does each image need to have its own cell? (See "Tutorial: Using Fixed Tables to Build the Home Page.")

9. What makes a table autostretch, fluid, or stretchy? (See "Tutorial: Using Autostretch Tables to Build the Interior Pages.")

10. List two advantages of using the Layout view. (See "Tutorial: Exploring the Layout View.")

In this session you built all the tables needed to lay out the home page, the inside pages, and a calendar. You learned that images and tables stack on top of each other automatically. These layouts are now ready for the image `<alt>` tags to be added as well as the remaining images and text links.

» Additional Projects

This is a project to expand your new skills learned in this session. You can build the table that is used for the database chapters of this course. A sample of the finished file (default.asp) and all the images you need are in the DatabaseChapter/Sample folder. If you didn't copy this folder to your hard drive (not in the CompleteCourse folder) and define a new site, then do it prior to this project.

1. **Add a new document to the Database Chapter/sample folder, and name it practice.asp.**

2. **Insert a table with these values:**
   Rows: **1**
   Columns: **3**
   Width: **100** percent

3. **Insert another table with these values:**
   Rows: **1**
   Columns: **3**
   Width: **100** percent

4. **Insert another table with these values:**
   Rows: **2**
   Columns: **2**
   Width: **100** percent
   Cell Padding: **0**
   Cell Spacing: **1**

5. **Click inside the second column and first row of this table and insert a nested table with these values:**
   Rows: **1**
   Columns: **2**
   Width: **100** percent
   You can add images to this project in the practice project for Session 4.

6. **Save your file.**

Working with Images

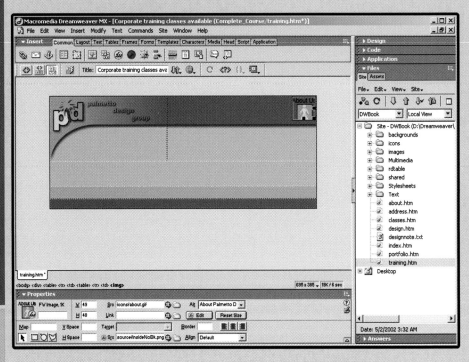

Tutorial: **Inserting Images**

Tutorial: **Replacing Images**

Tutorial: **Making a Rounded Table Using Images**

Tutorial: **Aligning Images**

Tutorial: **Using Background Images**

Placing and Aligning Images

Images are more than decoration. They can help locate content, navigate a site, evoke an emotional response, and provide a company identity. You should optimize and size your images in Fireworks or other image editor prior to laying them out in Dreamweaver, instead of relying on Dreamweaver to edit the bulk of your work. You should know something about the basic formats — GIF, JPEG, and SWF — that most browsers support.

GIF stands for *Graphic Interchange Format*, pronounced "jif." The GIF compression algorithm works best for line art and images with flat color, such as cartoons, logos, and type. GIF images are limited to 256 colors, but you can have a transparency in a GIF image, which is very important when you want to remove a background color. The GIF format is used for animation.

JPEG, pronounced "jay-peg," stands for *Joint Photographic Expert Group*. Because the JPEG compression algorithms excel at compressing millions of colors, photographs look best in JPEG format.

Although an exciting alternative created to combat patent holders who started charging for the GIF technology, PNG is only partially supported by Netscape and IE, which means it's not a viable option.

SWF, a vector format that Macromedia Flash uses, is viable because over 96% of all users have the Flash player plug-in. Vector graphics are usually much smaller than GIF and JPEG graphics due to their method of generation. They are also scalable, which means you can change their size without sacrificing image quality.

TOOLS YOU'LL USE
Property inspector, Assets panel, Insert Bar

MATERIALS NEEDED
Session 3 files from the CD-ROM added to your CompleteCourse root folder if you didn't do the previous tutorial

TIME REQUIRED
90 minutes

Tutorial
» Inserting Images

There are many ways to insert images into Dreamweaver. In this tutorial you use them all at least once, and then the instructions for the rest of this course use the methods I have found to be most convenient through experience.

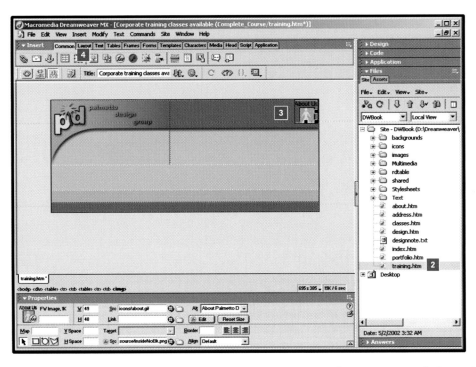

1. **Open the Site panel.**

2. **Double-click the training.htm page to open it.**

3. **Place the cursor in the top-right column.**

4. **Click the Insert Image icon in the Insert Bar.**

5. **Navigate to the icons folder and select about1.gif in the Select Image Source dialog box.**

   One advantage to using this insertion option is that you can not only see a preview of the image but the image's dimensions, file size, and approximate loading time in the Preview panel, as well.

6. **Be sure that Relative To: Document is selected.**

7. **Click OK.**

8. **Type** Information about Palmetto Design Group. **Click OK.**

   Notice how the icon is added to the top and it's positioned to the right. That's because you set this column to top and right positioning when you set up the table. As easy as that was, using the Assets panel as you learned in the previous session is the method I find the quickest.

9. **In the Assets panel, click classes.gif.**

10. **Click the Insert button.**

11. **Type** Online Classes Available **for the Alternative Text and click OK.**

12. **Click and drag the portfolio1.gif image from the Assets panel next to the design icon and drop it (release the mouse button).**

13. **Type** Our Portfolio **for the Alternative Text and click OK.**

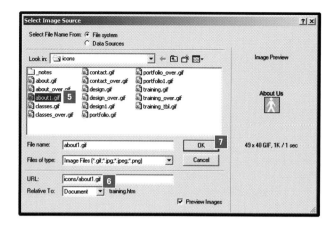

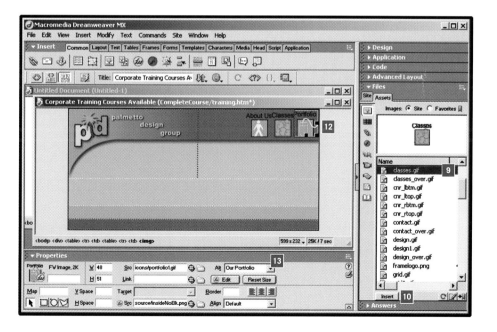

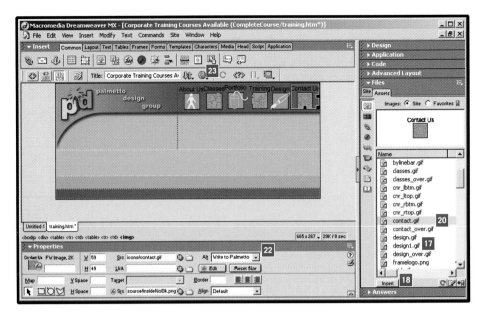

14. **Click Insert→Image.**
    The Select Image Source dialog box opens.

15. **Navigate to the icons folder and click training.gif and click OK.**

16. **Type** Corporate Training Options **for the Alternate Text and click OK.**

17. **Select design1.gif from the Assets panel.**

18. **Click the Insert button.**

19. **Type** Designs **for the Alternate Text and click OK.**

20. **Click the contact.gif image file in the Assets panel.**

21. **Click the Insert button.**

22. **Type** Write to Palmetto Design Group **for the Alternate Text and click OK.**

23. **Save and preview your file.**

Table 4.1: Alignment Attributes

Property	Function
Default	The browser default; usually denotes bottom alignment.
Baseline	Bottom-aligns the images with the baseline of the first line of text.
Top	Top-aligns the top of the image with the first line of text.
Middle	Middle-aligns the middle of the image with the baseline of the first line of text.
Bottom	Bottom-aligns the bottom of the image with the baseline of the first line of text.
TextTop	Top-aligns the top of the image with the top of the first line of text.
Absolute Middle	Middle-aligns the middle of the image with the middle of the first line of text.
Absolute Bottom	Bottom-aligns the bottom of the image with the bottom of the first line of text.
Left	Aligns the image flush left on the page or cell; text is on the right.
Right	Aligns the image flush right on the page or cell; text is on the left.
Low Src	A URL for the image file that loads before the main image. It's usually a black-and-white version or a very low-resolution version of the final image.

Tutorial
» Replacing Images

There are several ways to replace images. You replace the three icons with the yellow color using three methods.

1. **Double-click the About Us icon in the document window.**
   The Select Image Source dialog box will open.

<N O T E>
You navigate to the CD-ROM to get a few files in this tutorial. The images are accessed from outside your root folder intentionally. This shows you what to do if you need to use assets outside your currently defined site.

2. **Navigate to the Session4 New Icons folder on the CD. Open it and select about.gif. Click OK.**
   A dialog box opens that says:

   This file is outside of the root folder of site 'Complete_Course', and may not be accessible when you publish the site. Your root folder is: D:\DW_CC\Complete_Course\ *(your path name would be here)*

   Would you like to copy the file there now?

3. **Click Yes in the dialog box.**
   The Copy File As dialog box opens. Locate the icons folder in your CompleteCourse root folder and click Save. The new image file is now in the root folder.

4. **Look in the document window; the About Us icon has been replaced.**
   The image in the icon is now the same gold as the logo (instead of the former yellow color). Notice in the Assets panel that the new image is not listed in the list of image assets. The list needs to be re-created (step 6) in order for the changes to show up.

5. **Copy the images inside the New Icons folder from the Session4 folder on the CD-ROM and paste them all into the Icons folder with the other icon images.**

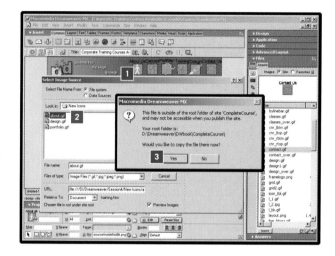

<N O T E>
Double-clicking the image name in the Assets panel does not produce the same result as in the document window. If you double-click the image in the Assets panel, your image editor opens.

6. **Click the Options pop-up menu in the Files panel group and click Recreate Site List.**
   Now look in the Assets panel; the new button names are all in the list.

7. **Open the Site panel.**

8. **Open the Icons folder.**

9. **Select the Portfolio icon in the document window.**

10. **In the Property inspector, click the Point-to-File icon to the right of the Src box. Drag from that icon to the portfolio.gif image in the Site panel.**
    If necessary, fill in the Accessibility information again. The image is then automatically replaced with the new one.

11. **Select the Design icon and click the yellow folder to the right of the Src box in the Property inspector.**
    The Select Image dialog box opens.

12. **Select the design.gif image from the Icon folder and click OK.**
    Once again, if necessary, fill in the Accessibility information. The Design icon has now been replaced. Table 4.2 shows a list of all the image attributes. You add or adjust all of these in this course.

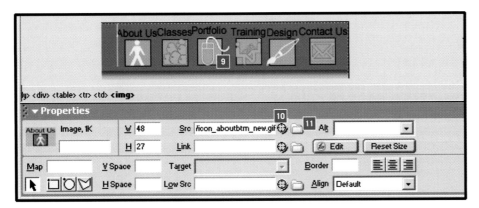

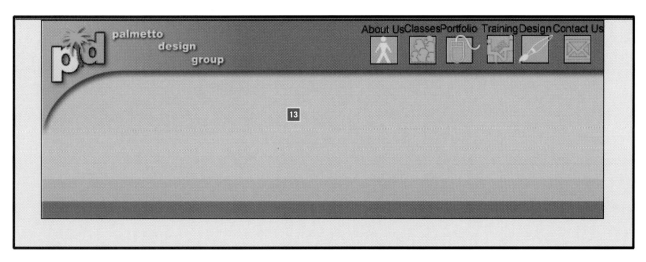

13. **Save and preview in your browser(s).**

Table 4.2: The Properties of the Image Tag

Property	Function
Src	Specifies the URL of the location of the image file.
Align	Aligns the image to the specified margin.
Border	The border around the image, measured in pixels.
Height	The height of the image measured in pixels. It's best if you use the actual (rather than resized) height of the image, which Dreamweaver adds automatically.
Width	The width of the image measured in pixels. It's best if you use the actual (rather than resized) width of the image, which Dreamweaver adds automatically.
Hspace	Horizontal whitespace around the image measured in pixels.
VSpace	Vertical whitespace around the image measured in pixels.
Alt	Text that displays when images can't be displayed due to the Images Off option in browsers (or for accessibility readers).
Link	URL for a hyperlink attached to the image.
Low Src	A URL for the image file that loads before the main image. It's usually a black-and-white version or a very low-resolution version of the final image.

Tutorial
» Making a Rounded Table Using Images

Tables with rounded corners are a popular table design. The rounded corners are achieved by using four corner images, and then background images for the outline. In this tutorial you make a fluid rounded table.

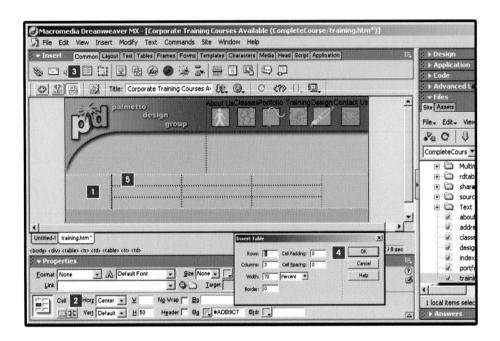

1. **Click in the second table to insert the cursor.**

2. **In the Property inspector, set the Horz value to Center.**
   Alignment is discussed in more detail in the next tutorial.

3. **Click the Insert Table icon and use these values:**
   Rows: **3**
   Columns: **3**
   Width: **70 Percent**
   Border: **0**
   Cell Padding: **0**
   Cell Spacing: **0**

4. **Click OK.**
   If necessary, fill in the Accessibility information. The table is added to the center of the center column.

<NOTE>
With your cursor placed in the table, look in the code area and notice all the `<td> </td>` tags. These tags indicate that this cell has a non-breaking space (` `) in it. Dreamweaver automatically adds this code so that there is content in each cell. When you add "real" content, such as an image or text, the non-breaking space is removed. In Netscape this space does not render properly unless there is real content.

5. **Click in the top-left cell of the first row.**

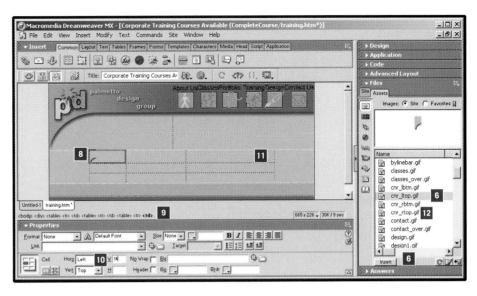

6. **In the Assets panel, select cnr_ltop .gif and click the Insert button.**

7. **Press the spacebar for the Alternate Text field of the Image Tag Accessibility Attributes dialog box and click OK.**
   The spacebar adds empty double quotes that are used for the alternate text, because this image is decorative and offers no valuable information.

8. **Click on the image in the top-left cell and look in the Property inspector at the Width; it's 14px wide.**

9. **Press the right arrow key once to place the cursor in the top-left cell.**

10. **In the Property inspector, add these values:**
    Horz: **Left**
    Vert: **Top**
    W: **14**
    Press Enter/Return.
    This collapses the entire column so you don't have to add the width value to the bottom-left corner.

11. **Click in the top-right cell of the first row.**

12. **In the Assets panel, select the cnr_rtop .gif and click the Insert button.**

13. **Press your space bar in the Alternate Text field of the Image Tag Accessibility Attributes dialog box and click OK.**

    Pressing the space bar or using double quotes produces an empty Alt field that won't come up as a missing field if you run a search for missing Alt tags.

14. **Look in the Property inspector at the Width. It's 14px wide, the same as the left corner.**

15. **Select the image and press the right arrow key once to place the cursor in the top-left cell.**

16. **In the Property inspector, add these values:**
    Horz: **Right**
    Vert: **Top**
    W: **14**
    Press Enter/Return.

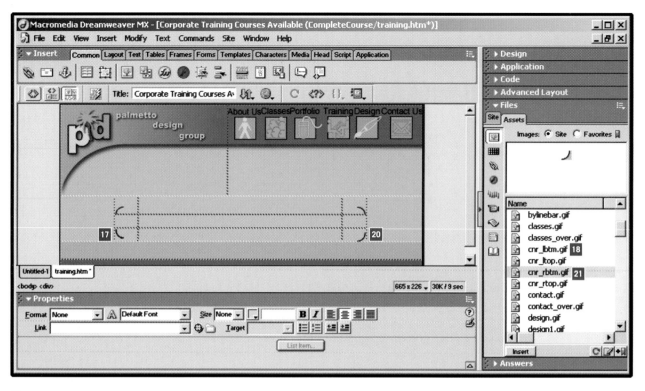

17. **Click in the bottom-left corner cell.**

18. **Insert the cnr_lbtm.gif from the Assets panel using the spacebar for the Alternative description.**

19. **Place your cursor in the cell or select the <td> tag and set these properties:**
    Horz: **Left**
    Vert: **Top**
    Width: **14**
    Press Enter/Return.

20. **Click in the bottom-right corner cell.**

21. **Insert the cnr_rbtm.gif image from the Assets panel using the spacebar for the Alternative description.**

22. **Place your cursor in the cell or select the <td> tag and set these properties:**
    Horz: **Right**
    Vert: **Top**
    Width: **14**
    Press Enter/Return. All the corners are added to the table. Now add the vertical and horizontal lines to the table. The lines are used as background images.

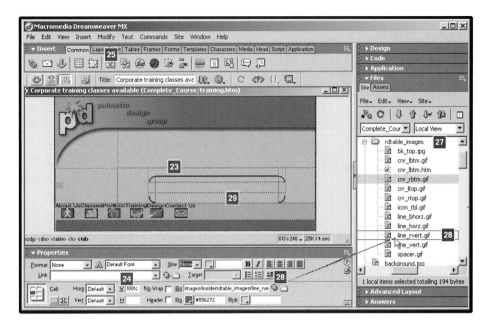

23. **Select the center cell of the top row.**

24. **Set the W to 100% — be sure to manually type in the percent sign.**

The center column now fills up 100 percent of the available space. The table itself uses 70 percent of the available space of the column it's in, and this cell uses 100 percent of the available space of this table.

< N O T E >

If you recall, when you started the table was set at 70 percent. The right and left columns are now both fixed-width columns set at 14px each. You make the center column fluid so that it stretches depending on the browser size.

25. **Select spacer.gif from the Assets panel and click the Insert button (press spacebar for Alt text).**

You can use the default of 1px by 1px. The reason you are adding a spacer is that it is considered real content. This cell is going to have a background image added. Without the spacer the image wouldn't render in Netscape.

26. **Open the Site panel.**

27. **Open the rdtable_images folder.**

28. **Place your cursor in the top row's center cell in the Property inspector, click and drag the Point-to-File icon for the Bg to the line_thorz.gif image in the rdtables folder and release the mouse.**

Notice the line from the Point-to-File icon to the selected image, which is indicated by the rectangular outline. When you click, this image is inserted where the cursor is positioned. Alternatively you can click the folder icon to the right of the Bg box in the Property inspector and select the image from the Select Image Source dialog box.

< N O T E >

This is actually a very small image; it's 2px wide by 26px high. By placing it in the background of the cell, it tiles to fill up the available space. The height was determined by the top corner images, which are 26px high.

29. **Place your cursor in the bottom row's center cell and repeat steps 24–28, except use the line_bhorz.gif image.**

You now have horizontal lines that connect the top and the bottom corners.

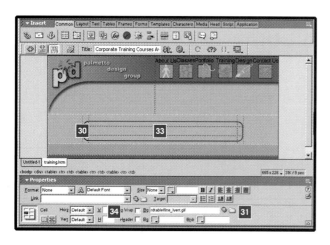

30. Click in the center row of the left column and insert a spacer image.

31. Set the Bg image using the Point-To-File method or by clicking the yellow folder and selecting the line_lvert.gif image.

32. Repeat steps 30 and 31 for the right side, except use the line_rvert.gif image.

33. Insert the cursor in the center cell of the center row.

34. Insert a spacer image and set the width and height to 20.
The reason a spacer image is being added to the center cell is to prevent the cell from collapsing until some real content is added.

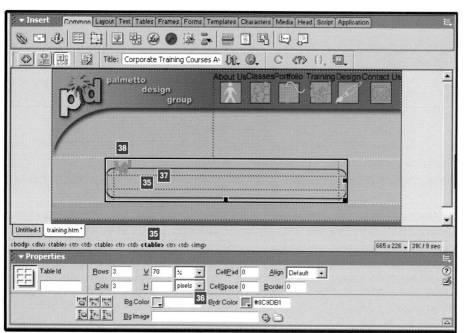

35. Click anywhere in the rounded cornered table, and click the `<table>` selector tag.

36. In the Property inspector, set the Bg color to #8C9DB1.

37. Click inside the center column of the top row.

38. Click the training_tbl.gif image in the Assets panel and click the Insert button.
This isn't where you want the icon, but it's fine for now. You align it in the next tutorial.

39. Preview in browsers.
Your table and background color should render properly in Internet Explorer 5.5 and Netscape 6.22. In Netscape 4.79 the cells are colored but the background lines won't show.

<NOTE>
If you have cells with no background color, you missed a spacer image. Add it and the cells show the background color.

Tutorial
» Aligning Images

You've done a good bit of aligning already, but in this tutorial you align images and add spacing using spacer images.

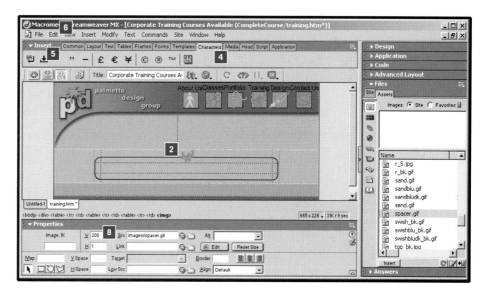

1. **Open the training.htm file if it isn't open by double-clicking it in the Site panel.**

2. **Click to the left of the green icon you added to the top of the table.**

3. **In the Property inspector, set the Horz to Center.**
   This aligns any content added to this cell to the center. The image is the center but what if you wanted it to the right just a little bit more? I'll show you two methods for doing so.

4. **Click the Characters tab in the Insert Bar.**

5. **Click the Non-Breaking Space icon.**
   This adds one space at the cursor location and moves the icon to the right one space. Look in code view and you see   added.

<NOTE>
This is not the preferred method of adding space, primarily because it is unreliable. The amount of space added is determined by the font used and its size. Because of this your layout could be considerably different than you expect if the users define their own fonts in their browsers.

6. **Click Edit→Undo to remove the non-breaking space.**
   I had you do this just so you'd see what it did. Non-breaking spaces can come in handy at times. For instance, Dreamweaver uses them in the table cells until you add real content to help maintain the table's integrity.

7. **Insert a spacer.gif before the icon.**
   You can insert the spacer using any of the image-insertion methods you prefer.

8. **In the Property inspector, set the width to 200.**
   The icon moved to the right by 200px. With this method you can get precise alignment of an image.

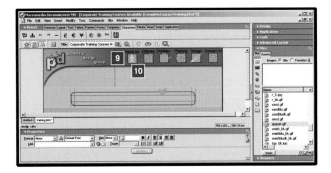

<NOTE>

The icons are now lined up to the right of the table, but they are much too close to each other. Each icon needs a small amount of space between them.

9. **Click in the cell of the row of icons.**
   Click the `<td>` tag in the Tag Selector or select an image and press the arrow key.

10. **Click the About Us icon.**

11. **Use the right arrow key to move to the cell off of the image.**

12. **Insert a spacer.gif.**

13. **Add the double quotes in the Alternative text box.**

14. **Set the width of the spacer to 10.**

15. **Repeat steps 11-14 for the remaining icons.**
    The Contact Us icon doesn't need a spacer after it because there are no other icons. There you have it—precisely aligned image icons. You work with more alignment features after you add some text to the layout in the next session.

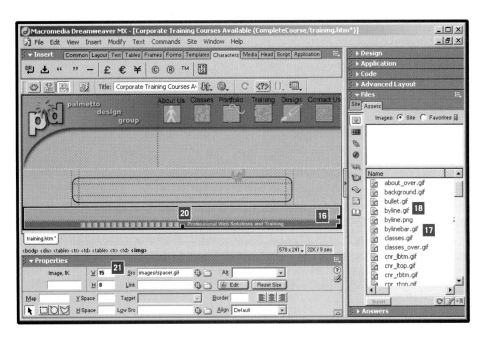

16. **Place the cursor in the bottom dark blue table and set the Horz alignment to Center.**

17. **Insert the bylinebar.gif from the Assets panel.**
    Use the spacebar for the Alternative text.

18. **Insert the byline.gif from the Assets panel.**

19. **Type** Professional Web Solutions and Training **for the Alternative text.**

20. **Place the cursor between these two images.**

21. **Insert a spacer and set its width to 15.**

Tutorial
» Using Background Images

Earlier in this session, you used background images in cells for the horizontal and vertical lines of the rounded cornered table. Now you learn how to use background images for an entire page or table.

1. **Choose Modify→Page Properties.**

2. **In the Page Properties dialog box, click the Browse button next to the Background Image box. Navigate to the images_backgrounds folder and click the background.gif image.**

3. **Click OK.**

4. **Preview your work in the browser.**
   This image is only 130px x 130px. Because it's applied as a background image, it tiles to fit the available browser space. Later in this course you learn how to use a background image that does not tile but that requires CSS styles.

5. **Click Edit→Undo to remove the background.**

< N O T E >
Background images can be GIF, JPEG, or PNG. If you want to use background images, be sure that they do not distract from the content of your pages. Very pale backgrounds work best. Whatever you do, don't put text on top of a colorful or busy background. This is the mark of an amateur designer. Pale pastels or textures work best as backgrounds.

6. **Choose Modify→Page Properties.**

7. **Navigate to the images_background folder and choose parchment_bk.gif.**
   Notice how much nicer and less distracting a texture looks?

8. **Click OK.**

9. **Repeat steps 5 and 6 for the other images in the folder, ending with swishblu_bk.gif.**
   The other images are provided simply so you can see how a variety of textures look as background images. We'll use the swishblu_bk.gif background.

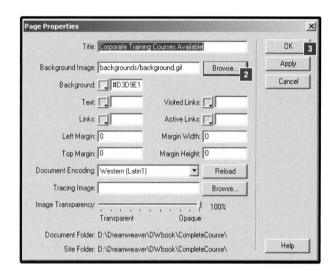

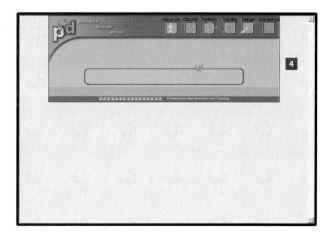

» Session Review

It's time to test out those newly acquired skills. If you find you don't know the answers to certain sections then it's a good idea to go back and rework that tutorial to expedite your learning curve.

1. Name three ways to insert an image. (See "Tutorial: Inserting Images.")

2. When selecting an image from the Select Image Source dialog box, there is an option to make the path Relative to the Site Root or Document. Which is the most often used method? (See "Tutorial: Inserting Images.")

3. If you have an image selected and insert another from the Assets panel, is the original image replaced? (See "Tutorial: Replacing Images.")

4. How do you collapse a column to fit the image size? (See "Tutorial: Making a Rounded Table Using Images.")

5. What type of image was used for the horizontal and vertical lines of the rounded corner table? (See "Tutorial: Making a Rounded Table Using Images.")

6. What is the best method for adding spaces between images? (See "Tutorial: Aligning Images.")

7. You used a background image of 130px by 130px; how can such a small image fill the entire canvas? (See "Tutorial: Using Background Images.")

In this session you added a rounded corner table with background images and special alignment options. You also added the icons, centered them, and added space between them. You also added a byline and a background image for the page.

» Additional Projects

If you'd like more practice with the techniques you've learned in this session, you can make a duplicate copy of the training.htm page and then add the icons to the table just above the byline, as follows:

1. Right-click/Control-click the training.htm page and choose Duplicate.

2. Double-click the new file to open it.

3. Add the icons to the medium blue table.

4. Center the icons.

5. Add about 10 pixels between each icon image.

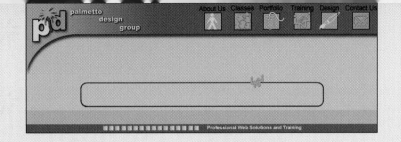

Adding Text

Corporate Training

Palmetto Design Group will develop a specialized course to fit your unique needs. Training your development team and setting up a usable workflow can cut your production costs considerably.

Certified Instructors

At Palmetto Design Group we employ only certified instructors to train your development team. Our instructors are Microsoft, Adobe, and Macromedia certified as well as numerous other certifications. The Instructor link to the left contains the bios of our current instructors.

Working with Text

Dreamweaver provides a few methods for formatting your text. You can use HTML styles, which apply a group of attributes at one time, or apply HTML formatting manually to selected parts of text. Cascading style sheets are now the preferred method of formatting. I'll explain that statement shortly and expand upon it in the CSS session.

With HTML styles or CSS styles, manual HTML formatting of individual elements overrides the applied style. In this session you will learn how to manually apply HTML formatting. If you find yourself in a position of having to code your pages for version 3 browsers, HTML formatting is what you'll need to use.

CSS styles are the preferred method of formatting your text. HTML formatting is now considered deprecated code. A *deprecated* element or attribute is one that has been outdated by newer constructs. Deprecated elements may become obsolete in future versions of HTML. The World Wide Web Consortium (W3C) oversees standards for the Internet.

Although HTML formatting is deprecated code, it is still widely used. You'll learn all the basic functions of applying formatting to your text.

TOOLS YOU'LL USE
Property inspector, Assets panel, Insert Bar, Flash Text, Spell Checker

MATERIALS NEEDED
Session 4 files from the CD-ROM added to your CompleteCourse root folder if you didn't do the previous tutorial

TIME REQUIRED
60 minutes

Tutorial

» Adding Text

This tutorial shows you how to insert text into your Web pages and how to format the text. It's good to know a bit of HTML when editing text so you know how the code should look. We'll be looking at code as we work with text in this session.

Refer to the O'Reilly reference guide for HTML help. You can click the Reference icon (<?>) on the toolbar; you can also find O'Reilly HTML Reference in the Reference panel, which is part of the Code panel group. The reference guide contains not only definitions and descriptions of HTML tags but many other topics as well, including reference material for CSS and CFML.

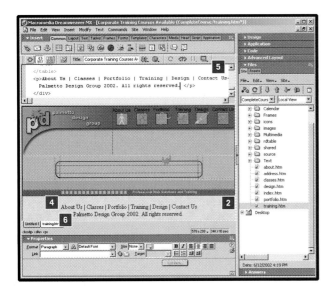

1. **Open the training.htm file from the CompleteCourse root folder in the Site panel.**

2. **Place your cursor outside the bottom table containing the byline.**

3. **Press Enter/Return to add a paragraph space.**
   Look in the code part of your document window and notice the `<p> </p>` that is added after `</table>` (closing table tag). This new tag is the `<p>` opening paragraph tag, ` ` is a non-breaking space, and then the `</p>` is the closing paragraph tag. The non-breaking spacer is removed when you add content in the paragraph.

4. **Type the following text for what will become text links:**
   About Us | Classes | Portfolio | Training | Design | Contact Us

5. **Press Shift-Enter/Return to add a single line break**.
   Look at the code. A `<br>` tag is added right after Contact Us.

6. **Type the following copyright notice:**
   Palmetto Design Group 2002. All rights reserved.

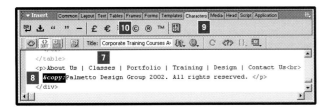

7. **Now look at the code that was added: Both lines of text are enclosed inside the paragraph tags.**

8. **Place the cursor in front of Palmetto.**

9. **Click the Characters tab in the Insert Bar.**

10. **Click the copyright symbol.**
    The copyright symbol is added in front of the copyright statement. This is all the formatting we will do in this area for now. This site will be formatted using CSS styles in a later session.

Tutorial
» Importing Text

This tutorial shows you how to import text from a text file and from a Microsoft Word document. This text has no formatting, but you'll see that the Word file has all kinds of markups, which need to be removed.

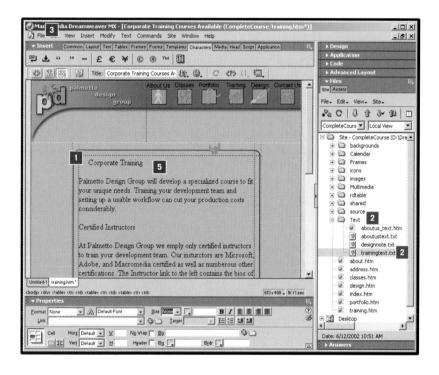

1. **Click in the center cell of the rounded table to place the cursor.** Don't select the spacer image; place the cursor in the cell itself.

2. **In the Site panel, open the Text folder and double-click the trainingtext.txt file to open it.**

3. **Click Edit→Select All (Ctrl-A/Option-A).**

4. **Copy by choosing Edit→Copy (Ctrl-C/Option-C).**

5. **Select the document and then paste into the center cell by clicking Edit→Paste (Ctrl-V/Option-V).**
   You might want to memorize the copy and paste keyboard shortcuts; they sure save a lot of time.

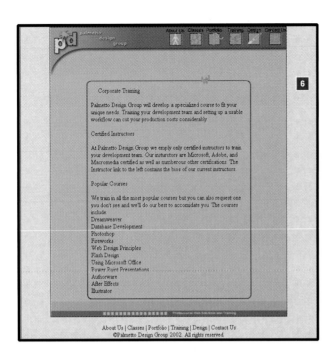

6. **Preview your work in all the target browsers.**

7. **Return to Dreamweaver and highlight and delete all the text in the center cell of the rounded table.**

8. **Place the cursor in the center cell of the table below the spacer image.**

9. **Choose File→Import→Word HTML.**
   The Select Word HTML File to Import dialog box opens.

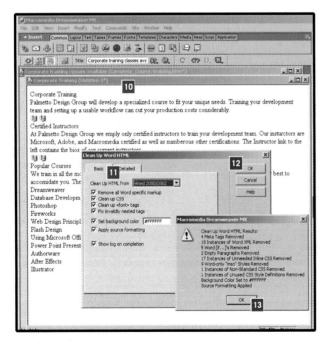

10. **Navigate to the Text folder and click the training_text.htm file, and then click Open.**
    The Clean Up Word HTML dialog box opens. Also notice that the Word document opened in a separate window.

11. **Leave everything checked in the Basic and Detailed tabs of the Clean Up Word HTML dialog box.**

12. **Click OK.**

13. **Click OK on the results dialog box that opens.**
    Notice that the little yellow icons indicating the markup text are gone and the text is automatically highlighted for you.
    If you don't see yellow icons, choose View→Visual Aids→Invisible Elements.

< N O T E >
There sure were a lot of items removed for just a text file. To see what the Microsoft code looked like prior to removing all the markup we didn't want, just open the training_text.htm file and look at the code.

14. **Copy the text using the keyboard shortcut of Ctrl-C/Option-C.**

15. **Close the text document, clicking No when the Save changes to Untitled opens.**

16. **Paste into the center cell of the rounded table using Ctrl-V/Option-V.**

17. **Select the spacer image that is in the center cell and delete it.**
This spacer was here simply to prevent the table from collapsing until we could add some real content in it. The final results look the same as pasting in the text. But I wanted you to know how to deal with Microsoft Word documents as well.

18. **Save your file.**

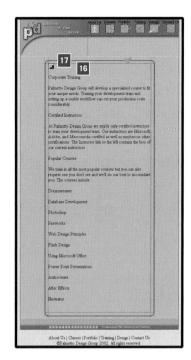

You are now ready to begin working with fonts, so take a moment to look at Table 5.1, which lists the font families available in Dreamweaver. In order for your text to appear as you've designed, you need to use fonts that are on everyone's machines. As this is difficult, Dreamweaver groups fonts into font families, so that if the user does not have the first font in the family, the next font is used. For example, if a user does not have Verdana, Arial is used. You can change fonts within the current font families or add new families by clicking the font field drop-down and choosing the Edit Font List option.

Table 5.1: Font Lists in Dreamweaver

Font	Type
Default Font	Usually Times New Roman or Arial
Arial, Helvetica, sans-serif	Proportional sans-serif font
Times New Roman, Times, serif	Proportional serif font
Courier New, Courier, mono	Mono-spaced serif font
Georgia, Times New Roman, Times, serif	Proportional serif font
Verdana, Arial, Helvetica, sans-serif	Proportional sans-serif font
Geneva, Arial, Helvetica, sans-serif	Proportional sans-serif font
Edit Font List	Add fonts

Tutorial
» HTML Formatting

Although much of the HTML formatting is handled effectively by CSS style sheets, the underlying formatting techniques are useful to understand. Also, HTML formatting is still used in style sheets for such things as heading tags.

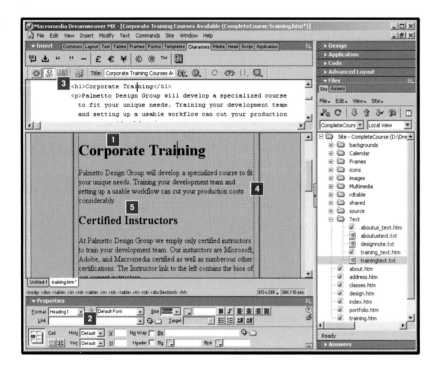

1. **Place the cursor in the words Corporate Training.**
   You don't have to highlight the text; just place the cursor within the text you want to change.

`<NOTE>`
If there were no paragraph spacing below the Corporate Training text, the entire section including the paragraph text would be changed.

2. **In the Property inspector, click the Format arrow and click Heading 1.**

3. **Look at the code you just added.**
   Notice the `<h1>` heading tag and the closing `</h1>` tag surrounding the words Corporate Training.

4. **Place the cursor in the paragraph text.**
   Notice it is already set for Paragraph; don't change it just yet.

5. **Place the cursor in the Certified Instructors text and set the Format to Heading 2.**

6. **Place the cursor in the Popular Courses text and set the Format to Heading 2.**

7. **Place the cursor in the first paragraph of text.**

8. **Click the `<p>` tag selector, which will select the entire paragraph.**

9. **Click the down arrow in the Font box area and choose Verdana, Arial, Helvetica, sans-serif.**

   You should list multiple fonts because you don't know what fonts a user may have. If users don't have Verdana, Arial is displayed. If there is no Arial, Helvetica or the default sans-serif font are used. Refer back to Table 5.1 for a list of the font groups in Dreamweaver along with the types of fonts. A sans-serif font is easier to read on the screen than a serif font (one that has little "feet"). A serif type font is best used for large text in perhaps a heading or title.

<NOTE>

You can also click Edit Fonts and specify your own. If you specify a custom font, one that may not be available on all computers, you should always specify a standard font as another choice. For example, say you really want to use Akzidenz Grotesk for a heading. If the viewing (or client) computer doesn't have that font installed, you could use Swiss721 . . . or as a last choice, Arial. You'd then set up your font list as Akzidenz Grotesk, Swis721, Arial.

10. **Click the down arrow in the Size box and click 2.**

<NOTE>

There are two types of font sizes. The Headings 1-7 get smaller as the number increases. The font size increases as the number gets higher — so font size 3 is larger than size 2. You can also use negative values, which are based on the default font size. The default is typically size 3 (unless the user has changed it) so a -1 size would be one less than size 3 making the font size 2, and so on.

11. **Click in the color box to the right of the Size box and select a red color.**

    We are not going to keep this color, I just want you to see how to use the tool and take a look at the code. Notice that after the paragraph tag there is a font tag with the color. Color is denoted by a # symbol, and then a combination of numbers and/or letters. This is the hexadecimal number. Then the size of the font and the font name are listed. At the end of the paragraph is a closing font tag added in front of the closing paragraph tag.

12. **Click and drag over the color number in the Property inspector and delete the color.**

    Black is the default text color so we don't need to add the code to make it black.

13. **Click the B icon to bold the text and click outside the text to see the change.**

    If you want to remove the bolding, highlight the word again and click the B icon.

14. **Save your file.**

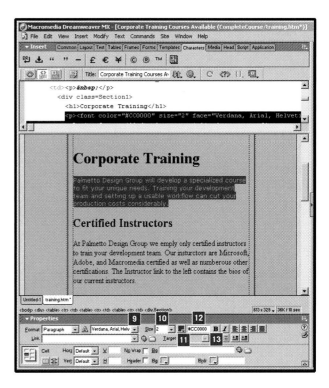

<NOTE>

The code you just looked at, specifically the font tags, is deprecated code. Deprecated means it has been outdated by newer constructs. Deprecated elements may become obsolete in future versions of HTML. In general, authors should use style sheets to achieve stylistic and formatting effects rather than HTML presentational attributes. HTML presentational attributes have been deprecated when style sheet alternatives exist. Because of this we will do very little HTML text formatting in this course. The final text formatting will be done in the session on CSS style sheets.

Tutorial
» Wrapping Text Around an Image

There are many ways to position text around images and you'll be doing that in this tutorial using the text alignment options as well as with vertical and horizontal spacing.

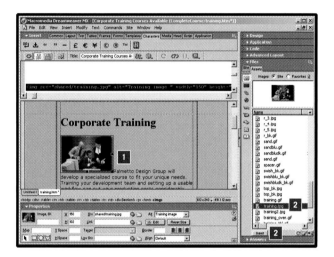

1. **Place the cursor in front of the first word of the first paragraph (Palmetto).**

2. **In the Assets panel, click the training.jpg image and click the Insert button.**

3. **In the Alternative text box, type** Training image **and click OK.**
   Notice how the text is aligned with the bottom of the image. It doesn't look very attractive. Dreamweaver has nine alignment options; refer to the table on page 76.

4. **Click the image.**

5. **Click the down arrow in the Align box in the Property inspector.**

6. **Click Left.**
   Notice how the text wraps around the image on the right.

7. **With the image still selected, type** 5 **where you see H Space in the Property inspector.**
   H Space adds the desired amount of pixels around the right and left sides of the image. V Space adds space to the top and bottom of the image.

< N O T E >

The Left alignment is just one of nine alignment choices. The best way to understand these effects is to try each one and see the effect. When you are done, continue with step 8.

8. **Place the cursor in front of the word At in the second paragraph.**

9. **Click the training2.jpg image in the Assets panel and click the Insert button.**

10. **Add the Alternative text of** Instructor image.

11. **Click right in the Align drop-down in the Property inspector.**

12. **Set the H Space to 5.**

13. **Preview your work in a browser and make the browser window large.**

    Notice how the text and images change position according to the size of the browser. This is because this middle cell, which contains the content, is a fluid column. The images are also considered floating images and move with the text as it moves.

14. **Go back to Dreamweaver and click Text→Check Spelling.**

    The word **employ** is displayed in the Change To box; click Change.
    Click Change for instructors.
    Click Change for numerous.
    Click Change for accommodate.
    Click OK for spelling check completed.

    Don't forget to run the spell checker whenever you have text in a document. Misspelling a word is real easy. Of course these mistakes were made on purpose.

15. **Save your file.**

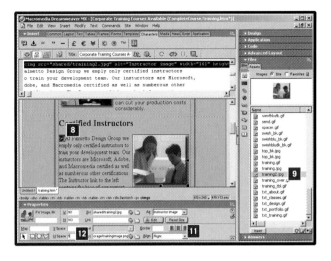

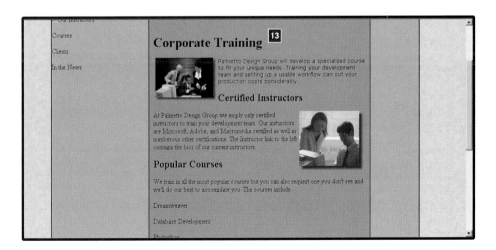

Tutorial
» Making a List

There are several kinds of lists in Dreamweaver. We'll add one to our training page and you can try out the others.

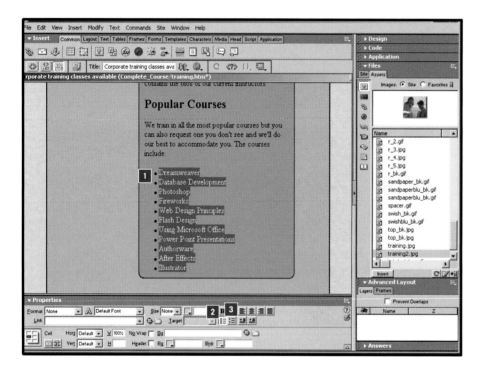

1. **Place the cursor in front of the word Dreamweaver in the list below the Popular Courses paragraph and drag to highlight the remaining text.**

2. **Click the Unordered List icon in the Property inspector.**
   Notice how Dreamweaver automatically adds the bullets.

3. **Now click the Ordered List icon.**
   See how the list is now numbered.

4. **Click the Unordered List icon again.**
   This is the type of list we want for this document.

5. **Save your file.**

Tutorial
» Adding Flash Text

Macromedia Flash has quickly become the number one software program for generating vector-based animations. Because vectors are based on mathematical formulas, the file sizes are normally smaller and faster loading. We'll add some simple Flash text in this tutorial.

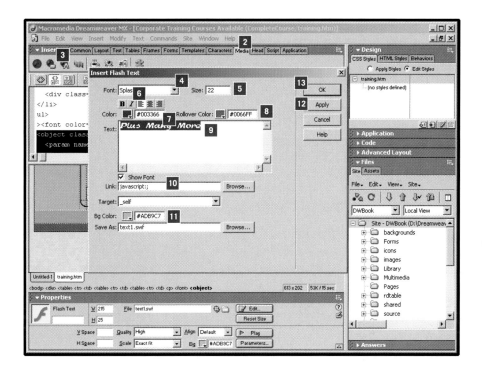

1. **Click to place your cursor below the last line of text in the training document.**

2. **Click the Media tab in the Insert Bar.**

3. **Click the Add Flash Text icon.**

4. **Click the down arrow in the Font box and choose a decorative font. I have Splash, so it's what I choose.**
   One advantage of Flash text is that the users don't have to have the font installed.

5. **Type a size. I used 22 but the size will depend on the font you use.**

6. **Click the Left align icon.**

7. **Type** #003366 **for the Color field.**

8. **Type** #0066FF **for the Rollover color.**

9. **Enter the text of** Plus Many More **in the Text box.**

10. **Type** javascript:; **in the link field for a null link.**

11. **Click in the Bg Color box and use the eyedropper to sample the blue background of the table color.**

12. **Click the Apply button to see if the text looks like you want it to.**
    Is it the correct size? If not make changes until you are satisfied.

13. **Click OK and type** Plus many more classes available **in the accessibility box.**
    The text may look jaggy in Dreamweaver, but when you preview it in a browser, you will see that the edges look great.

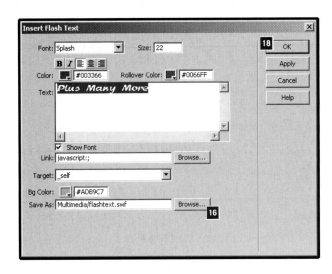

14. **Click the Flash text to select it.**

15. **In the Property inspector click the Edit button.**
    The Insert Flash Text dialog box will open.

16. **Click the Browse button for the Save As field and name it flashtext.swf.**

17. **Navigate to the Multimedia folder and select it.**

18. **Click OK to close the dialog box.**

19. **Preview your work in the browsers.**

20. **Save the file.**

» Session Review

You probably found this session on the easy side. Adding and formatting text isn't difficult in Dreamweaver. Test your skills:

1. What is the difference between a paragraph space and a break? (See "Tutorial: Adding Text.")

2. What is the tag for paragraph and for break? (See "Tutorial: Adding Text.")

3. Where do you find the copyright symbol? (See "Tutorial: Adding Text.")

4. How do you clean up the text imported from Microsoft Word? (See "Tutorial: Importing Text.")

5. Do you need to select the entire title to change the formatting of it? (See "Tutorial: HTML Formatting.")

6. Why do the font choices list several different fonts in the list? (See "Tutorial: HTML Formatting.")

7. How do you wrap text around an image? (See "Tutorial: Wrapping Text Around an Image.")

8. What are the two kinds of lists you practiced with in this session? (See "Tutorial: Making a List.")

9. When you add Flash text, does the user have to have the font on their machine to view it properly? (See "Tutorial: Adding Flash Text.")

INTRANET HOME

GO TO >>

[Intranet Home ▼]

Lorem ipsum dolor sit amet, consectetaur adipisicing elit, sed do eiusmod tempor incididunt ut labore et dolore magna aliqua. Ut enim ad minim veniam, quis nostrud exercitation ullamco laboris nisi ut aliquip ex ea commodo consequat. Duis aute irure dolor in reprehenderit in voluptate velit esse cillum dolore eu fugiat nulla pariatur. Excepteur sint occaecat cupidatat non proident, sunt in culpa qui officia deserunt mollit anim id est laborum Et harumd und ilet, dereud facilis est er expedit distinct.

New Classes Online

Gonsectetaur adipisicing elit, sed do eiusmod tempor incididunt ut labore et dolore magna aliqua. Ut enim ad minim veniam, quis nostrud exercitation ullamco laboris nisi ut aliquip ex ea commodo consequat. Duis aute irure dolor in reprehenderit in voluptate velit esse cillum dolore eu fugiat nulla pariatur. Excepteur sint occaecat cupidatat non proident, sunt in culpa qui officia deserunt mollit anim id est laborum Et harumd und ilet, dereud facilis est er expedit distinct.

Beating the Commute
Lex ea commodo consequat. Duis aute irure dolor in reprehenderit in voluptate velit esse cillum dolore eu fugiat nulla pariatur.

What's New
Lorem ipsum dolor sit amet, consectetaur adipisicing elit, sed do eiusmod tempor incididunt ut labore et dolore magna aliqua.

Human Resources
Excepteur sint occaecat cupidatat non proident, sunt in culpa qui officia deserunt mollit anim id est laborum Et harumd und ilet, dereud facilis est er expedit distinct.

Adding Navigational Links

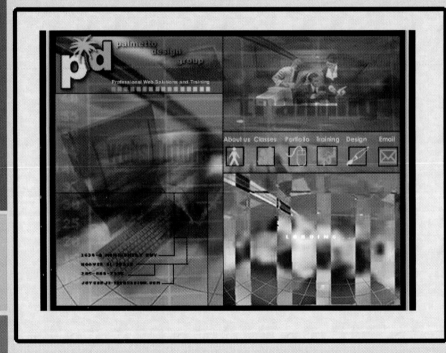

Tutorial: **Adding Links**

Tutorial: **Adding Rollovers**

Tutorial: **Making an Image Map**

Tutorial: **Adding a Flash Button**

Links and Rollovers

This session looks at some of the more common types of navigational links. So far your Web site is a simple and clean format, which can be viewed in older browsers. The type of linking you do in this session fits with this simple design. You make a rollover, in which one image is swapped for another, and an image map, which is one image with multiple links attached to it. You also add an e-mail link and a Flash button.

Some of the more sophisticated navigation schemes require layers or frames, so they are discussed in those sessions. But because of the layers and frames, these pages are compatible with version 4 browsers and later.

TOOLS YOU'LL USE
Property inspector, Insert Bar, Flash button, Hotspot tools

MATERIALS NEEDED
Session 5 files from the CD-ROM added to your CompleteCourse root
folder if you didn't do the previous tutorial

TIME REQUIRED
75 minutes

Tutorial

» Adding Links

Actually adding the links is quite easy. A link is a behavior that tells the browser, "When a user clicks here, open this page or go to this part of this page." You add some of the links in this tutorial and more in some of the other tutorials in this session.

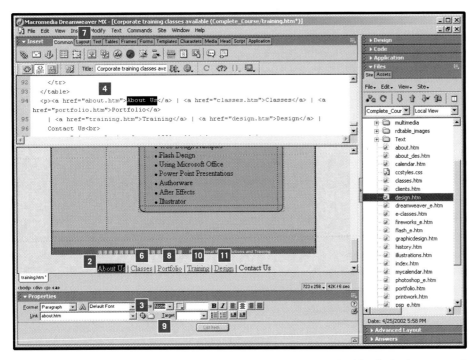

1. **Double-click the training.htm file in the Site panel.**

2. **Place your cursor in front of the About Us text at the bottom of the page below the tables, and drag to highlight About Us.**
   Don't highlight the pipe symbol, just the text.

3. **Add a link in the Property inspector. The easiest way is to drag the Point-to-File icon to the about.htm file in the Site panel.**
   You can also click the yellow folder to the right of the Link box and navigate to the appropriate file.

4. **Click split view or code view (if you're in Design view) and look at the code.**
   The code is:

   ```
   <p><a href="about.htm">About Us</a> | Classes
   | Portfolio | Training | Design |
   Contact Us<br>
   ```

   Notice the anchor tag (<a>) added before and after the About Us text.

5. **Click in the document to deselect the text.**
   Notice that the link is now blue and is underlined. The CSS session shows you how to remove the underline.

6. **Highlight the word Classes.**

7. **Click Modify→Make Link, navigate to the CompleteCourse folder, select the classes.htm file, and click OK.**
   Now you see another way to add a link. Personally, I think the Point-to-File method is the quickest and easiest.

8. **Highlight the Portfolio text.**

9. **In the Property inspector, click the yellow folder and navigate to the portfolio.htm file, and then select it and click OK**.

10. **Highlight the word Training and link to design.htm using your favorite method.**

11. **Highlight the word Design and link to training.htm using your favorite method.**

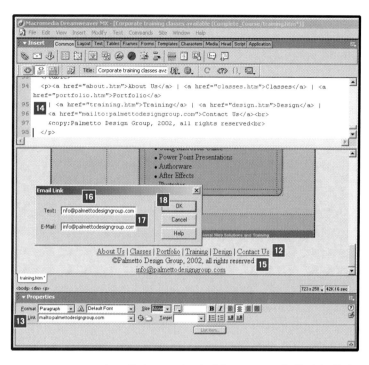

12. **Highlight the Contact Us text.**
    This time you make an e-mail link, which is a bit different than regular links. With an e-mail link the user's default e-mail client opens.

13. **In the Link box of the Property inspector, type the words** mailto:info@palmettodesigngroup.com **to quickly add a link.** Just type mailto: and add any e-mail address to it. Don't use any spaces between the mailto: and the e-mail address.

< N O T E >

To automatically include a subject line, use this text:

mailto:info@palmettodesigngroup.
com?Subject=Yoursubjectline.

14. **Look at the code.**
    Notice the e-mail link still uses the <a> tag; the only difference is that the mailto: is added before the e-mail address.

15. **Place the cursor to the right of the copyright line and add a line break (Shift-Enter/Return).**

16. **Click Insert→Email Link.**
    The Email Link dialog box opens.

17. **Type in the e-mail address for both the Text and the E-mail fields.**
    You don't need to type in the mailto: for the e-mail address. The reason you typed the e-mail address instead of a link

name is so that users who don't have an e-mail client for their Web browser can see the address so they can type it manually.

< N O T E >

Of course you can add this e-mail link the same way you did the Contact Us. This is just an optional method of adding text links.

18. **Click OK.**

19. **Preview your work in a browser.**

20. **Pass your cursor over your new links.**
    The cursor changes into a hand to indicate that these are links. The blue text and underline also indicate that these are links. When you pass your mouse over a link it shows up in the status bar.

21. **Save your file.**

< N O T E >

Open the Assets panel and click the URL icon. You see two links that you've used so far in this site. The first one you didn't actually add, it was added with the Flash text. It's a link to the Flash player. But notice the e-mail link is now in the Assets panel. You can use this just like any other asset. Also click the Colors icon to see the colors used in your site. You can use these colors when choosing new ones. It's a great way to keep a specific color palette for a site.

Tutorial
» Adding Rollovers

A rollover is a behavior that causes one image to swap with another one when the mouse cursor passes over it. Users normally recognize that an image that changes is a link to another page or section. In this tutorial you will add rollover images and links to the navigational icons in the training.htm page.

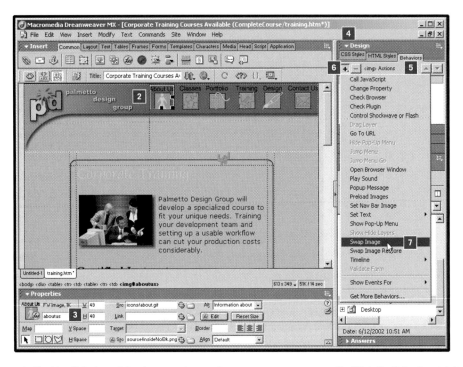

1. **Double-click the training.htm page to open it.**

2. **Select the About Us icon.**

3. **Type** aboutus **in the Image box of the Property inspector.**
   You need a name for the image when you attach different behaviors to it. It's a good habit to get into.

4. **Click the expander arrow in the Design panel group.**

5. **Click the Behaviors tab to open the Behaviors panel.**

6. **Click the plus (+) sign.**

7. **Click Swap Image.**
   The Swap Image dialog box opens. Notice that the selected image is highlighted. You have a lot of unnamed images in the document, but you remedy that shortly.

8. **Be sure that the image called "aboutus" is, in fact, highlighted.**

9. **Click the Browse button and navigate to the Icons folder. Select the about_over.gif image.**

10. **Click OK to close the Swap Image dialog box.**

11. **Preview your work in a browser.**

12. **Pass your mouse over the About Us icon.**
    You should see the text change from black to gold.

13. **Check the code.**
    Just in front of the $\langle img \rangle$ tag you'll see the JavaScript behavior:

    ```
    <a href="javascript:;"
    onMouseOver="MM_swapImage

    ('aboutus','','icon/about_over.gif',1)"
    onMouseOut="MM_swapImgRestore()">
    ```

    This says that when the mouse passes over the image called aboutus, the program swaps it with about_over.gif. When the mouse moves off the icon, the program restores the icon to the original state.

14. **Click the Classes icon and delete it.**
    You are deleting it so you can learn another way of inserting both the original and the swap image at the same time. Because I normally add my icons first, there wasn't anything to demonstrate this technique.

15. **Click the Rollover Image icon from the Common category of the Insert Bar.**
    The Insert Rollover Image dialog box opens.

16. **Type** Classes **in the Image Name box.**

17. **Click the Browse button next to the Original Image box and navigate to the Icons folder. Select classes.gif and click OK.**

18. **Click the Browse button to the right of the Rollover Image box and navigate to the Icons folder. Select the classes_over.gif image and click OK.**

19. **Type** Classes PDG Offers **for the alternate text.**

20. **Click the Browse button to the right of the "When Clicked, Go To URL:" box, navigate to the classes.htm file, select it, and click OK.**

21. **Click OK to close the Insert Rollover Image dialog box.**

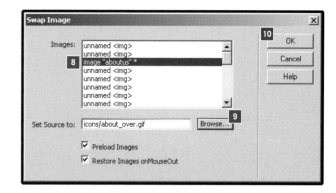

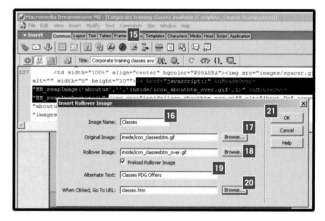

< N O T E >
Preload Images is checked by default. It's a good idea to leave it this way. The rollover image loads with the rest of the page's graphics and is available as soon as the user's mouse passes over the icon. If you uncheck this option the image has to load before it appears on mouseover.

The Restore Images onMouseOut is also checked by default. This allows the icon to go back to the original state once the mouse cursor leaves the icon.

< N O T E >
All this code for the swap image was added automatically; you didn't have to do any manual hand coding. But it's still a good idea to understand what is going on under the hood.

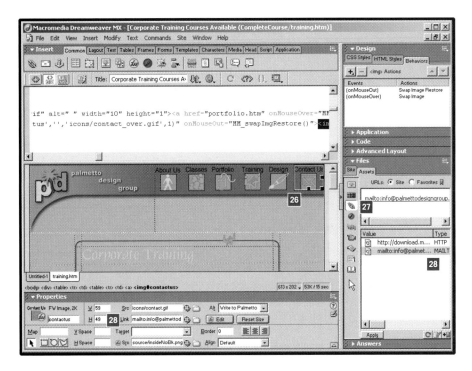

22. **Preview in a browser and mouseover both the About Us and Classes icons.**

23. **Repeat the method you prefer on the remaining icons in the top navigation area.**
    Because the icons are already in place, using the Behavior panel is the easiest method. Also remember to name each icon in the Property inspector before you add the Swap Image behavior.

24. **Open the Site panel.**

25. **Click each of the icons and use the Point-to-File method of adding links.**
    Drag the Point-to-File link icon to each .HTM file for the respective icons.
    About Us to about.htm
    Classes to classes.htm
    Portfolio to portfolio.htm
    Training to training.htm
    Design to design.htm

26. **Select Contact Us.**

27. **Open the Assets panel and click the Link icon.**

28. **Click the e-mail address and drag it on top of the Contact Us icon.**
    Notice in the Property inspector that the link has been added.

29. **Save your file and close training.htm for now.**

Tutorial

» Making an Image Map

An image with many links is an image map. Links are attached to different areas of the same image by using hotspots. Clicking the hotspot takes you to the respective link.

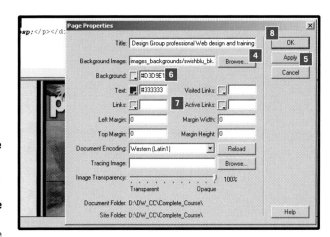

1. **Double-click the index.htm file.**

2. **Click the Show This File When Opened option for the design note (to deselect) so it doesn't open automatically anymore**.

3. **Click Modify→Page Properties.**
   Before you work on this page, make a few alterations to the Page Properties you set in an earlier session. Now that you know how to add a background image, you can do so.

4. **Click the Browse button for the Background Image, navigate to the Background folder, select swishblu_bk.gif, and click OK.**

5. **Click the Apply button to see the background.**

6. **Click the Background color box and click in the background of the document to select a light blue color.**
   The light blue background color appears in a browser while the background loads so the user doesn't have to see a white screen.

7. **Highlight all the link colors and click Delete to remove them.**
   You add link colors for the entire page using CSS Styles in the next session.

8. **Leave the text and margin settings as they are and click OK.**

9. **Click the area that contains the navigation icons.**
   Notice that the icons are all one image.

10. **Click the expander arrow in the Property inspector to see the image map properties.**

11. **Select the Rectangular Hotspot tool.**
    In the bottom-left corner, you see three blue shapes. These are the Rectangular Hotspot tool, the Oval Hotspot tool, and the Polygon Hotspot tool. You use the Rectangular Hotspot tool for this tutorial.

12. **In the Map field enter a name of mainnav.**
    It's especially important to name your image maps with unique names when you have more than one image map on a page. Notice I said a unique name; this does not give you the option to skip this step. If you don't enter a map name of some sort you are unable to use the Hotspot tools.

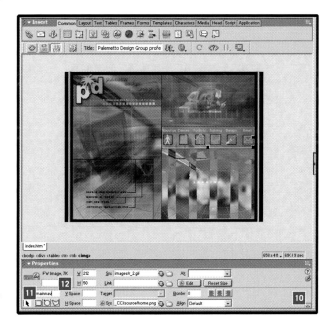

Hotspot Tool Tips

The Rectangular and the Oval Hotspot tools work by clicking and dragging out the shape. The Polygon Hotspot tool differs in that you click around an irregularly shaped area. As you click, the points are connected. Continue to click until the area is defined, and finish by clicking the Arrow tool to close the shape.

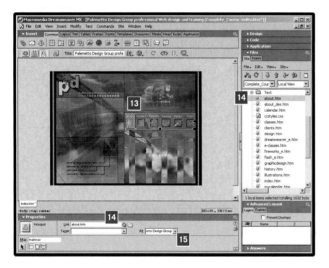

<NOTE>

You can edit a shape by dragging any one of its corners. You can move a shape by simply dragging it. You also can copy and paste shapes to place them in new locations.

13. **Place the cursor at the top-left corner of the About Us icon and drag toward the bottom-right of the icon to define the shape.**
    Once a hotspot is defined you see the hotspot properties in the Property inspector.

14. **Click and drag the Point-to-File icon for the Link field to the about.htm file in the Site panel.**

15. **Enter the Alt text of** About Palmetto Design Group.

16. **Repeat steps 13-15 for the rest of the icons, replacing the alt text with:**
    Classes: **Online Classes Available**
    Portfolio: **Portfolio**
    Training: **Corporate Training Available**
    Design: **PDG Design Concepts**
    Email: **Contact Us**

    You can copy and paste the first hotspot area for all the rest since the icon sizes are all pretty close. Just move the pasted shape over another icon.

17. **Drag the e-mail link from the Assets panel on top of the Contact Us icon after the hotspot for Contact Us is defined.**

18. **Take a look at the code.**
    Notice that the map information is located at the bottom of the .HTML file, just before the closing body tag. This code shows the map name and the specific coordinates (yours may vary) of the hotspots, with the Alt text included.

```
<map name="mainnav">
  <area shape="rect" coords="177,1,208,47"
href="mailto:info@palmettodesigngroup.com"
  alt="Contact Us">
  <area shape="rect" coords="145,2,176,48"
href="design.htm" alt="PDG Design Concepts">
  <area shape="rect" coords="108,1,139,47"
href="training.htm"
alt="Corporate Training Available">
  <area shape="rect" coords="72,2,103,48"
 href="portfolio.htm" alt="Portfolio">
  <area shape="rect" coords="35,2,66,48"
href="classes.htm"
alt="Online Classes Available">
  <area shape="rect" coords="2,2,33,48"
href="about.htm"
alt="About Palmetto Design Group">
</map>
```

19. **Save the file, and then preview and close it.**

Tutorial
» Adding a Flash Button

In this tutorial, you will learn how to add a Flash button to your page, which adds personality to your site. Don't overdo it with Flash, though, because it can make it harder for search engines to recognize your site.

1. **Double-click the training.htm page in the Site panel to open it (or the training.htm tab at the bottom of the document if you still have it open).**

2. **Click to the right of the Plus Many More Flash text at the bottom of the rounded table.**

3. **Click the Media category tab of the Insert Bar.**

4. **Click the Flash Button icon.**
   The Insert Flash Button dialog box opens.

5. **Choose the Navigation-Next (Green) style.**
   If you click the style in the preview window, you can see what the button looks like in a browser.

6. **Leave the Button Text area blank because you are using an arrow instead of a text button.**
   If you click the style sample in the preview window, it does not reflect the text change. The changes appear in Design view after you insert the button.

7. **Click the Apply button to insert the button in the document immediately.**

8. **If you use a button that needed text you would choose any font style.**
   It doesn't matter which font you use since it is embedded in the Flash movie. The user doesn't have to have it on their system. I used Splash since it's the one I used for the Flash text.

9. **If you are using a button, select a size of text that will fit on the button.**

10. **Enter a null link of javascript:;.**

11. **Click in the Bg Color box and use the eyedropper to sample the light blue of the table background.**
    The background color is the color that shows through transparent areas of the Flash button.

12. **Click the Browse button for the Save As field and save in the Multimedia folder. Name the image flashbutton.swf.**
    The Get More Styles button takes you to the Macromedia Exchange site to download more styles.

13. **Click the Apply button to see the updated button in the document.**
    The advantage of clicking Apply first is that you keep the dialog box open and you can make alterations if needed.

14. **Click OK to close the dialog box.**

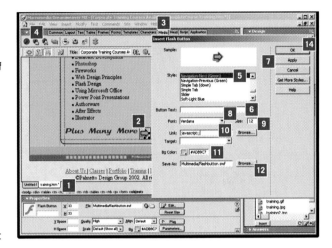

<NOTE>

Site root relative links are not recognized with Flash movies so use an absolute URL (www.palmettodesigngroup.com/media/ buttonname.swf). You can also save the .SWF file in the same folder as the .HTML file. To save the .SWF in the root folder with the .HTML file, click the Browse button to the right of the Save As field. Navigate to your root folder and save the file there.

<NOTE>

If you notice that the sample color shift or doesn't look accurate be sure that you have Snap to Web Safe color option turned off. To do this, click the color box in the Property inspector and click the right-pointing arrow and if you see a check mark next to Snap to Web Safe, click it to turn it off.

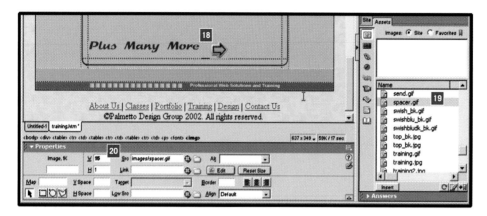

15. **Type** More Courses Available **for the alternate text and click OK.**

16. **Notice how the Property inspector has changed.**
There are no loop and autoplay options. Now there is an Edit button, which opens the Insert Flash Button dialog box.

17. **Preview in your browsers.**
Notice how the button lines up with the Flash text even though it appeared lower in Dreamweaver. But the arrow is too close to the text.

18. **Place your cursor in front of the arrow.**

19. **In the Assets panel, click on spacer.gif and the Insert button.**

20. **Change the Width of the spacer to 15 and press Enter/Return.**

21. **Preview your work again.**

» Session Review

Well, it's that time again. Time to see how much of this information has stuck in your head. Roll up your sleeves and let's get started.

1. What kind of tag is used for links? (See "Tutorial: Adding Links.")

2. How do you add an e-mail link? (See "Tutorial: Adding Links.")

3. Where can you look for additional help with .HTML code? (See "Tutorial: Adding Links.")

4. What is a rollover? (See "Tutorial: Adding Rollovers.")

5. Where do you find the Swap Image behavior? (See "Tutorial: Adding Links.")

6. How is an image map different from other images or links? (See "Tutorial: Adding an Image Map.")

7. Do you have to name the image map, or can you skip this step? (See "Tutorial: Adding an Image Map.")

8. Where do you find the code for the image map? (See "Tutorial: Adding an Image Map.")

9. What type of URL do you have to use for a Flash button? (See "Tutorial: Adding a Flash Button.")

10. How can you preview a Flash button? (See "Tutorial: Adding a Flash Button.")

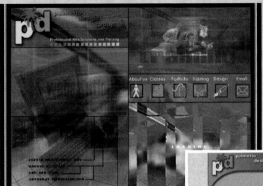

Corporate Training

 Palmetto Design Group will develop a specialized course to fit your unique needs. Training your development team and setting up a usable workflow can cut your production costs considerably.

Certified Instructors

At Palmetto Design Group we employ only certified instructors to train your development team. Our instructors are Microsoft, Adobe, and Macromedia certified as well as numerous other certifications. The Instructor link to the left contains the bios of our current instructors.

Popular Courses

We train in all the most popular courses but you can also request one you don't see and we'll do our best to accommodate you. The courses include:

- Dreamweaver
- Database Development
- Photoshop
- Fireworks
- Web Design Principles
- Flash Design
- Using Microsoft Office
- Power Point Presentations
- Authorware
- After Effects
- Illustrator

Plus Many More

Part III:
Automating the
Design Process

Using Cascading Style Sheets (CSS)

Adding Some Style

The use of cascading style sheets (CSS) is on the rise. Dreamweaver MX includes a lot of new and improved CSS features that are compatible with the World Wide Web Consortium (W3C) standards.

Style sheets are formatting rules that control the appearance of content in a Web page. Style sheets are a collection of formatting rules — known as styles — that control the appearance of content in a Web page. These style rules are governed by a cascading hierarchy that uses the principles of inheritance, specificity, and importance to determine which rule applies when a conflicting rule exists.There are three ways to implement CSS styles. One is *inline,* which is placed directly in the code of your Web page. This is similar to *embedded,* which embeds the entire style sheet into an individual document. Neither of these methods is recommended, however. They increase the download time because of all the extra code written to the file. They also defeat the ease of updating your styles site-wide.

External style sheets are the way to go for the most part. With this method, you actually link your page or template to the CSS and it becomes accessible to the entire site. Making modifications is as easy as changing one file. Some of the benefits include maintaining a consistent look across all pages that link to the style sheet, easily updating the look of all pages by changing the values in one file, and making your pages much smaller and quicker to download, because all of the style information is in one file.

TOOLS YOU'LL USE
CSS Styles panel, Tag Selector, Quick Tag Editor, Property inspector

MATERIALS NEEDED
Session 6 files from the CD-ROM added to your CompleteCourse root folder if you didn't do the previous tutorial.

Optional but important: Any browser your target audience might be using. The minimum testing should be done with Netscape 4 (which causes the most problems) and Internet Explorer.

TIME REQUIRED
90 minutes

Tutorial
» Redefining the BODY Tag

In this first tutorial, you redefine the `<body>` tag using an external style CSS. You can do this using the Modify→Page Properties dialog box but the purpose of using CSS is to remove the page formatting from the HTML and use styles instead for better control and easier updating.

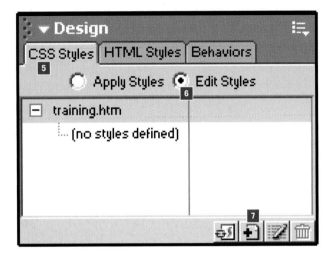

1. **Open the Site panel and double-click training.htm.**

2. **Highlight the first paragraph of text beginning with Palmetto.**
   You are removing the font tags that you added in Session 5. It wouldn't hurt to leave them but your goal is to have your site as uncluttered as possible, plus the extra code just adds to the page's total weight.

<NOTE>
Look at the code before going to the next step. Notice the `<p>` tag, and then font color, size, and face preceding the image and the paragraph text.

3. **Click Text→HTML Styles and then click Clear Paragraph Style.**
   Look at the code again and notice that all that is left are the opening and closing paragraph tags. Now you set the body style declarations.

4. **Click the expander arrow of the Design panel group.**

5. **Click the CSS Styles panel tab to make it the active panel.**

6. **Click the Edit Styles radio button.**

7. **Click the Add (+) button.**
   The New CSS Style dialog box opens.

8. **Click the Redefine HTML Tag radio button.**

<NOTE>
An HTML tag is a selector, but the redefine HTML label tells you that you are going to change the default properties of the HTML tag you select.

9. **Choose body from the Tag drop-down menu.**

10. **Click (New Style Sheet File) in the Define In box.**

11. **Click OK.**
    The Save Style Sheet File As dialog box opens.

12. **Navigate to your CompleteCourse root and add a new folder called stylesheets. Name the style sheet pdg and save it in the stylesheets folder.**
    The CSS Style Definition for body in pdg.css dialog box opens.

CSS Rules

Each rule has two parts, a selector and the declaration. The selector is most often an HTML element such as `<H1>`, `<body>`, `<p>` and so on. The declaration is a combination of properties and values. A declaration is always formatted as a property followed by a colon, a value, and then a semicolon. Each

style sheet is made up of a series of rules. You don't need to know how to actually write the rules (although understanding how they work is a good idea), because DW has a great interface that lets you choose the properties and values you want. DW writes all the code for you.

13. **Set the following properties for the Type category:**
    Font: Verdana, Arial, Helvetica, sans-serif
    Size: 12 pixels
    Color: #333333
    Leave the default settings for everything else.

14. **Click the Background category.**

15. **Click in the Background Color box and use the eyedropper to sample the blue from the background in the document.**
    I like to use a background color with a background image in case someone has a slow connection and the background image doesn't appear right away. That way they at least see a color that complements the page while they wait for it all to load.

16. **Click the Browse button for the Background Image and navigate to the Backgrounds folder. Select swishblu_bk.gif and click OK.**
    Leave all the other fields blank. This is all you set for the `<body>` tag.

17. **Click OK to close the dialog box.**

18. **Look at the CSS Styles panel.**
    Notice the pdg.css style has been added and the new rule for `<body>` is there as well.

19. **Look at your document.**
    Notice how all of the body text is now in Verdana. You did not have to do anything to apply this style. It was applied automatically because of the selector you redefined, in this case, the `<body>` tag.

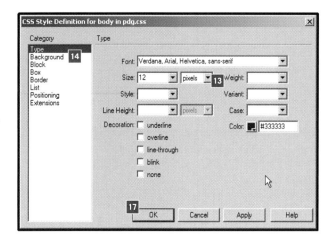

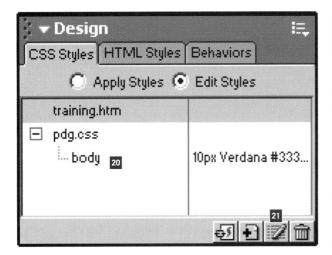

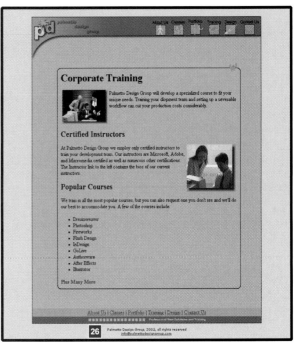

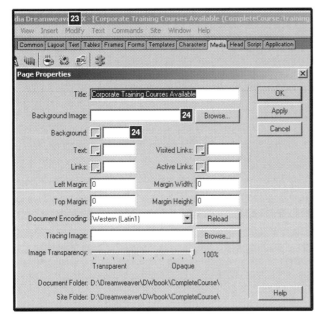

<NOTE>

Did you notice that the font size still didn't change? The `<body>` tag style did in fact set the Font attribute but it isn't controlling the paragraph and heading tags. That's why the font didn't change. Look at the link text at the bottom of the document; the text inside the body and not inside the table is Verdana and 10px. You defined the `<body>` tag, not the `<p>` or `<td>` tags (more on this later).

20. **In the CSS Styles panel, click the body definition to select it.**

21. **Click the Edit Style Sheet button to open the CSS Style Definition for body in pdg.css dialog box.**

22. **Change the Size from 12 to 10 and click OK.**
That's all there is to editing a style. You can also edit a style by double-clicking the name in the CSS Styles panel to open the CSS Style Definition dialog box.

23. **Click Modify→Page Properties.**

24. **Delete the Background Image and the Background color.**
You are deleting these because they are now defined in the CSS styles. Plus they need to be deleted so you can test the results of setting these values using CSS in a browser test instead of using the page properties.

25. **Test your page in Internet Explorer 5 and in Netscape 6.**
It renders as expected. The text in the body (copyright and e-mail address) has been changed to 10 pixels and the background is visible.

26. **Test the page in Netscape 4X.**
The background isn't visible because of the way Netscape 4 wants to access the background image. You learn how to fix that problem later in this session.

27. **Save your page.**

Tutorial
» Embedding a Style Sheet

In this tutorial you use an embedded style to fix the Netscape 4 problem of recognizing the background image.

1. **Open the training.htm file if you've closed it.**

2. **Open the CSS Styles panel.**

3. **Click training.htm to select it.**

4. **Using the Edit Style mode, click the Add (+) button.**

5. **Click the Redefine HTML Tag radio button in the New CSS Style dialog box.**

6. **Select or type** body.

7. **Click the radio button to select This Document Only.**
   This option embeds the declaration into the head of this document.

8. **Click OK.**

9. **Click the Background category to make it active.**

10. **Click the Browse button for the background image and navigate to the Backgrounds folder. Select the swishblu_bk.gif image and click OK.**
    The path to the image is now relative to the document, which will satisfy Netscape 4X.

11. **Click OK and save the document.**

12. **View the results in both browsers.**

13. **If you can't see the background in Netscape 4, look at the code in the head of the document.**
    It should look like this:

```
<link href="Stylesheets/pdg.css"
 rel="stylesheet" type="text/css">
<style type="text/css">
<!-
body {
 background-image:
 url(backgrounds/swishblu_bk.gif);
}
->
</style>
```

The link needs to precede the style type. If it doesn't, change to Code View, highlight the code, and drag it on top as seen here. Test again, and it works.

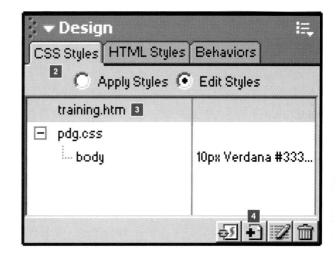

<NOTE>

This is just one reason why knowing a little bit of coding helps. If you didn't know what to look for you wouldn't know how to fix it. Dreamweaver is great but it sometimes puts things in the wrong place.

Tutorial
» Grouping Selector Tags

In this tutorial you group the paragraph tag (<p>) and the table cell tag (<td>) in order to define the text that is contained inside the table. You re-declare the text properties.

1. **Click the pdg.css style sheet in the CSS Styles panel to select it.**

2. **Click the New CSS Style icon.**

3. **Click the Use CSS Selector radio button in the New CSS Style dialog box.**
   You are actually redefining a selector but in Dreamweaver you are only allowed to group selectors using the Use CSS Selector option, not the Redefine HTML option.

4. **In the Selector field, type** p, td **(p comma space td).**

5. **Click the radio button to Define In: pdg.css.**
   If you had more than one style sheet and the proper one wasn't listed by default, you'd select the one you wanted from the drop-down menu.

6. **Click OK.**

7. **Set the following properties for the Type category:**
   Font: Verdana, Arial, Helvetica, sans-serif
   Size: 10px
   Color: #333333
   Leave the default settings for everything else.

8. **Click OK.**

9. **Save your page and then view it in both of the browsers.**
   It renders properly in Internet Explorer and Netscape 4X and above.

Tutorial

» Applying Custom Classes

So far you haven't applied any styles. In this tutorial you will define some custom classes and then apply them to different selectors.

1. **Open training.htm.**

2. **Open the CSS Styles panel.**

3. **Click pdg.css.**

4. **Click the plus sign to add a new style.**
   The paragraph tag has already been defined for font, size, and color. Now you are going to add a class that will be applied to the content paragraphs to add space around them.

5. **Click the Make Custom Style (Class) radio button.**

6. **Click the Define In radio button.**
   Because we only have one style sheet, the pdg.css will be shown by default.

7. **Type** .para **in the Name field.**

8. **Click OK.**

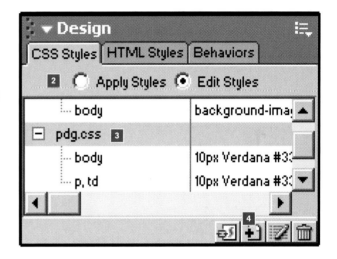

<NOTE>
Notice that the name begins with a period. Custom classes always begin with a period. They can't start with a number or include spaces and special characters.

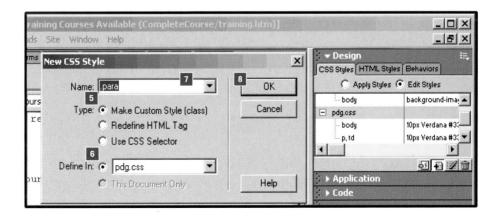

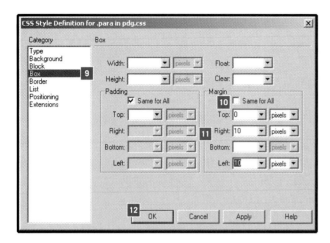

9. **Click the Box category to make it active.**

10. **In the Margin values, uncheck the Same for All check box by clicking it.**

11. **Set the following values:**
    Top: **0px**
    Right: **10px**
    Bottom: **blank**
    Left: **10px**

12. **Click OK.**

13. **Place your cursor inside the first paragraph and click.**
    You will now apply the new Custom Class of .para to the paragraph.

14. **In the CSS Styles panel, click the Apply Styles radio button.**
    The Apply Styles and the Edit Styles modes are new to Dreamweaver MX.

15. **Click para.**

16. **Repeat steps 13-15 for the remaining paragraphs.**
    You might notice that the Certified Instructors title is positioned incorrectly. Don't worry about it for now. It will be fixed in the next few steps.

< N O T E >

Notice how extra space is added around the paragraph. If you look closely, though, you will notice that there is not a 10px margin (which you defined in the box values of the .para style) around the pictures. That's because the picture is part of the paragraph and the 10px is added to the left side of the top image and to the right side of the second image.

Background Images and Netscape 4

The CSS specification states that background image URLs should be relative to where the style rule is defined. But Netscape 4X wants the URL relative to where the style is used. There are several ways to alleviate this problem.

You can use an absolute URL if you know what it is (www.whatever.com/backgrounds/bk.gif), but then you can't view it on your local machine.

You can also save your style sheets in the same folder as the HTML page. The simplest way, however, is to add another declaration for <body> in the head of the document, which sets only the URL attribute. This is what you do here.

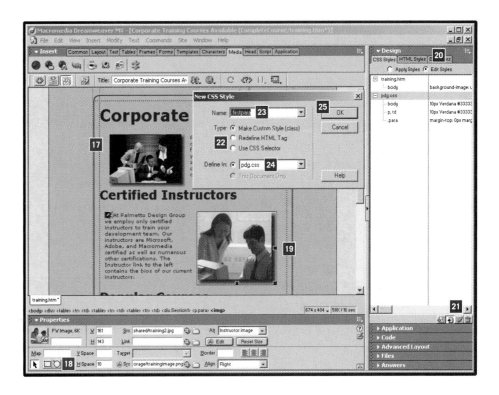

17. **Select the first image that is left aligned.**

18. **Change the H Space to** 10.
    This will move the text away from the edge of the picture a bit more and move the Certified Instructors title down.

19. **Select the second image and change the H Space to** 10 **as well.**

20. **In the CSS Styles panel, click the Edit Styles radio button.**

21. **Click the Add New Style button.**
    This time you will define a custom class that will add some space between the lines of text for the first paragraph only.

22. **Click Make Custom Style.**

23. **Type** .firstpara **in the name field.**

24. **Set Define In to pdg.css.**

25. **Click OK.**

Cascading

Netscape 4 can now find the image. Internet Explorer continues to work fine. All you did was add a declaration to the head of the document for Netscape. You didn't have to repeat the other declarations because Netscape can find the actual style sheet. Netscape, however, ignored the URL it didn't recognize and proceeded to the embedded style it did recognize instead. This is the cascade effect. If the same style is defined in both the internal and external style sheets, the definition closest to the affected tag wins. For the <body> tag, the embedded declaration is closer in hierarchy than the external style sheet.

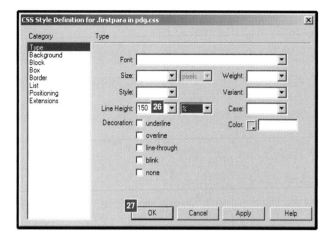

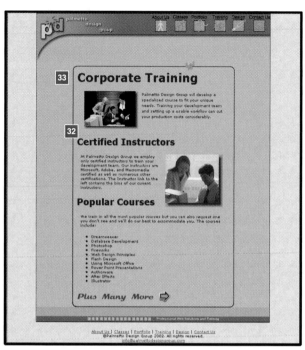

26. **In the Type category, type** 150 **in the Line Height field, and choose percent (%) from the drop-down menu.**

27. **Click OK to close the dialog box.**

28. **Select the entire first paragraph.**

29. **Press Ctrl-T/Command-T to access the Quick Tag Editor.**

30. **Type the word** span **(or select from the menu) and press Enter/Return to close the Quick Tag Editor.**
    The opening and closing span tags are now added in front of and at the end of the selected text.

31. **Right-click/Ctrl-click the** <span> **tag in the Tag Selector and Set Class to** .firstpara.
    The first paragraph now has more space between each line and lines up nicely with the image.

32. **Click in front of the word Certified and add a line break (press Shift-Enter/Shift-Return).**

33. **Save your page and preview it in both browsers.**

< N O T E >

Now the style is defined. You can't, however, just apply it to the paragraph because it already has a style applied to it. What you will need to do is add a <span> tag that will wrap around the specific text that you have selected. Then the new style will be applied to that. This same method is how you add bold or change the format of one or several words in a sentence.

Tutorial
» Using Pseudo-Class Selectors

Pseudo-class selectors change the appearance of all hyperlinks using the `<a>` tag. In the CSS1 specification, the only pseudo-class selectors include `:visited`, `:link`, and `:active`. Notice that pseudo-classes begin with a colon. What makes pseudo-class selectors different is that they are dynamic. They can be used to add rollover effects without images in browsers that support them. You see in this tutorial that pseudo-class selectors work in Internet Explorer 5.5 and Netscape 6.2.

When defining more than one of the pseudo-class selectors, you need to do it in this order: `a:link`, `a:visited`, `a:hover`, `a:active`. Be sure to test your styles in all your target browsers. To test unvisited links you need to clear your link history (in IE 5 use Tools→Internet Options→General→Clear History and in NN4 use Edit→Preferences→Navigation→Clear History) and then refresh the browser page.

1. **Select the row of text links at the bottom of the document and cut it (Ctrl-X/⌘-X). You are going to move the text links into the medium blue table of your layout.**

<NOTE>
I thought it looked too busy at the bottom of the page and you have a perfectly good table just sitting there unused. Your code automatically moves when you cut it from the old location.

2. **Paste (Ctrl-V/⌘-V) into the medium blue table above the byline.**

3. **In the Property inspector, set the table's Horz setting to Center.**

4. **Place your cursor in the area where you cut the text and press Delete to remove the extra space.**

5. **In the CSS Styles panel, select pdg.css and click the Add (+) button to make a new style.**

6. **Click Use CSS Selector.**

7. **Click Define In, pdg.css.**

8. **Name the Selector a:link (type it or choose it from the drop-down menu).**

9. **Click OK.**

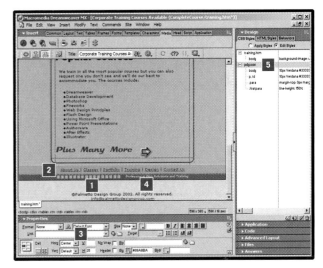

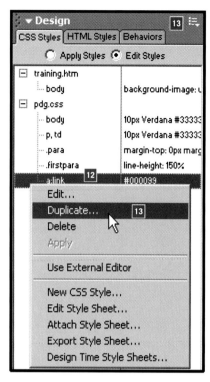

10. **In the Type category set the color to #000099.**
Because the font size is already 10px and the font style of Verdana is set, and I like both, nothing else has to be done. Inheritance will take care of the rest. But if you'd like your links to be a different size, font, and the like, you can change them.

11. **Click OK.**
This style will be applied to all links regardless of their location. There are times when you might have links on a page that need to be different colors to be visible. That can be accomplished by using contextual styles, which you will do later in this tutorial.

12. **In the CSS Styles panel, Edit Styles mode, select the a:link style you just made.**

13. **Click the panel option pop-up and click Duplicate.**
Alternatively you can right-click/Control-click the name and the same menu is available.

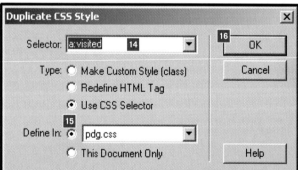

14. **In the Duplicate CSS Style dialog box, type or select** a:visited.

15. **Make sure that the Define In box lists pdg.css as the style sheet.**

16. **Click OK.**

17. **Double-click a:visited to edit it.**

18. **In the Type category, change the color to a lighter blue (use #0066FF).**

19. **Click OK.**

20. **Make a duplicate of a:visited (refer to step 13).**

21. **In the Duplicate CSS Style dialog box type or select** a:hover.

22. **Click OK.**

23. **Double-click a:hover to edit it.**

24. **Change the color to gold (#FFCC00).**

25. **Click OK.**

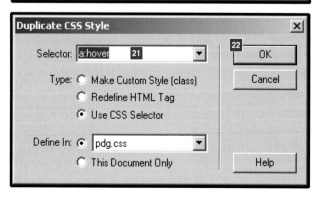

Tutorial
» Using Contextual Selectors

In this tutorial you set up a class that is used to designate a specific region to accept a style. This is beneficial if you want certain tags to have one style while the rest have another. Contextual selectors use rules that apply whenever the specific selector occurs within a container using a class style. For instance, the <p> tag or the <a> tag can only have one style applied, but by adding a contextual style you can format each paragraph or link differently.

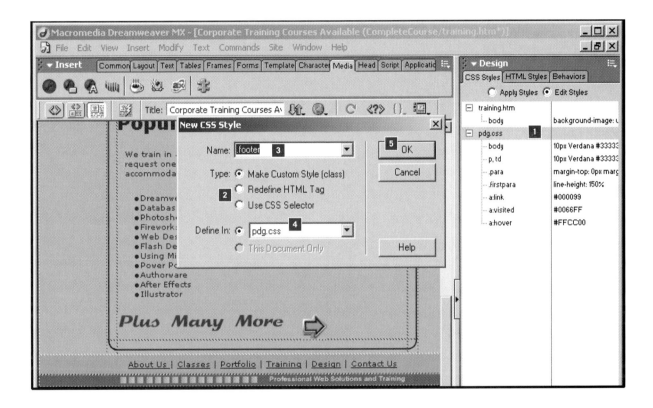

1. In the CSS Styles panel, click pdg.css and add a New Style.

2. Click the Make Custom Style radio button.

3. Enter .footer in the Name field.

4. Make sure that the pdg.css style sheet is selected.

5. Click OK.

6. In the Type category, select the Weight value and click Bold.

7. Click OK.

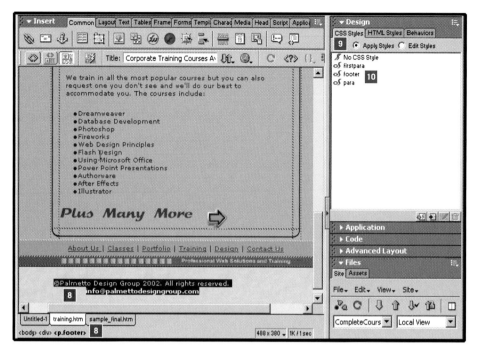

8. **Click in the copyright and e-mail area. Click the** $\langle p \rangle$ **tag in the Tag Selector.**

9. **In the CSS Styles Panel, click Apply Styles mode.**

10. **Click footer.**

11. **Notice the code,** `class="footer"`, **added to the** $\langle a \rangle$ **tag.** You just designated the footer area as a class.

12. **Save the file.**

13. **Click the Edit Styles radio button in the CSS Styles panel.**

14. **Add a new style.**

15. **Click the Use CSS Selector radio button.**

16. **Type** .footer a:link **into the Selector field.**

17. **Be sure Define In is set to the pdg.css style sheet.**

18. **Click OK.**

19. **In the Type category, click Decoration none.**

    This removes the underline from the e-mail address.

20. **In the Color field, type** #000099 **(a dark blue).**

21. **Set the Weight to Bold.**

22. **Click OK.**

23. **Add a New Style (be sure pdg.css is selected in the CSS Styles panel).**

    This setting won't affect the copyright line even though it is part of the footer because this contextual selector only affects the <a> tag.

24. **Click the Use CSS Selector radio button.**

25. **Type** .footer a:visited **into the Selector field.**

26. **Be sure Define In is set to the pdg.css style sheet.**

27. **Click OK.**

28. **In the Type category, click Decoration none.**

29. **In the Color field type** #0000FF **(a lighter shade of blue).**

30. **Click OK.**

31. **Add a new style.**

32. **Click the Use CSS Selector radio button.**

33. **Type** .footer a:hover **into the Selector field.**

34. **Be sure Define In is set to the pdg.css style sheet.**

35. **Click OK.**

36. **In the Type category, click Decoration underline.**

37. **In the Color field, type** #000099.

38. **Click OK.**

39. **Save the file and do a browser check.**

    The hover does not work in Netscape 4X but it does in Internet Explorer and Netscape 6. The footer is all blue instead of black and the e-mail link is bold, the only effect being an underline for the hover.

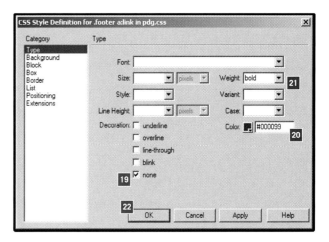

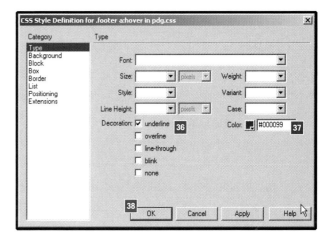

» Session Review

If you've never used CSS styles before then I'm sure your mind is probably boggled at this point. Go ahead and do your best with these questions. You may want to repeat this session a time or two until you get the hang of it.

1. When you redefine the `<body>` tag, can you change all the font attributes for the entire page? (See "Tutorial: Redefining the BODY Tag.")

2. How do you apply a redefined body style? (See "Tutorial: Redefining the BODY Tag.")

3. Name two ways to edit a style. (See "Tutorial: Redefining the BODY Tag.")

4. How can you get Netscape 4X to recognize a background image? (See "Tutorial: Embedding a Style Sheet.")

5. What happens if the same style is defined in both an internal and an external style sheet? (See "Tutorial: Embedding a Style Sheet.")

6. How do you define the text within a table? (See "Tutorial: Grouping Selector Tags.")

7. Can you add a style to just one word in a paragraph that already has a style applied? (See "Tutorial: Applying Custom Classes.")

8. Name the three pseudo-class selectors. (See "Tutorial: Using Pseudo-Class Selectors.")

9. Can you have links in different locations of the document with different styles applied to them? (See "Tutorial: Using Contextual Selectors.")

10. Which browser doesn't recognize hover? (See "Tutorial: Using Contextual Selectors.")

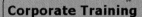

Corporate Training

 Palmetto Design Group will develop a specialized course to fit your unique needs. Training your development team and setting up a usable workflow can cut your production costs considerably.

Certified Instructors

At Palmetto Design Group we employ only certified instructors to train your development team. Our instructors are Microsoft, Adobe, and Macromedia certified as well as numerous other certifications. The Instructor link to the left contains the bios of our current instructors.

Popular Courses

We train in all the most popular courses but you can also request one you don't see and we'll do our best to accommodate you. The courses include:

- Dreamweaver
- Database Development
- Photoshop
- Fireworks
- Web Design Principles
- Flash Design
- Using Microsoft Office
- Power Point Presentations
- Authorware
- After Effects
- Illustrator

Plus Many More

Professional Web Solutions and Training

Session 8

Using Templates and Libraries

Design with Templates

Using templates in your site saves a lot of time and aggravation. By using a template, you can determine which elements should appear on each page and which elements can be edited. This assures the designer/developer that others adding content can't alter the design.

Another benefit of templates is that changes can be made directly to the template. Once it is saved, you can automatically update all the pages attached to the template. This is particularly important when a site swells to hundreds of pages.

Be sure to test any design in multiple browsers prior to making it into a template to assure that it is performing as you expect.

TOOLS YOU'LL USE
Assets panel, Library category, Templates category, CSS Styles panel

MATERIALS NEEDED
Session 7 files from the CD-ROM added to your CompleteCourse root folder if you didn't complete the previous tutorial

TIME REQUIRED
60 minutes

Tutorial

» Using an Existing Document as a Template

You use the training.htm file as a template for the rest of the site. The navigation, header, and footer are all in place. Now is the perfect time to make it into a template.

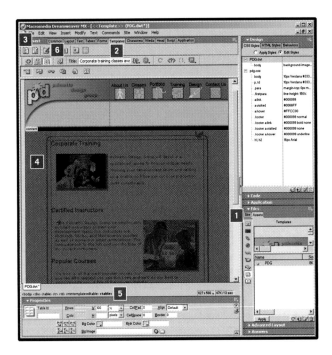

1. **Open the Site panel and double-click training.htm to open it.**

2. **Click the Templates category tab in the Insert Bar.**

3. **Click the Make Template icon and name the template PDG. Click on Save.**
   All regions of the document are locked by default except for the title. In order to use this template we need to set a region that is editable.

4. **Click just to the outside of the rounded table.**

5. **Select the** `<table>` **tag.**
   Be sure the selected table is the one that the rounded table is in.

6. **Click the Editable Region icon in the Insert Bar.**

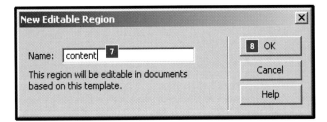

7. **Type** content **into the New Editable Region dialog box.**

8. **Click OK.**
   Notice an overlay over the table that is editable as well as a label that says content. This is the only part of this document that can be edited when the template is applied to documents in the site.

9. **Open the Assets panel.**

10. **Click the Templates icon.**
    You see a preview of the template in the preview pane.

11. **Save the template file.**

12. **If you get a message to update all files using the template, just click No since there are none yet.**

Tutorial
» Applying a Template

In this tutorial you apply the PDG template to the training.htm page and the rest of the site's pages as well.

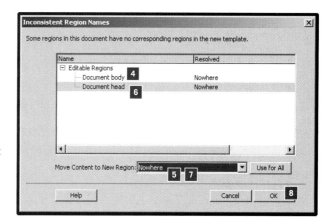

1. **Open training.htm again.**
   Your other open file was converted into the template file.

2. **In the Assets panel, click PDG to select the template.**

3. **Click Modify→Templates→Apply Template to Page, click PDG, and click Select.**
   The Inconsistent Region Names dialog box opens. This happens when a document has never had a template applied before or if it has another template applied with different regions. In this case your document has content that it doesn't know what to do with.

4. **Click Document body.**

5. **Click Nowhere in the Move Content to New Region drop-down menu.**
   You choose Nowhere because the body content is already in the template you are applying. If you put it anywhere else, there would be two copies of the page.

6. **Click Document head.**

7. **Click Nowhere in the Move Content to New Region drop-down menu.**

8. **Click OK.**

9. **Notice the top-right corner of the document window.**
   A template marker is added to the entire document. Yellow indicates it is not editable. Also notice the blue marker titled content. This one is editable. Move your cursor over the icons; you get the no symbol. But if you place your cursor in the content area you can change the content.

10. **Save the file.**

11. **In the Site panel, double-click about.htm.**

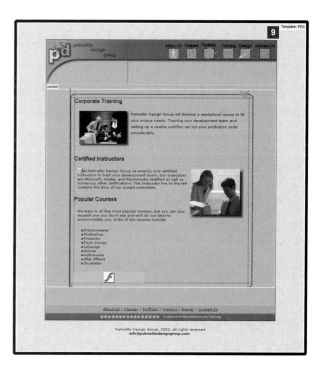

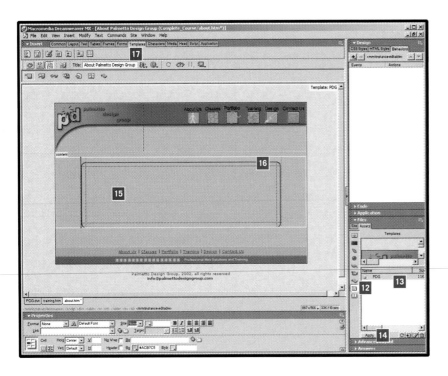

12. **In the Assets panel, click the Template icon.**

13. **Select the PDG template.**

14. **Click Apply.**
    No dialog box opens this time because you have no content to deal with.

15. **Highlight the content in the center table and delete it.**

16. **Delete the little green icon on top of the table.**

17. **Type the following page title:** About Palmetto Design Group.
    The title area is the only area other than the content area that is not locked. Adding a title right away is a good habit to get into. It's very easy to forget and there is nothing worse than seeing Untitled Document in the Browser title bar and in the Favorites list.

18. **Repeat steps 11-17 for the other main site pages using these titles:**
    classes.htm: **Online graphic design classes**
    portfolio.htm: **Professional Web site design portfolio**
    design.htm: **Brochures, illustration, magazines and print designs**

19. **Save all the files.**

< N O T E >
Getting some of your main keywords into your title is a good idea. Some of the search engines use the title text to help index your content.

Tutorial
» Editing a Template

There are a few keywords used in the page titles that aren't in our Meta keywords. You add a few to the template. Once you are done you can see how the change is done automatically to the entire page you applied the template to.

1. **In the Assets panel, double-click the PDG template to open it.**

2. **In either Split view or Code view, locate the Meta keywords in the head of the document.**
   Although this part of the document is locked, you can edit directly into the code.

3. **Highlight the words: Flash animation, animation,**

4. **Press Ctrl-X/⌘-X to cut the selection.**

5. **Place your cursor in front of the words "information design" and paste (Ctrl-V/⌘-V) the selection.**
   Be sure there is a space after the comma.

6. **At the beginning of the keywords, add:** Online graphic design classes, online classes.

```
<!DOCTYPE HTML PUBLIC "-//W3C//DTD HTML 4.01 Transitional//EN">
<html>
<head>
<!-- TemplateBeginEditable name="doctitle" -->
<title>Corporate training classes available</title>
<!-- TemplateEndEditable -->
<meta http-equiv="[2]ntent-Type" content="text/html; charset=iso-8859-1">
<meta name="keywords" conten[6] Online graphic design classes, online classes, business, business consultant,
  creation, designers, developer, development, ebusiness, e-business, graphic design, Flash animation, animati[5] information design,
  interactive design, internet, multimedia, website, webpage, corporate training, Dreamweaver, Fireworks, Flash, training, classes">
<meta name="description" content="Headquartered in Florida, Palmetto Design Group is a leading web solution developer specializing
in Ebusiness, Web Design and Corporate training">
<link href="../Stylesheets/pdg.css" rel="stylesheet" type="text/css">
<style type="text/css">
```

7. **Save the template (File→Save).**
   The Update Template Files dialog box opens with a listing of all the documents that are using the PDG template.

8. **Click Update to apply the changes to all the pages.**
   The Update Pages dialog box opens and reports which files were updated, including how many were examined and how many were updated. If for any reason files can't be updated you are told so in this dialog box.

9. **Click the Close button to close the Update Pages dialog box.**

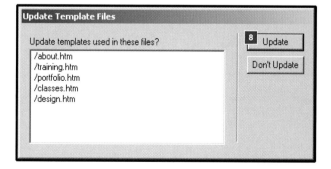

> 141

Tutorial
» Detaching a Template

You want to edit pages in a site separately from the rest of the site. For instance, you may want to make changes to one page that don't conform to the template. To do this you need to detach the template from the page. In this tutorial you detach the template because you are going to make a few library elements from some of the content. You then attach the template again.

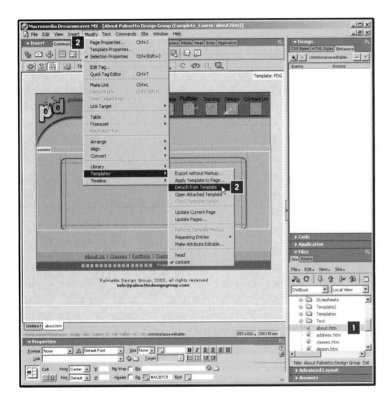

1. **Double-click the about.htm file in the Site panel to open it.**

2. **Click Modify→Templates→Detach From Template.**
   That's all there is to it. If you want your page to remain without the template, you should save now. (You don't, so don't save the page.) If you close and save this page before completing the next tutorial, you need to apply the template again.

<N O T E>
When a page is detached from the template, it no longer updates when a change is made to any of the un-editable areas of the document. You can even make design changes and make a new template if you want to. Many sites have more than one template.

Tutorial

» Making a Library Item

This tutorial shows you how to make three library items. Library items can be added to individual pages and updated just as easily as templates. Library items contain the necessary code with them so you can insert, for example, a table with specific formatting with the click of your mouse.

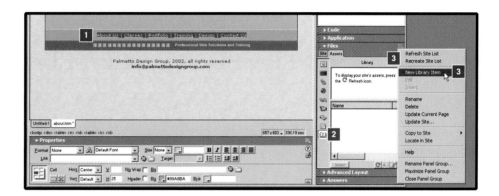

1. **Select the text navigation in the PDG.dwt template document.**

2. **Click the Library icon in the Assets panel.**

3. **Click the Options pop-up menu and click New Library Item.**
   A warning dialog box opens that says, "This selection may not look the same when placed in other documents because the Style Sheet information is not copied with it." That's okay; you can edit it later. The links do remain with the library item.

4. **Click OK.**
   In the Assets panel you see a preview of the new library item.

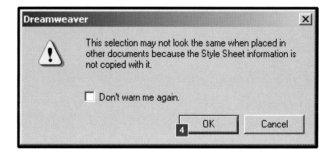

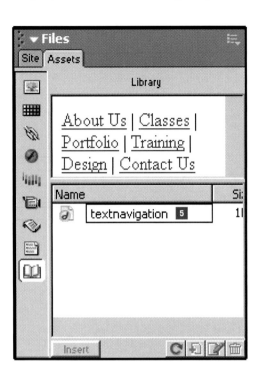

5. **Type** textnavigation **for the name of the item and press Enter/Return.**
   The new library item is now available for use.

6. **Highlight the copyright and e-mail address in the about.htm document.**

7. **Click the Options pop-up menu and click New Library Item.**

8. **Name it** copyright **and press Enter/Return.**
   You now have two library items in the library of this site.

9. **Close the about.htm file without saving it.**
   This way, the template is still attached.

10. **In the Site panel, click Site→Recreate Site Cache to see the library items added to the Site panel.**

< N O T E >
Notice that there are two new folders added that you didn't make. One is templates, the other is library. These folders are automatically generated by Dreamweaver. You don't upload these to your server; they are strictly internal folders for Dreamweaver's use.

Tutorial
» Inserting Library Items

This tutorial shows you how to add the text navigation and the copyright library items to the index page of the site.

1. **Double-click the index.htm file in the Site panel to open it.**

2. **Place your cursor below the layout.**

3. **Click the Library icon in the Assets panel.**

4. **Click textnavigation.**

5. **Click the Insert button.**

6. **Add a paragraph space (Enter/Return) after the navigation.**

7. **Click the copyright library item.**

8. **Click the Insert button.**

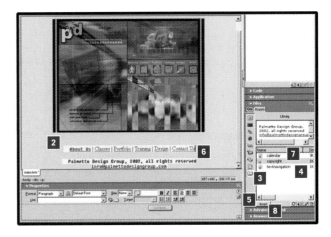

<NOTE>

That's all there is to inserting library items in a document. The items are highlighted with yellow to indicate they are library items. Also notice the code — it is highlighted as well. You can't edit the library item in an individual document unless you detach it first. Detaching it does not allow the items to be updated if the original library item is updated or changed.

Library Item Facts

You can also copy a library item to another site. Select the library item in the Assets panel and click the Options pop-up menu. Click Copy to Site and choose the site you want to copy it to. This works great for library items such as the ones you made, because they are text-only. But if you make a library item that contains images, the images don't move with the library. You'll need to copy the images or the folder with the images and paste into the new site.

Be sure you keep the same structure so the links work. A library item is actually linking to the images in your site. If you want to copy a library item to another site you can do that and then separately place the images in a folder into the new site. Be sure, though, that the folder has the same name as the original so the links work properly.

Tutorial
» Editing Library Items

You can edit any library item by double-clicking it in the Assets panel. Once you are done you are prompted to save the file and update any uses of the item. In this tutorial you make a separate style sheet for each of the library items you added to the home page.

1. Open the index.htm page and double-click the textnavigation library item in the Assets panel.

2. Click the expander arrow in the Design group.

3. Make the CSS Styles panel active.

4. Select the navigation text.

5. Add a new style in the CSS Styles panel.

6. **In the New CSS Style dialog box, click Make Custom Style.**

7. **Name the style .nav.**

8. **Click Define In (New Style Sheet File).**

9. **Click OK.**

10. **Name the style sheet** homepage, **navigate to the Stylesheet folder, and save.**

11. **In the Type category select the font Verdana, Arial, Helvetica, sans-serif.**

12. **Choose a size of 10.**

13. **Click OK.**

14. **Click Apply Styles mode in the CSS Styles panel.**

15. **Click .nav.**

16. **Save the library item.**

17. **If prompted to update, click the Update button.**

18. **Add the .nav style to the copyright item.**
    You don't have to make a new style for the copyright lines. You can just highlight it and apply the .nav style from the CSS Styles panel as you did in step 15.

19. **Refer to Session 7 to add the pseudo-link styles if you'd like.**

20. **Click Modify→Page Properties.**
    The index.htm page doesn't have the background image added to it.

21. **Click the Browse button for the Background Image.**
    Navigate to the Backgrounds folder and select swishblu_bk.gif.

22. **Click OK to close the dialog box.**

23. **Save the file and preview your work in a browser.**

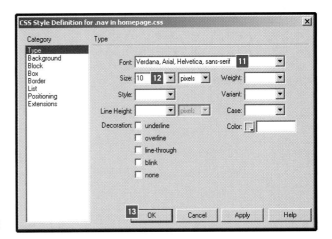

» Session Review

This session should have been pretty easy for you. But just in case, go ahead and take this little test.

1. What is editable in a new template by default? (See "Tutorial: Using an Existing Document as a Template.")

2. Does a document have to have content in it to have a template applied to it? (See "Tutorial: Applying a Template.")

3. How do you edit a document that has a template attached to it? (See "Tutorial: Editing a Template.")

4. Why would you want to detach a template from a document? (See "Tutorial: Detaching a Template.")

5. Where are library items stored? (See "Tutorial: Making a Library Item.")

6. Why are library items useful? (See "Tutorial: Making a Library Item.")

7. Once you insert a library item, how do you edit it? (See "Tutorial: Editing a Library Item.")

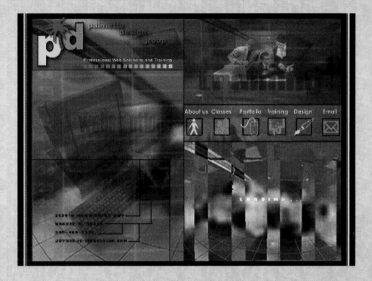

About Us | Classes | Portfolio | **Training** | Design | Contact Us

Palmetto Design Group, 2002, all rights reserved
info@palmettodesigngroup.com

Part IV:
Adding Interactivity

Adding Dimension with Layers

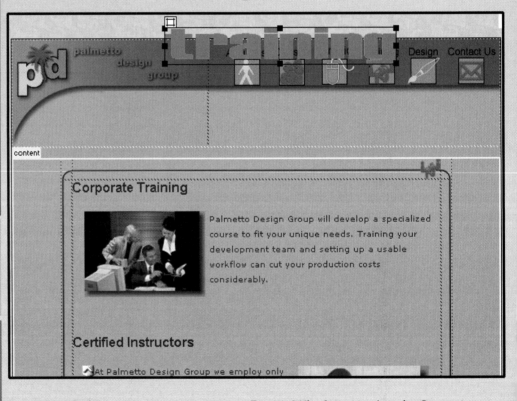

The Power of Layers

Layers are a very flexible element you can add to your Web pages. You can drag them, you can make them invisible, and you can animate them along a timeline. Layers can be positioned where you want them. You can place content in a layer above content in a table. They are very powerful tools.

In this session you begin using layers. Because they are so closely tied to using behaviors, timelines, and even forms, you won't do all the layer exercises for the Palmetto Design Group site in this session. You learn how to draw a layer and some of the basics, but actually using all the features of layers carries over into the next few sessions as well.

There are two types of layer formats: CSS and Netscape. CSS layers allow you to use layers using the <div> and the <span> tags. This markup allows your layers to be usable in all version 4 and later browsers. The Netscape tags <layer> and <ilayer> are only good for Netscape. For this reason, Dreamweaver uses the CSS tags by default.

Because older browsers don't support layers, you may want to convert your layers into tables if you know that users are using older browsers. In order to successfully convert layers into tables, you just need to be sure that the layers don't overlap. Of course Dreamweaver provides a "Prevents Overlap" option if you need to use it.

TOOLS YOU'LL USE
Draw Layer tool, Assets panel, and Templates category

MATERIALS NEEDED
Session 8 files from the CD-ROM added to your CompleteCourse root
folder if you didn't complete the previous tutorial

TIME REQUIRED
70 minutes

Tutorial
» Layer Basics

This tutorial helps you discover the basics of using layers. A new layout is used just to look at the features of layers here. In the next tutorial, you add a layer with content to the Palmetto Design Group Web site.

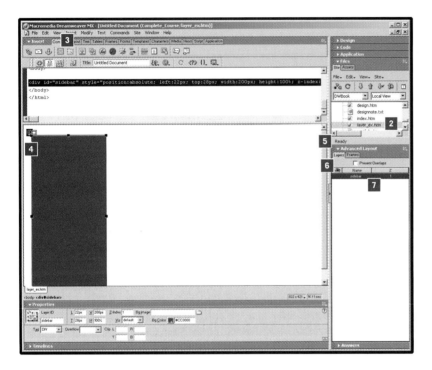

1. **Right-click/Control-click the root name of your site in the Site panel and click New File.**

2. **Name the file layer_ex.htm and double-click it to open it.**

3. **Click the Draw Layer icon from the Common category of the Insert Bar.**

4. **Drag anywhere on the document to draw a layer; size doesn't matter for now.**
   Notice the yellow anchor added just above the layer.

<NOTE>
If you can't see the anchor, click View➔Visual Aids➔Invisible Elements. You can click an anchor to select the element it represents. You can also select the layer by clicking it, or by selecting it in the Layers panel.

5. **Click the expander arrow of the Advanced Layout panel group.**

6. **Click the Layers tab to make it the active panel.**
   Notice the default name of your layer—layer1. It's very important to give your layer a distinctive name. It becomes important when you want to add a behavior to a layer. You'll do this in another session.

7. **In the Layers panel, double-click the name Layer1 and type sidebar for the name.**

8. **Look at the Property inspector. Locate Layer ID in the left corner; the new name is also present here.**

   You can change the layer name either in the Layers panel or in the Property inspector. Notice the other controls available in the Property inspector. You use some of these next.

9. **Highlight the W (width) field and type** 200px.

10. **Type** 100% **for the H (height) field.**

11. **Click the color box for the Bg Color and click a red.**

12. **In the L (left) field, type** 0px.

< N O T E >

This places the layer to the left of the browser window. You can control positioning of the left and top easily since they are the same no matter what size the browser window is. It's much more challenging to position layers based on the right side or bottom since they vary greatly.

13. **Type** 0px **for the T (top) field to place the layer at the absolute top.**

14. **Preview in at least Netscape 4X and Internet Explorer.**

< N O T E >

Notice how the layer is positioned to the very top and the extreme left. If this were a table it would have a default border around the top and left edge. You did not change the border to 0 in the Page Properties. But the layer positioning is not affected by the default border of the browser. Are you beginning to see some of the power and flexibility you have with layers?

Layer Basics

Layers are considered to be real content. You can set the height and width in pixels and percentage values. Layers are compatible with version 5 and above browsers. If you need to design for older browsers than this, your layers can be converted into tables as long as you don't have any overlapping layers.

15. **Save the file but leave it open for the next tutorial.**

Tutorial
» Using Layers for Layout

In this tutorial you continue with the layer basics but add two more layers that define all the areas of a page layout.

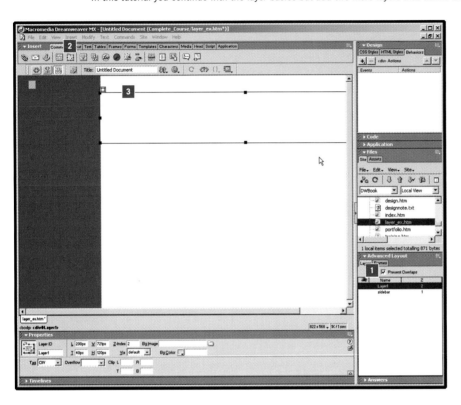

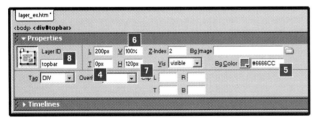

1. **Check the Prevents Overlaps option in the Layers panel.**

2. **Click the Draw Layer icon.**

3. **Draw a layer any size.**
   Notice you can't draw over the other layer because the Prevents Overlap option is turned on.

4. **Type** 0px **into the T (top) field and set the visibility to visible.**

5. **Click the color box for Bg Color and choose a blue.**
   The colors we are using are for demonstration only to easily distinguish the separate layers when drawn and viewed in a browser.

6. **Type** 100% **for the Width.**

7. **Type** 120px **for the Height.**

8. **In the Layer ID field or the Layers panel, name this layer** topbar.

9. **Preview your efforts in different browsers.**

<**N O T E**>
When viewed in Internet Explorer 5.5 and Netscape 6.2, the layers perform as expected. The sidebar expands to the height of the browser window and the top bar expands to the width of the browser. But in Netscape 4.7 the top bar does not expand to fill the entire width. This is why you need to check various browsers. If you have Web stats available to you and you can determine that your audience isn't using Netscape 4.7, you can disregard this behavior. Otherwise you have to use a set width for the top bar to assure that it looks the way you want it to.

10. **Draw another layer in the center.**

11. **Name this layer** content.

12. **Set the Width to** 100%, **the Height to** 100%, **and the visibility to visible.**

13. **Click the Bg Color box and choose a green.**

14. **View your work in different browsers.**

<**N O T E**>
Netscape 6.2 and Internet Explorer 5.5 are the same, but notice that the red sidebar doesn't expand all the way down. Netscape 4.7 almost gets it right. There is a border on the right side that the top bar and content layers don't fill up. These can be minor issues if you design for them. For instance, if the content of the layer is transparent or the same color as the page background, the areas that don't expand to fill the browser window won't be noticeable.

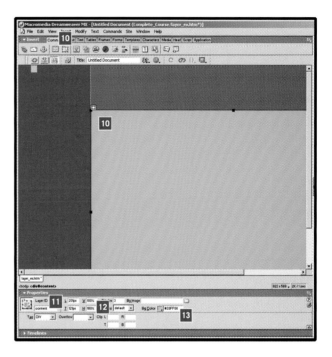

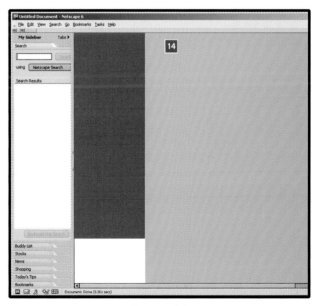

Netscape 6.2

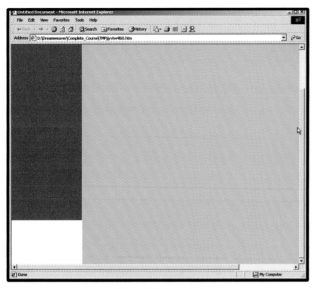

Internet Explorer 5.5

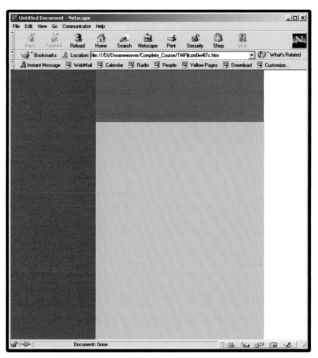

Netscape 4.7

Layer Facts

You use some of these layer facts in this session and in future sessions but this serves as a quick reference.

Positioning: You have dealt with the left and top or the x- and y-axis so far in your layouts. But layers introduce the z-axis. The z-axis (see the Property inspector) determines the positioning of the layer in terms of stacking order. Position 1 is the bottom. The higher the number, the closer it is to the top. Layers can share the same z-axis but this only makes sense if they don't overlap each other.

Layers and tables: A table can be placed in a layer but a layer can't be placed or nested inside a table.

Visibility: You can set a layer to be visible or hidden. If you want it to be visible, be sure to actually set it to visible. Don't rely on default.

Nested layers: Layers can be nested inside of layers. The main layer is the parent and the nested layer is the child. The child inherits some of the values of the parent, such as visibility and alignment, unless you change the child's properties.

The Overflow and Clip properties work properly in Internet Explorer only. You can clip portions of an image using Clip properties, and you can determine how to handle content that doesn't fit in the layer with the Overflow property, such as scrolling.

Tutorial
» Adding a Layer to the Template

In this tutorial you add a layer for a graphic you animate in Session 10. You also learn how to resize layers.

1. **In the Assets panel, click the Template icon.**

2. **Double-click PDG to open it.**
   Because the layer you are going to add is used on all the main pages, you add it to the template. Plus it is going in an uneditable area so it has to be added to the template. It remains blank in the template so if it weren't used on a page, no one would see it anyway.

3. **Click the Draw Layer icon.**
   Here, you use the Draw Layer icon for a very specific reason. When you use the Insert Layer icon, Dreamweaver does, at times, insert the code wherever your icon is instead of in the beginning of the ⟨body⟩ tag.

4. **Draw a layer at the top of the document.**

5. **Click the white handle to select the layer.**

6. **In the Property inspector name the layer** title.
   You could set the width and height if you knew the dimensions but you change this later when you learn to resize a layer manually.

7. **Be sure the layer is selected and click the Templates category in the Insert Bar.**

8. **Click the Editable Region icon.**

9. **Enter** title **for the Region name.**

10. **Click OK.**

11. **Click File→Save.**

12. **Click the Update button, and then click Close when the results dialog box opens.**

13. **Close the template file.**

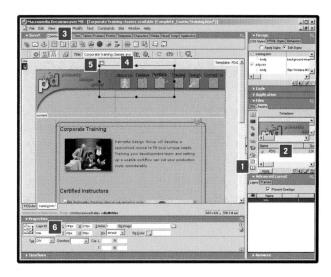

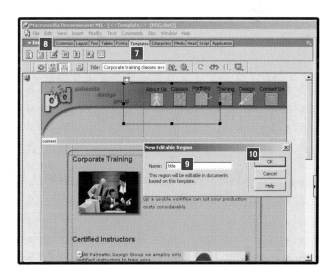

Tutorial
» Adding Content to a Layer in a Document

In this tutorial, you add the title text to the layer you just added in the template. You see how you can manipulate this layer in the document since it is an editable area.

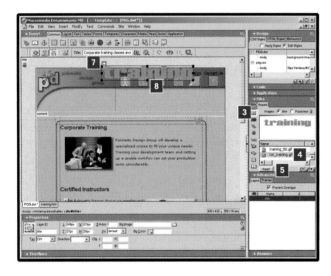

1. **Double-click the training.htm file to open it.**

2. **Place your cursor inside the title layer and click.**

3. **Click the Images icon in the Assets panel.**

4. **Click txt_training.gif.**

5. **Click the Insert button.**

6. **Type** Corporate Training **in the Alternate text field and click OK.**
   Notice how the layer expanded to fit the content. The width is also reflected in the Property inspector. The same would happen for the height if the image were taller than our layer.

7. **Select the layer in the Layers panel or click the white handle.**

8. **Place your cursor over the bottom center square of the layer and drag up to resize the height.**
   The layer snaps to the height of the image if you drag up all the way to the image. You can even drag into the image and the height snaps to the correct size.

9. **Set the Top to** −100px **in the Property inspector.**
   This puts the layer 100px above the table. At this point the layer isn't visible in Dreamweaver either. The only way to select it is to click the invisible icon or the layers name in the Layers panel.

10. **Set the Left alignment to** 270px.

11. **Set the visibility to** visible.
    Don't worry that you can't see anything. This is all you do with this layer right now. In Session 10, you animate the layer to come down and fall into place above the rounded table.

12. **Save the file and close it.**

Tutorial
» Nesting Layers

This is a short tutorial to demonstrate nesting layers. There may be times when you want to put a layer inside a layer to suit your design, but it can be unpredictable in browsers. Just be sure to check any browser your target audience is using.

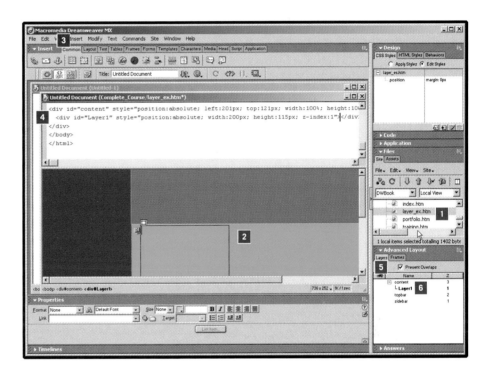

1. **Double-click the layer_ex.htm file you were practicing on earlier.**
   If you didn't save it, that's okay. There is a copy in the Session9 final folder.

2. **Click inside the content layer.**

3. **Click Insert→Layer.**
   If you were to simply draw the layer with the Draw Layer tool, the layer would be placed on top, not inside, the content layer.

4. **Look at the code in Split view.**
   Notice the <div id="content"... code. Just below it and indented is <div id="Layer1".

5. **Look in the Layers panel.**
   Notice that Layer1 is connected to the content layer and indented.

6. **Double-click the Layer1 name in the Layers panel and type** image.
   This layer could be used for different images in a layout.

<NOTE>
Use nested layers with caution. Although nested layers or child layers inherit properties from the parent, they don't always work properly in Netscape 4X browsers. Be sure to test in Netscape 4X if it's a browser your visitors use. You can compensate by setting the values you want to the nested layer and not relying on inheritance.

» Session Review

In this session you learned how to add layers that could be used for a layout instead of tables. In the process you learned a lot of layer basics such as sizing and positioning. You also nested a layer inside of the content layer. In the training.htm page you added a layer with content. This layer is not seen in the final file because you placed it above the page content. It was lowered for the illustration. Well, it's that time again. Time to see how much of the layer information stuck. If you get most of the answers correct you are ready to move on to the next session, which builds on this session.

1. What are the two types of layers available in Dreamweaver? (See "The Power of Layers.")

2. Where are the two places you can name your layers? (See "Tutorial: Layer Basics.")

3. Can layers be placed inside of tables? (See "Sidebar: Layer Facts.")

4. What layer properties do not work in Netscape 4X? (See "Sidebar: Layer Facts.")

5. Do any of the browsers tested support 100% values for layers perfectly? (See "Tutorial: Using Layers for Layout.")

6. Can you make a layer added to a locked portion of a template editable? (See "Tutorial: Adding a Layer to the Template.")

7. Is a layer added to a template flexible in documents using the template? (See "Tutorial: Adding a Layer to the Template.")

8. What happens if the content you add to a layer is larger than the layer? (See "Tutorial: Adding Content to a Layer in a Document.")

9. How can you resize a layer? (See "Tutorial: Adding Content to a Layer in a Document.")

10. How do you nest a layer inside of another layer? (See "Tutorial: Nesting Layers.")

11. How can you tell if a layer is nested? (See "Tutorial: Nesting Layers.")

content

Corporate Training

Palmetto Design Group we develop a specialized course to fit your unique needs. Training your development team and setting up a usable workflow can cut your production costs considerably.

Certified Instructors

At Palmetto Design Group we employ only certified instructors to train your development team. Our instructors are Microsoft, Adobe, and Macromedia certified as well as numerous other certifications. The Instructor link to the left contains the bios of our current instructors.

Popular Courses

We train in all the most popular courses but you can also request one you don't see and we'll do our best to accommodate you. The courses include:

- Dreamweaver
- Database Development
- Photoshop
- Fireworks
- Web Design Principles
- Flash Design
- Using Microsoft Office
- Power Point Presentations
- Authorware
- After Effects
- Illustrator

Plus Many More

Professional Web Solutions and Training

Session 10

Dynamic HTML (DHTML)

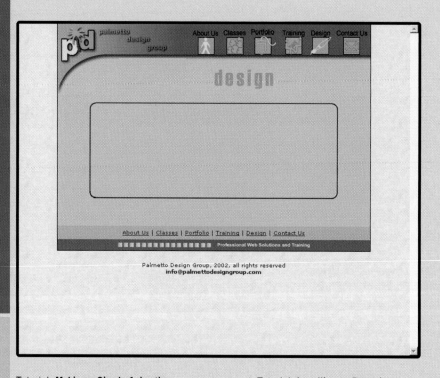

Making Animations

In this session you learn how to make a simple animation. Although the animation is an easy one, you learn a lot different techniques, such as how to add an animation to a template. This animation is editable, to a degree, in the individual pages of the site.

DHML is the use of HTML scripting with a scripting language that allows you to change the style or properties of HTML elements. For example, Timelines, in Dreamweaver, use dynamic HTML to change the properties of layers and images over time. But don't confuse the dynamic as in Dynamic HTML with dynamic Web pages. Dynamic Web pages are generated dynamically using server-side code. You make a dynamic intranet application in Sessions 17 and 18.

You work with the Timeline and its frames and keyframes as well as setting the timing of the animation. A powerful tool in Dreamweaver is the ability to add behaviors to the Timeline, which in turn affects your animation. You not only learn how to add a behavior to the Timeline, but you use a third-party extension to do so. You download and install the extension, which teaches you how to use the Extensions Manager, a vital tool to managing all the great extensions (behaviors) available to you.

TOOLS YOU'LL USE
Behaviors panel, Timeline, Layers panel, Extensions Manager

MATERIALS NEEDED
Session 9 files from the CD-ROM added to your CompleteCourse root folder if you didn't complete the previous tutorial

TIME REQUIRED
90 – 120 minutes

Tutorial
» Making a Simple Animation

In this tutorial, you move the title from off the screen into the area below the icon. The animation plays as soon as the browser loads. You also use a third-party extension to snap the title layer to a specific location.

1. **Double-click the PDG.dwt template file to open it (in the Templates folder).**
   You are animating the layer you added in Session 9. If you recall, this layer is set to be editable, so you can change images in it on the individual pages.

2. **Open the Layers panel (Advanced Layout panel group) if it isn't already open.**

3. **Double-click the name title and rename it** titlemove.
   You are renaming this layer because it conflicts with the name of the editable region, which is title as well.

4. **Click Window→Others→Timelines to open the Timeline.**
   The Timeline opens below the Property inspector.

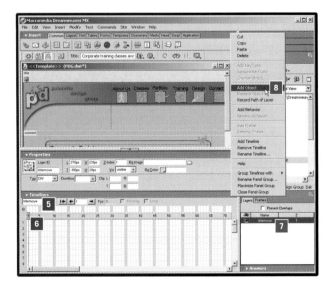

5. **Click on the expander arrow to open the Timeline and type** titlemove **for the title.**

6. **Click Frame 1 (a red box will be around the number 1) in the Timeline.**

7. **Click the titlemove name in the Layers panel.**

8. **Click the Options pop-up menu in the Timelines panel and click Add Object.**

9. **Check the Don't show me this message again option by clicking it once.**
   Notice the dialog box tells you what you are able to do to this layer. You can safely animate the Left and Top since it's the same on all browsers, but it's impossible to determine where the right or bottom of a browser window is. You can also animate the Width, Height, Z-index, and the Visibility.

10. **Click OK in the dialog box.**

11. **Click the keyframe (white circle) in Frame 15 to select it.**
   You will now position this keyframe to the location you want it to be.

12. **In the Property inspector, change the T value to 100. Just delete the minus sign.**
   You are changing the position in the Property inspector only so you can see the layer to drag it into position. Because you have selected Frame 15 this change doesn't affect Frame 1, which has the layer at a top position of -100, off the screen.

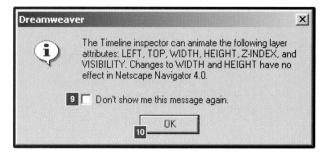

Using the Timeline

Take a look at the Timeline. Notice how two white circles are added with a dark blue bar. The first circles are keyframes. Keyframes are added whenever you want a change in the appearance of the animation. The first one shows the starting position of the animation; the last one shows the ending position of the animation. You can add keyframes to your Timeline if needed. Some complex movements require a keyframe in every frame.

Look along the top of the Timeline. Notice the title, and then the arrows that can be used to move the playhead (red rectangle) to different frames. Or you can simply click the frame number to select it. The fps stands for frames per second. This number determines how many frames per second the animation plays.

The default of 15 may be too high. The higher the number, the more stress it puts on slower computer systems. If your animation plays too fast or if it is jerky, change the fps number and test it.

If you want your animation to play longer than the default of 15 frames, click and drag the last keyframe to another number. For instance, you could set the fps to 5 and extend the Timeline to 30. At 5 fps, 30 frames would take 6 seconds to play.

You would check Autoplay to have the movie or animation begin when the browser loads. Loop is checked if you want the animation to keep playing over and over.

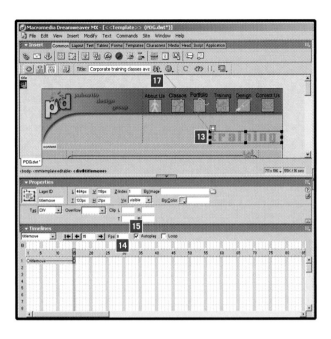

13. **Drag the layer to the right of the document below the icons.**
Don't worry about the exact position right now. It varies depending on the size of your working document. You do this step as a learning method and change it shortly.

14. **In the Timeline, change the Fps to** 8.

15. **Check the Autoplay option in the Timeline.**
A dialog box opens. It tells you that a Play Timeline action is being added to the document using an `onLoad` event. This enables the Timeline to start when the page loads.

16. **Click OK to close the dialog box that opens telling you that the Timeline action is being added.**

17. **Notice the line in your document.**
The line is connected to the layer that is off-screen and is showing the path the animation follows.

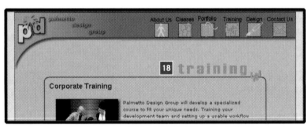

18. **Save and click Update when prompted. Preview your work in a browser.**
Watch the animation to determine whether it is smooth and moves at the appropriate speed. You can adjust the fps to your own preference. Also take note of where the animation ends.

19. **Resize the browser window by dragging the right side to make it larger.**

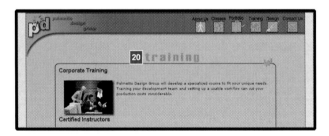

20. **Press the Refresh or Reload button in the browser.**

< N O T E >

Notice how the title is in the same position but it appears in a different location depending on the size of the browser window. This could work since the location from the top is acceptable. It isn't vital that the title be in an exact position to look good. This title is to let the users know which page they are currently viewing.

Tutorial
» Editing an Editable Region

In this tutorial, you make a repair to the template. When you changed the title of the title layer to titlemove, this change was not applied to the other pages. The reason is because it's an editable region, so the change wasn't updated. Why was this error left in the book? It was left because you inevitably encounter similar situations in your own workflow.

1. **Open the PDG template file.**

2. **Select the titlemove layer by clicking its name in the Layers panel.**
   Because the layer is not on the screen, the easiest way to select it is from the Layers panel.

3. **Click Modify→Templates→Remove Template Markup.**
   You just made this editable region uneditable. Because it is no longer editable, the associated pages update with the new title name. Don't worry, you make it editable again in a little bit.

4. **Save the document and update the associated pages.**

5. **Click titlemove in the Layers panel again to select it.**

6. **In the Template category of the Insert Bar, click the Editable Region icon.**

7. **Name the editable region title and click OK.**

8. **Save and update the pages.**
   Now all the associated pages have the title layer name changed to titlemove.

Tutorial
» Downloading an Extension

In this tutorial, you go to Dreamweaver Exchange (`www.macromedia.com/exchange/Dreamweaver`) to obtain an extension, which gives you an additional behavior to work with. Third-party developers provide these extensions.

< N O T E >

When you arrive at the results page, take a look at the information available. You see the category of the extension, which can help in your search for other similar extensions. You also see the name of the extension, the author, date, and version. The rating is pretty important. This is determined by previous users of the extension. The approval shows whether or not it is a Macromedia-approved extension. Lastly you can see how many others have downloaded the extension from this location. I say from this location specifically because Al Sparber has a very active Web site which offers extensions as well. Plus, when a Web site is given you want to check and be sure you have the most current version of the extension. Extension authors don't always get a chance to update the Macromedia list of extensions.

1. **If you aren't online, connect to the Internet now.**

2. **Access the Dreamweaver Exchange using any one of these methods:**

   » Click Help→Dreamweaver Exchange.

   » Click Commands→Get More Commands.

   » In the Behaviors panel, click the plus sign (+) and click Get More Behaviors.

   » Click Commands→Manage Extensions to open the Extensions Manager. Click File→Go to Macromedia Exchange.

   » Go directly to the exchange by typing `www.macromedia.com/exchange/Dreamweaver`.

   Wait while the Dreamweaver Exchange Web site loads.

3. **Register if you need to.**

4. **When you arrive on the Exchange page, and if you are registered and logged in, you see** Welcome (your name). **Look around to see what is available.**

5. **Click the down arrow for Browse Extensions.**
   Notice they are listed by category. But because you know the name of the extension you are looking for, use Search Extensions instead. But do take the time to browse the Extensions list. There are a ton of them and some are quite interesting.

6. **In the Search Extensions field type** snap layer **and press Go.**

7. **Click the Snap Layers by PVII.**

   The page that loads gives you a lot of information. You see the features; the developer's URL; support that's available, if any; a discussion forum; reviews; and a sample URL.

<NOTE>

The developer's URL is very important. You want to check the specific developer's site to be sure you are getting the latest and greatest extension. For example, there is a new version to the extension you are downloading now (although this one works fine). You can continue to see how getting extensions are done but you want to get the latest version later.

8. **Click the Windows or Macintosh green links to download the extension.**

   You can read the installation instructions if you desire, but you install in this tutorial. Don't worry about the Warning if you are using Dreamweaver MX because the Extensions Manager is already installed.

9. **Click OK for the Save This File to Disk option.**

10. **Navigate to the Dreamweaver MX program folder and open the Downloaded Extensions folder. Click OK.**

11. **Now would be a good time to go to Project Seven and get the newest version, which is 2.63 (specifically for Dreamweaver MX).**

    Here is the direct link so you don't have to search for it. Save it in your Downloaded Extensions folder: www. projectseven.com/extensions/listing.htm.

Downloading Extensions

There are numerous ways to access extensions, some of which you see in this tutorial. When you arrive at the Dreamweaver Exchange you are asked to register for free if you haven't done so already. If you've never registered you need to do that first. Most of the extensions are free; there are a few commercial ones. You see this information on the extension explanation page. Some may offer a lite version or a 30-day trial version.

Dreamweaver MX ships with a standalone application called the Extensions Manager, which is used to manage your extensions.

When you download third-party extensions you should save them in a folder other than your root folder. Normally you would save them in a folder named Downloaded Extensions, which is located in the Dreamweaver MX program folder. By keeping the extensions together, it is easy for you to locate them when you want to install or remove them.

Tutorial
» Installing an Extension

In this tutorial, you install the snap layers extension you downloaded.

1. **Click Commands→Manage Extensions.**
   The Extensions Manager opens.

2. **Click the down arrow next to the program field, and click Dreamweaver MX if it isn't selected already.**
   You can select the program you want to manage the extensions for. If you only have Dreamweaver MX installed, it is selected by default. If not, the list shows other Dreamweaver applications, as well as Flash applications and Fireworks MX.

3. **Click File→Install Extension and navigate to the Downloaded Extensions folder if it doesn't open automatically.**

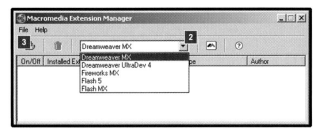

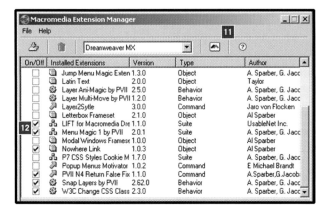

4. **Select the MX267082_P7_Snap.mxp file (P7_Snap_263.mxp if you downloaded the update from the developer's site).**

5. **Click Install.**

6. **Click the Accept button for the disclaimer.**

7. **Click OK when the dialog box opens telling you it was successfully installed.**

8. **Look at the great information listed in the Extensions Manager about the extension.**
   With Snap Layers by PVII selected, you can read what the extension does, what browsers it's compatible with, and how to access the action. Not all extensions provide this much information, if any.

9. **Close Dreamweaver and re-open it so that the extension is available for use.**

10. **There are other ways to install extensions, such as:**
    - » With the Extensions Manager open, press the Ctrl-I (⌘-O) keys to open the Select Extension to Install dialog box.
    - » In Windows you can click the Install Extension icon in the Extensions Manager.
    - » Go directly to the .MXP file and double-click it to install for Windows. This works for Macs as well if the file's hidden file type is set to MmXm.
    - » You can also Import extensions from other Dreamweaver or UltraDev installations by clicking File→Import Extensions in the Extensions Manager.

11. **Look at this illustration. It shows a large list of extensions in the Extensions Manager.**
    I imported my extensions from Dreamweaver UltraDev 4 into Dreamweaver MX. Too many extensions can slow Dreamweaver down. But you can disable the ones you don't need.

12. **Click the check boxes of the extensions you don't need to disable them.**

13. **Click OK for the dialog box that opens stating The extension has successfully been disabled.**
    In order for the changes to take effect, you must close and then restart Dreamweaver. You can continue disabling other extensions before you close and restart Dreamweaver.

Tutorial
» Using an Extension

In this tutorial, you change the title animation so that it snaps to a specified location based on an image in the document instead of a specified location of the layer itself.

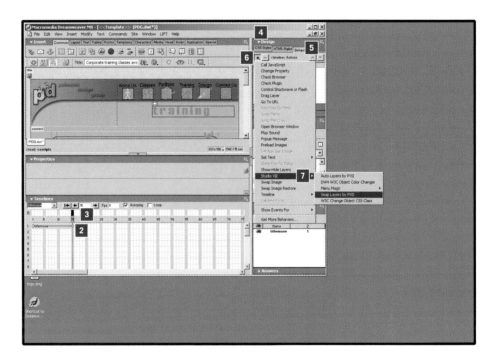

1. **Open the pdg.dwt template file.**

2. **Click Frame 15.**
   You are going to add a behavior to this frame, which makes the layer snap to a specified location based on the contact icon image.

3. **Click in the Behavior line above Frame 15.**

4. **Click the expander arrow of the Design panel group.**

5. **Click the Behaviors panel to make it the active panel.**

6. **Click the plus sign (+).**

7. **Click Studio VII and then click Snap Layers by PVII.**

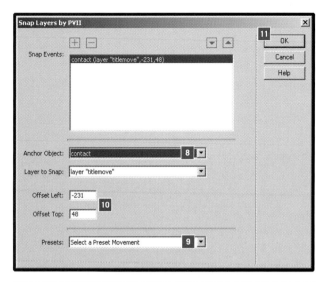

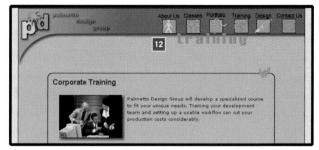

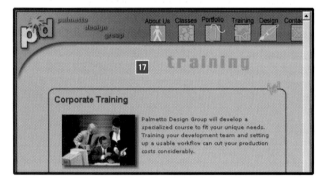

<NOTE>

Notice the title stays in the same place when you resize the window instead of keeping the same relationship with the contact icon. That's okay, though, because the title will look fine no matter where it is located. The only way it will look bad is if the users make the browser window extremely small. Note that these position changes occur only if the window is resized after the page loads. When the page loads, the title will be positioned according to the location of the contact icon.

8. **In the Snap Layers by PVII dialog box, click the down arrow for the Anchor Object and click contact.**

9. **Click the down arrow for the Presets field to select a preset movement.**

10. **Click the To Bottom Left of Image option.**
    Notice the Offset Left and the Offset Top fields are automatically filled in.

11. **Click OK.**

12. **Save and click Update when prompted. Preview your work in a browser.**
    Notice that the image is positioned a bit high on the page.

13. **Double-click the Snap Layers by PVII Action in the Behaviors panel.**
    This re-opens the Snap Layers by PVII dialog box so you can make alterations to the behavior.

14. **Highlight the number in the Offset Top field and type** 75.
    This value positions the title 75 pixels from the top of the document.

15. **Click OK.**

16. **Check in a browser again.**
    That's better. Leave the browser open for the next step.

17. **Resize the browser window to make it larger.**

18. **Click the titlemove file in the Layers panel.**

19. **If you aren't using Split Code view, then click the Show Code and Design Views icon to view the code.**

20. **Save the template file.**

21. **Click Update to update all the pages using the template file.**

22. **Close the template file.**

Tutorial
» Editing the Animated Image

In this tutorial you change the image in the animation for the design.htm page.

1. **Double-click design.htm to open it.**

2. **In the Layers panel, click the titlemove layer to select it.**
   You selected it so you could see the Layers properties in the
   Property inspector. Because you want to change the image,
   you need to be able to see the layer, which requires changing
   the top position.

3. **Delete the minus sign in the Top field in the Property inspector.**

4. **Double-click the training text image inside the layer.**
   The Select Image Source dialog box opens.

5. **Navigate to the shared images folder and select txt_design.gif.**
   Click OK.
   The design text is now in the layer.

6. **Select the tilemove layer and type the minus sign in front of the**
   100 in the Top field again.

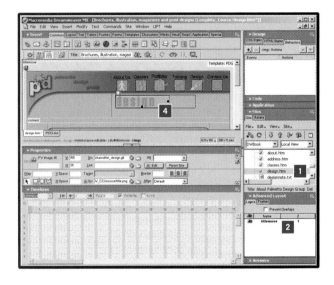

7. **Preview your work in a browser.**

8. **Save and close the document.**
   Did you notice when you saved, you weren't ask to apply the
   changes to all the documents? That's because you made the
   change to this page only and not to the template itself. You
   were allowed to edit the layer because it is an editable region.
   If you had attempted to edit the animation itself in the
   Timeline you would not have been allowed to do that.

9. **You can repeat this tutorial for the other pages of the site if you'd**
   like.
   There is a text image file in the shared folder for each page.

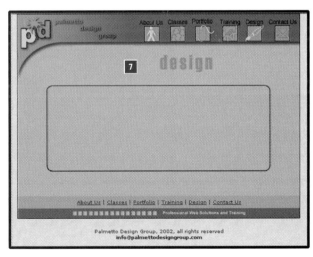

» Session Review

To discover how much information you retained from this session, give yourself this brief quiz. The information sticks better if you go back to the referenced tutorials for the questions you aren't sure of.

1. To add an animation to all of the sites pages, which file do you use? (See "Tutorial: Making a Simple Animation.")

2. What type of frame is added to the Timeline for the beginning and ending image? (See "Tutorial: Making a Simple Animation.")

3. What part of the Timeline determines the speed the animation plays? (See "Tutorial: Making a Simple Animation.")

4. Where do you go to get additional extensions to use? (See "Tutorial: Downloading Extensions.")

5. Name one way to access the Extensions Manger. (See "Tutorial: Installing an Extension.")

6. Name one way to install an extension. (See "Tutorial: Installing an Extension.")

7. What is the extension name of an extension? (See "Tutorial: Installing an Extension.")

8. How do you apply the extension you downloaded to the animation? (See "Tutorial: Using an Extension.")

9. Can you edit any part of the animation in a document other than the template? (See "Tutorial: Editing The Animated Image.")

10. Can you edit the Timeline of the animation in another document? (See "Tutorial Editing The Animated Image.")

In this session, you learned how to use the Timeline, add behaviors to it, and alter the timing of an animation. You also acquired a new extension for the snap layers behavior and installed it using the Extensions Manager. You have just experienced a taste of designing with DHTML!

design

About Us | Classes | Portfolio | Training | Design | Contact Us

Professional Web Solutions and Training

Palmetto Design Group, 2002, all rights reserved
info@palmettodesigngroup.com

Session 11

Making a Pop-Up Menu

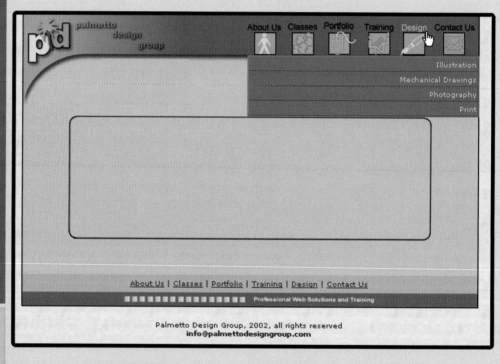

Using Pop-Up Menus

Pop-up menus, drop-down menus, DHTML menus, fly-out menus — they are all basically the same concept but with different names. Dreamweaver MX now ships with a very cool pop-up menu behavior that enables you to make very nice pop-up menus with little effort. Sure, you can make your own without this behavior and, for certain effects, you might want to. But this new behavior, which first appeared in Fireworks 4, is a fantastic timesaver.

Now when your client asks for a DHTML menu, you can say, "no problem" and whip one up in no time at all. Just don't tell anyone how easy it was!

TOOLS YOU'LL USE
Show Pop-Up Menu behavior

MATERIALS NEEDED
Session 10 files from the CD-ROM added to your CompleteCourse root
folder if you didn't complete the previous tutorial

TIME REQUIRED
90 minutes

Tutorial

» Adding the Show Pop-Up Menu Behavior

In this tutorial, you add the Show Pop-Up Menu behavior and configure the menu for the About Us link.

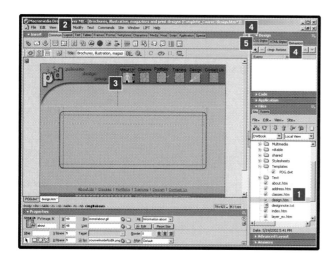

1. **Double-click the classes.htm file to open it.**

2. **Click Modify→Templates→Detach from Template.**
   Since the Show Pop-Up Menu behavior won't work in the template file, you add it to this page just to learn how to make this menu. If you decide this is the type of menu you want, make it prior to making the template or add the menu to the template file.

3. **Click the About Us icon to select it.**

4. **Click the Design panel expander arrow and click the Behaviors panel to make it active.**

5. **Click the plus sign and click Show Pop-Up Menu.**
   The Show Pop-up Menu dialog box opens.

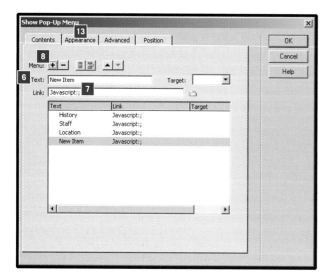

6. **In the Text field, type** History.

7. **In the Link field, type** Javascript:;
   If you recall, this is a null link, which you can change at any time.

8. **Click the plus sign (+) to add the menu item.**
   Notice the first menu item is in the Text field in the main window. A New Item is listed and will be replaced with the next entry.

9. **In the Text field, highlight New Item and type** Staff.

10. **Click the plus sign.**

11. **Highlight New Item and type** Location.

12. **Click the plus sign.**

13. **Click the Appearance tab.**

Tutorial
» Setting the Menu's Appearance

In this tutorial, you determine the appearance of the menu items.

1. **Click the down arrow in the first field.**
   Notice that you have two options: the Vertical Menu and the Horizontal Menu. Leave the default of Vertical Menu selected.

2. **Click the down arrow for the Font field and click Verdana, Arial, Helvetica, sans-serif.**

3. **Highlight the Size and type** 10.

4. **Click the B icon if you want the text to be bold and the I icon if you want the text to be italic.**

5. **Check the preview to see how the text looks.**

6. **Leave the default alignment at left-align.**

7. **Click the color box for the Up State Text field.**

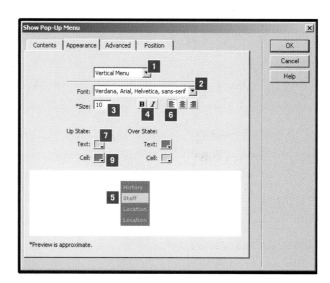

8. **With the Eyedropper tool, click a gold color.**
   The color clicked here is the second gold color from the right of the seventh row from the top, Hex #FFCC00. You can also click on the System Color Picker for more color options. You can't add a Hex number like you can in the Fireworks Pop-Up menu.

9. **Click the color box of the Cell field in the Up State and click a blue color.**
   The color clicked here is Hex #666699, the fourth row from the top and the fourth color from the right.

10. **Repeat for the Over State except reverse the colors.**
    Sample the colors with the Eyedropper from the Text and Cell boxes you selected in the Up State.

11. **Click the Advanced tab.**

12. **Don't close the dialog box yet.**

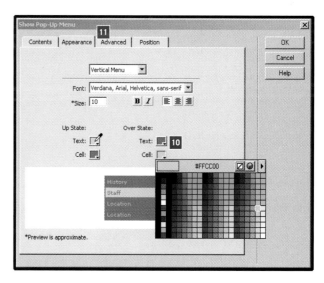

Tutorial
» Setting the Advanced Settings

In this tutorial you set the width and height of the cells as well as the border and shadow properties.

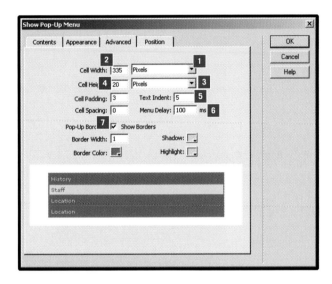

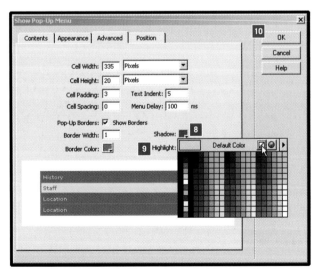

1. **Click the down pointing arrow of the Cell Width field and click Pixels.**

2. **Type** 335 **for the Cell Width amount.**

3. **Click the down pointing arrow of the Cell Height field and click Pixels.**

4. **Type** 20 **for the Cell Height.**
   You can see the changes in the Preview part of the window.

5. **Type** 5 **for the Text Indent.**
   This indents the text by five pixels from the left of the menu's edge.

6. **Delete the last 0 in the Menu Delay to change the number from 1000 to 100.**
   This setting determines how fast the menu closes when you mouse off.

7. **Leave the Show Borders box checked.**

8. **Click in the Shadow color box and click the symbol for no.**

9. **Click in the Highlight color box and click the symbol for no.**

< N O T E >

To determine the size of the cells it may take some trial and error. You can click OK at any time and preview in a browser. To continue editing you simply select the About Us icon again and double-click the Show Pop-Up menu behavior to open the Show Pop-Up Menu dialog box.

10. **Click OK.**

11. **Preview your work in the appropriate browser(s).**

12. **Mouse over the About Us icon.**
    You can see a couple of problems here. First, the menu isn't positioned correctly. Second, the menu goes under the classes title. You fix the title problem now and the position problem in the next tutorial.

13. **Open the Layers panel (Window→Others→Layers).**

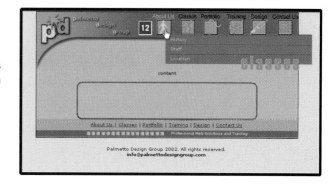

14. **Double-click the layers Z-index and change it to 0.**

15. **Preview again and mouse over the About Us icon.**
    The menu now opens over the design title.

16. **Save the file, but keep it open.**

Submenu Items

Because we are aligning this table to the right of the document window, you won't be using submenus. You might at some point want to have a menu system with submenus. A submenu item is added the same way as you just inserted the first three items. To make a submenu entry, type the name in the text field, click the plus sign, and then select the entry and click the Indent Item button. The item appears indented. Be sure to add the submenu items below the associated menu item. If you add a menu item and it appears indented, be sure to click the Outdent Item

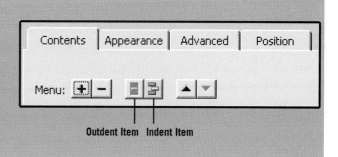

Tutorial
» Setting the Menu's Position

In this tutorial you set the menu's positioning. You set the position relative to the trigger button, which in this case is the About Us icon.

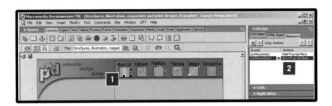

1. **Click the About Us icon.**

2. **Double-click the Show Pop-Up Menu action in the Behaviors panel.**

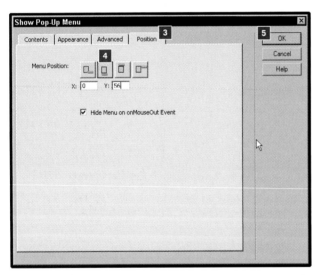

3. **Click the Position tab and type in 0 for x and 56 for y.**
   The bottom-right corner position is selected by default. The x and y coordinates are set automatically but you can adjust these values if needed.

4. **Click the Below and at Left Edge of Trigger icon (the second icon from the left).**

5. **Click OK.**

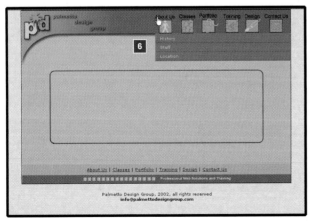

6. **Preview your work in the appropriate browser(s).**

7. **Save the file but keep it open.**

Tutorial
» Adding the Rest of the Menus

In this tutorial you add the rest of the menus. Because this is a right-aligned menu, it poses a few problems that you wouldn't encounter in a center-aligned menu. But because of this you learn how to use the menu-positioning tools to their fullest extent.

1. **Click the Classes icon.**

2. **Click the plus sign in the Behaviors panel.**

3. **Click the Show Pop-Up Menu.**

4. **Add the following menu items (using a null link) as you did in the "Adding the Show Pop-Up Menu Behavior" tutorial:**

   » Dreamweaver Beginner

   » Dreamweaver Intermediate

   » Photoshop

   » Fireworks

5. **Click the Appearance tab.**
   The settings are the same as the last time you used it. But if by any chance they aren't correct, use the same settings that you did in the appearance tutorial.

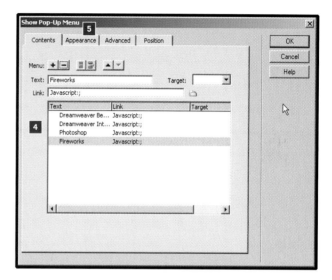

6. **Click the Advanced tab and use the same settings as the tutorial for the Advanced tab except for the indent.**
   Often times the No shadow and highlight switch back to the default, so be sure to change it to none.

7. **Change the Text Indent setting to 54.**
   This indents the text to line up under the Classes icon.

<NOTE>
The indent value was determined by adding the size of the About Us icon to the indent amount and then previewing. It takes some browser checking and tweaking to get your values where you want them. This menu loses the no shadow setting everytime you open it to edit, so be sure to check it.

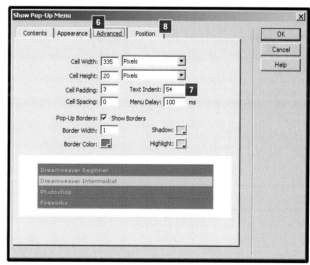

8. **Click the Position tab.**

9. **In the x field, type** -60.
   By typing a new value, no Menu Position icon is selected because the custom setting overrides it. The value was determined by trial and error during preview.

10. **Click OK.**

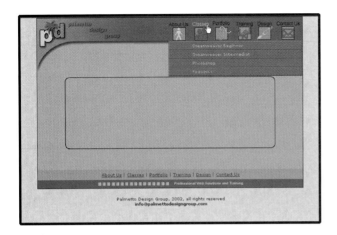

11. **Preview your work in the appropriate browser(s).**

12. **Save the document.**

13. **Click the Design icon and add the Show Pop-Up Menu behavior.**
    The portfolio and training icons don't need menus so you can skip those two.

14. **Add these menu items:**
    >> Illustration
    >> Mechanical Drawings
    >> Photography
    >> Print

15. **Click the Appearance tab and change the alignment to right.**

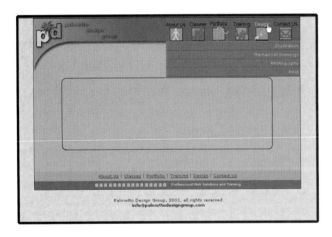

16. **Click the Advanced tab and set these settings:**
    >> Cell Width: **335 pixels**
    >> Cell Height: **20 pixels**
    >> Text Indent: **0**
    >> Shadow: **None**
    >> Highlight: **None**

17. **Click the Position tab and change the x-axis to** -223.

18. **Click OK.**

19. **Preview your work in the appropriate browser(s).**

20. **Now for the best part of all. Make the browser window larger and mouse over the menus.**
    Look at that! The menus are still aligned properly because they are positioned relative to the trigger.

Tutorial
» Making a New Template Page

You now make another template. This one can be used if you want to have pop-up menus on your pages. Instead of applying pdg.dwt, you would apply this template to any pages you want the pop-up menu on. Normally, you wouldn't have more than one menu system on a Web site. This template page gives you options when you design your own site.

1. With the classes.htm still open, click File→Save as Template.

2. Type popup in the Save As field.

3. Click Save.

4. Select the Template category from the Insert menu.

5. Click in the area outside the rounded table area.

6. Click the Editable Region icon and name it content.

7. Click the titlemove Layer to select it and add an Editable region named title.

8. Save the template.
   You get a message about updated pages linked to the template. That's OK, only classes change and you take care of that in a moment. You now have a template available to use if you'd rather use it than the pdg.dwt.

9. Double-click classes.htm to open it.
   It's no longer open because it was changed to the popup.dwt file. You now return this file to the original template.

10. Click Modify→Templates→Apply Template to Page.

11. In the Select Template dialog box, click PDG.

12. Click Select.
    You are reapplying the original template to classes.htm; you only used it to make the alternative menu template.

13. Click Document body.

14. In the Move Content to New Region menu, click Nowhere.

15. Click Document head.

16. In the Move Content to New Region menu, click Nowhere.

17. Click OK.

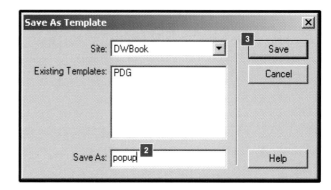

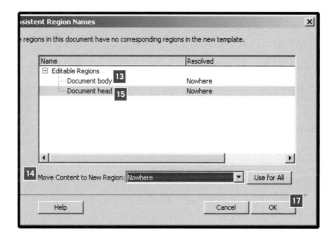

» Session Review

Aren't these menus fun? The best part is they are so quick to do and you have a ton of flexibility. Test yourself now and see how much you retained.

1. How do you add a null link? (See "Tutorial: Adding the Show Pop-Up Menu Behavior.")

2. What do you do if you want to add a submenu item? (See "Tutorial: Adding the Show Pop-Up Menu Behavior.")

3. Can you change the color of the menu cells? (See "Tutorial: Setting the Menu's Appearance.")

4. What are the two options for the menu types in the Appearance category? (See, "Tutorial: Setting the Menu's Appearance.")

5. What are the two options for the Cell Width and Height? (See "Tutorial: Setting the Advanced Settings.")

6. How did you make the menu go over the design title? (See "Tutorial: Setting the Advanced Settings.")

7. Which position icon do you click for a custom x or y setting? (See "Tutorial: Setting the Menu's Position.")

In this session, you learned how to add layers that could be used for a layout instead of tables. In the process you learned a lot of layer basics such as sizing and positioning. You also nested a layer inside of the content layer. In the training.htm page you added a layer with content. This layer is unseen in the final file since we placed it above the page content. It was lowered for this illustration.

» Additional Projects

Try making a menu using submenus. You couldn't do so in this design because of the position of the icons.

1. Type a few text links for navigation or start with a few buttons.

2. Add the Show Pop-up Menu behavior.

3. Add the menu items and use the indent button for the submenu items.

4. Set the Appearance of your menus. Try changing the border or adding a shadow and highlight.

5. Set the Advanced settings for the menu size to Automatic.

6. Choose the positioning you'd like.

7. Test your new menu.

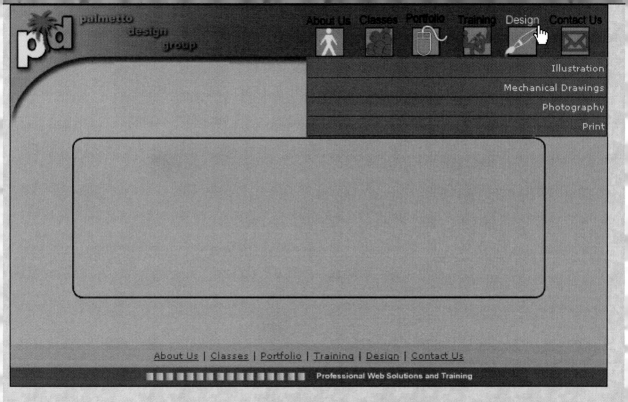

About Us Classes Portfolio Training Design Contact Us

Illustration
Mechanical Drawings
Photography
Print

About Us | Classes | Portfolio | Training | Design | Contact Us

Professional Web Solutions and Training

Palmetto Design Group, 2002, all rights reserved
info@palmettodesigngroup.com

Adding Forms and Behaviors

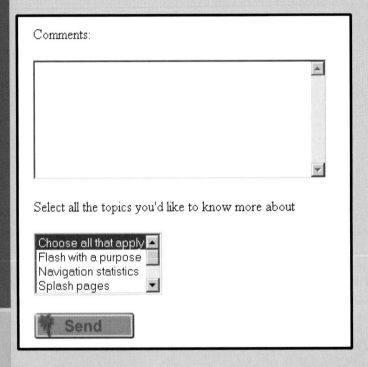

Tutorial: **Building a Basic Form**

Tutorial: **Inserting Radio Buttons**

Tutorial: **Inserting Check Boxes**

Tutorial: **Inserting a Textarea and a List**

Tutorial: **Using Jump Menus**

Form Basics

HTML forms are used to collect data from users. That data is then sent to the server. There are three form attributes that allow the form to interact with a program on your server. They are the Form Name, the Actions, and the Methods. The Form Name can be referenced by scripts to perform different actions. Actions are taken when the Submit button is clicked. There are two Methods: GET and POST, which are used to submit the forms data. GET is limited to ASCII data, which is no larger than 8KB, and it is a bit insecure. POST is the preferred method. It sends the data to the processing agent that the Action attribute specifies; it can handle encrypted files.

When you use a form to collect personal data you should also include a link to a Privacy policy. If you are dealing with children, there are laws about how to collect data from them and how and when to verify their age.

In this session you learn how to insert and label form objects. You make several forms on blank pages so that you can insert them into any document you'd like. Forms need to be linked to a CGI script to actually work, so I walk you through the steps you need to take to set up a script. But you need to have a server that supports CGI, as well as have a CGI script or get one of the free scripts in order to make your forms fully functional. You learn how to validate your forms in Session 18.

TOOLS YOU'LL USE
Form insertion icons, Property inspector, Behaviors panel

MATERIALS NEEDED
Session 11 files from the CD-ROM added to your CompleteCourse root folder if you didn't complete the previous tutorial

Access to a CGI script on a server

TIME REQUIRED
60 minutes

Tutorial
» Building a Basic Form

In this tutorial, you add a form field, a form element, and a Submit button. You build the form on a blank page so you can copy and paste it into other documents or make a library item of it.

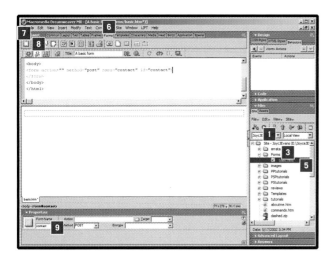

1. **In the Site panel, right/Control-click the root folder name and click New Folder.**

2. **Name the folder** Forms.

3. **Right/Control-click the Forms folder and click New File.**

4. **Name the file** basic.htm.

5. **Double-click basic.htm to open it.**

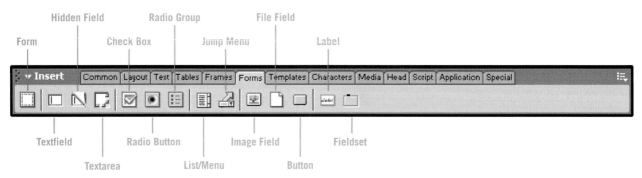

Form   Hidden Field   Check Box   Radio Group   Jump Menu   File Field   Label

Insert | Common | Layout | Text | Tables | Frames | Forms | Templates | Characters | Media | Head | Script | Application | Special

Textfield   Radio Button   Image Field   Fieldset
Textarea   List/Menu   Button

6. **Click the Forms category in the Insert Bar.**
   Pass your mouse cursor over each icon to familiarize yourself with what is available. You use many of these options in this session.

7. **Click the Form icon.**
   You see a red dotted line box; this is the empty form. If you can't see the red box, click View→Visual Aids→Invisible Elements.

8. **Click the Split view (Show Code and Design views) to see the code.**
   Notice the code added after the `<body>` tag. It says `<form name="form1" method="post" action=""> </form>`. Your form is between these opening and closing form tags.

9. **In the Property inspector, change the Form Name to** contact.
   If you look at the code now the form name has changed to `name="contact"`.

10. **Click your cursor inside the red lines that define the form area.**
    You are going to insert a table inside the form area to make the form objects look nicer. You don't have to use tables to organize form objects.

11. **Click the Insert Table icon in the Insert Bar, Common category.**

12. **Type these values in the Insert Table dialog box:**

    » Rows: **13**   » Border: **0**
    » Columns: **2**   » Cell Padding: **0**
    » Width: **340 Pixels** » Cell Spacing: **0**

13. **Click OK.**
    You now need to fill in the accessibility options for Forms if you have them turned on. You can turn on or off the accessibility options in the Preferences panel (Edit→Preferences→Accessibility). Give the form a label and then fill in the other options each time this dialog opens.

14. **Place your cursor in the first cell of the first row and type** Last Name.
    You can use the Tab key to move between cells.

15. **Place your cursor into each of the remaining rows on the left side of the column and enter these entries:** First Name, Address 1, Address 2, City, State, Zip or Regional Code, Country, Home Phone, Work Phone, Fax Number, Email Address

16. **Place your cursor in the first cell of the right column and click.**

17. **Click the Textfield icon in the Forms category of the Insert Bar.**
    Notice that a textfield is now visible in your document. If you have left the Accessibility options on, use No Label and type a letter for the Access key. This letter, when used with the Control key, tabs through the form fields.

18. **In the Property inspector, leave the Max Chars (Maximum Characters) blank.**
    By leaving the Maximum Characters blank, you eliminate the possibility of cutting a large last name.

19. **In the Char Width field enter a value of** 25.
    If you click in the document or press Enter/Return to activate the changes, you notice that the textfield box got a little larger after you changed the width. By specifically changing the character width you can control the appearance of all the text fields.

20. **Click the Single Line radio button (if it isn't selected already) to select it.**
    It's selected if you see a black dot in the radio button.

21. **Type a textfield name of** lastname.
    Avoiding spaces in field names is best.

22. **Repeat steps 16-21 for the rest of the entries, replacing the textfield name with an appropriate name for the entry.**

< N O T E >

A quick way to add numerous textfields with the same values is to select the first field and copy it. Then paste it into each of the desired rows. Select the pasted field and change the name.

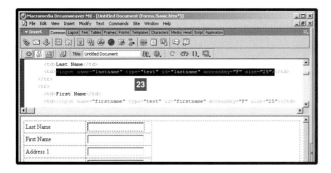

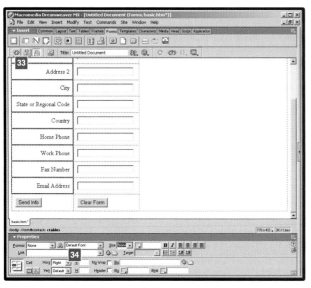

23. **Look at the code.**
    Notice that each textfield has an input name; you can see the properties of each.

< N O T E >
The input name helps you identify the entered information when you receive the form. You set up a database application in Part V of this course. I provide the actual database, but your form's input is entered into the database.

24. **Select the table.**
    The table content is much too close to each other. Add some padding to the cells.

25. **In the Property inspector type** 10 **in the Cell Padding field. Press Enter/Return.**
    The form looks much better now. You can add more or less padding depending on your taste.

26. **Click in the left column of the last row.**

27. **Click the Button icon in the Forms category of the Insert Bar.**
    For accessibility, I used No Label and an Access key of F.

28. **In the Property inspector, change the name from Submit to** info.

29. **Change the Label name to** Send Info.

30. **Leave the Action set to Submit form. Press Enter/Return.**
    Notice how the button expands to fit your text. You can type anything meaningful for the buttons.

31. **Place your cursor in the right column of the last row and add another button.**

32. **Name it and then clear and change the Label to** Clear Form. **Change the Action to Reset form and press Enter/Return.**

33. **Click in the Last Name cell and drag down to select all the text in the first column.**

34. **In the Property inspector, change the Horizontal alignment to Right.**
    The form looks much better but it needs some text formatting. When you use this form on a Web page, use CSS styles to format the text.

35. **Save the file.**

36. **Preview your work in the appropriate browsers.**

< N O T E >
You can enter text at this point into the form but it won't work because it needs to have a CGI-BIN set up with a CGI script with your ISP. I show you how to link a form to a CGI script in the "Inserting a Textarea and a List" tutorial. This particular form connects to a database in Part V.

Tutorial

» Inserting Radio Buttons

In this tutorial you insert three radio buttons with options. The user can choose just one of the options.

1. **Right/Control-click the Forms folder and click New File.**

2. **Name the file** survey.htm **and double-click the file to open it.**

3. **Click the Form icon to insert the form field. In the Property inspector, change the Form Name to Survey.**

4. **With the cursor inside the form (inside the red box), choose Insert→Table and use these values:**

» Rows: **12**	» Border: **0**
» Columns: **3**	» Cell Padding: **0**
» Width: **400**	» Cell Spacing: **0**

   Click OK.

5. **Click into the first left cell and drag horizontally to select the entire first row.**

6. **Right/Control-click and click Table→Merge Cells.**

7. **Type** What Do You Think?

8. **Place your cursor in the first row and set Horz to Center.**

9. **Place your cursor in the first cell (on the left) of the second row.**

10. **In the Forms tab of the Insert Bar, click the Radio button icon.**

11. **In the Property inspector, below the text RadioButton, type a name of** location.

12. **In the Checked Value field, type** Top.

13. **Click the Initial State of Checked.**

14. **In the document, to the right of the radio button, type** Top.

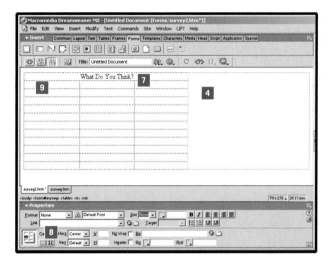

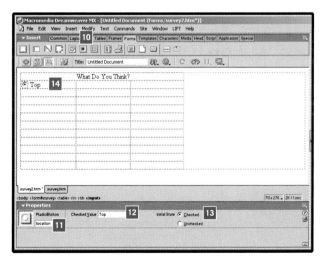

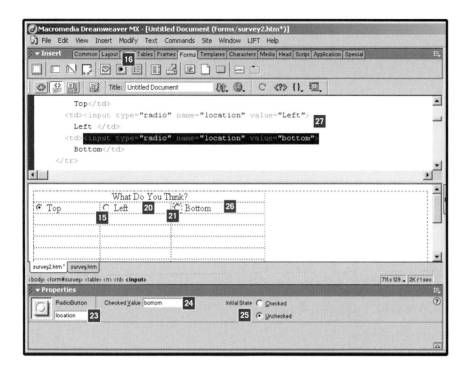

15. **Place your cursor in the center cell of the second row.**

16. **Click the Radio Button icon to insert the radio button.**

17. **Name it** location **again**.
    The buttons have the same names because you want readers
    to only be able to select one button. If each radio button had a
    different name, the users could select all of the options.

18. **In the Checked Value field, enter** left.

19. **For the Initial State, click Unchecked.**

20. **In the document, to the right of the center radio button, type** Left.

21. **Place your cursor in the right cell of the second row.**

22. **Click the Radio Button icon to insert the radio button.**

23. **Name it** location **again**.

24. **In the Checked Value field, enter** bottom.

25. **For the Initial State, click Unchecked.**

26. **In the document, to the right of the right radio button, type**
    Bottom.

27. **Look at the code.**
    Notice the input type is "radio", the name is "location",
    the value is "left", and so on.

28. **Save the document and leave it open.**

Tutorial
» Inserting Check Boxes

In this tutorial you add a series of check boxes that the users can check as many of as they want.

1. Select the table and enter 10 for the CellPad.

2. Merge the third row (select the row, and then right/Control-click and click Table→Merge Cells).

3. With the cursor in the third row, set the Horz to Left.

4. Type Check all the features that you'd rather not see on a business Web site?

5. Place your cursor inside the first cell of the fourth row.

6. Click the Check Box icon in the Forms Bar.

7. In the Property inspector, change the CheckBox name to splash.

8. Type Splash Page for the Checked Value.

9. Click Unchecked for the Initial State.

10. In the document, to the right of the check box, type Splash Page.

11. Repeat for these values, entering each value for the CheckBox name and the Checked Value name. For the initial state, leave them all unchecked: Sound, Flash Movies, Flash Interface, Sound-no Off Option, Difficult Navigation, Amateur Design, GIF Animation

    The location of each check box entry is not important.

12. To improve the appearance of the form, merge the center and last cells of all the check box rows.

13. Drag the column centerline to the right to allow the text in the first column to be on the same line.
    To move a column line, place your cursor over the line (you see double lines and arrows), and then click and drag.

14. Place your cursor in the first cell of the second row (Top radio button) and set the Horz to Center.

15. Save the file and leave it open.

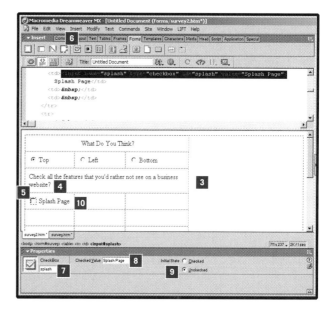

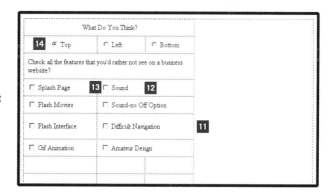

Tutorial
» Inserting a Textarea and a List

In this tutorial, you add a textarea that can be used for comments and a list that the users can select multiple options from.

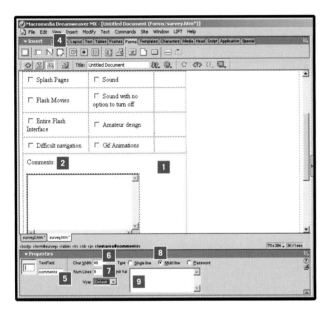

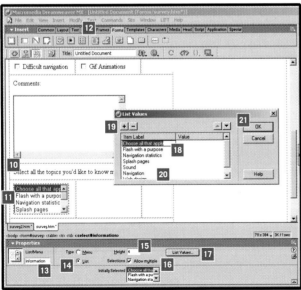

1. **Merge row 9 (under the last check boxes).**

2. **Type** Comments:.

3. **Press Enter/Return.**

4. **Click the Textarea icon in the Forms Bar.**

5. **Name the textfield** comments.

6. **Set the Char Width to** 40.

7. **Set the Num Lines to** 8.

8. **Leave Multiline option checked.**

9. **Leave the Init Val field empty.**
   The Initial Value field is where you can explain how the textarea is being used. In this case, the word Comments above the form object is sufficient.

10. **Merge the next row and type** Select all the topics you'd like to know more about.

11. **Place your cursor in the first cell of the next row.**

12. **Click the List/Menu icon in the Forms Bar.**

13. **Change the List/Menu name to** information.

14. **Click List for the Type.**

15. **Set the Height to** 4.

16. **Click Allow multiple selections.**
    You see a check mark, indicating the option is selected. This option allows the users to choose more than one option.

17. **Click the List Values button.**

18. **Type** Choose all that apply.

19. **Click the plus sign.**

20. **Repeat steps 18 and 19 for the following values:**

    » Flash with a purpose, Navigation statistics, Splash pages, Sound, Navigation, Web design

21. **Click OK and click for the Initially Selected field. Click Choose all that apply.**

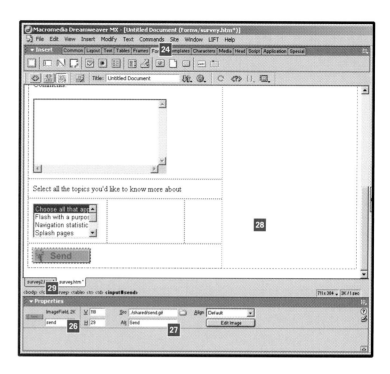

22. **Merge the last row.**

23. **Insert your cursor in the last row.**

24. **Click the Image Field icon in the Forms Bar.**
    The Image Field allows you to use a graphical button for the
    Submit and Reset buttons. You won't use the File field but it
    adds a Browse button to enable the user to send a file to you.

25. **Navigate to the shared folder and click send.gif. Click OK.**

26. **In the Property inspector, name the Imagefield** Send.

27. **Set the Alt tag to** Send.

28. **Click inside the form but outside the table.**

29. **In the Tag Selector, click form#survey.**

30. **In the Property inspector choose a Method of POST.**

31. **The Action field is where you'd enter the path to a CGI-BIN folder
    with a CGI script in it.**

32. **Save and close this form.**

CGI Scripts

The path to a script can be obtained from your hosting service if
they allow CGI and if they provide the script. There are also free
scripts you can find on the Internet. Just be sure that you get them
from a reputable source. I have provided a couple of links on the
CD-ROM.

Tutorial
» Using Jump Menus

In this tutorial you make a jump menu (whereby you click an item from a list and go somewhere else). You discover how similar jump menus are to list menus. In fact, you make the list menu you made earlier into a jump menu.

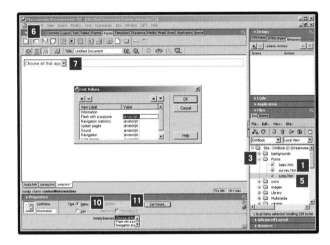

1. **Double-click survey.htm in the Forms folder to open it.**

2. Select the list form object and copy it.

3. **In the Site panel, right/Control-click the Forms folder and click New File.**

4. Name the new file jump.htm.

5. **Double-click jump.htm to open it.**

6. **Click the Form icon in the Forms Bar.**

7. **Insert your cursor inside the form box.**

8. Click Edit→Paste (or Ctrl/Command-V).

9. Select the list form.

10. **In the Property inspector, click Menu for the Type.**
    Notice that the list box has changed to a single line.

11. **Click the List Values button.**

12. **Click the Choose all that applies text and change it to**
    Information.

13. **Click Flash with a purpose and press the Tab key.**
    This puts you into the Value field. This is where you enter the URL that activates when the user clicks on the Flash with a purpose text.

14. **For now enter a null link of** javascript:;.

15. Copy the javascript:; **text.**

16. **Press the Tab key two times and paste the text.**
    This puts the focus into the value field of Navigation statistics.

17. Repeat the two tabs and paste for the remaining text items.

18. **Click OK.**

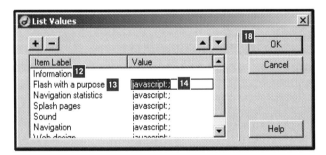

19. **In the Property inspector, click Information for the Initially Selected item.**

20. **This menu has no behavior attached to it yet, so open the Behaviors panel (in the Design panel group).**

21. **Click the plus sign and click Jump Menu.**

22. **When the Jump Menu dialog box opens, click one of the entries.** Notice that the null links are already entered. If you hadn't done this from the Property inspector you could also add the link fields here in the When Selected, Go To URL: field.

23. **Click Select First Item After URL Change if you'd like the Information entry to show after the page loads again.**

24. **Click OK.**

25. **Look at the behavior added to the Behaviors panel.** The Event should read `onChange`. You can always change the event that triggers the behavior by selecting the Jump Menu behavior and clicking the little arrow to choose a new event.

26. **Save the file and preview your work in the appropriate browsers.**

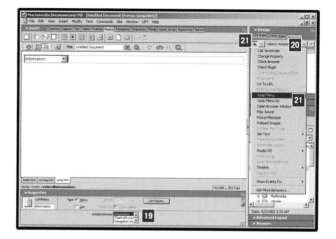

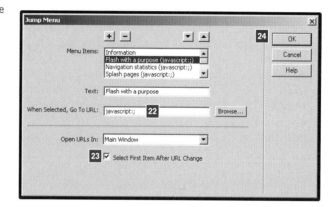

Jump Menu Form Object

I choose to show you how to convert a list object into a jump menu by adding the links and a behavior. If you want to, you can accomplish the same thing by clicking the Jump Menu icon in the Forms Bar. The dialog box that opens is almost identical to the one with the Jump Menu behavior. You have the additional option of adding a Go button. You don't have to add a behavior manually when you use the Jump Menu form object because it is added automatically.

» Session Review

Now that you know how to add various forms, you can give yourself this quick test to evaluate how much you can recall.

1. Where do you find the form objects? (See "Tutorial: Building a Basic Form.")

2. What tags are required for every form object? (See "Tutorial: Building a Basic Form.")

3. What technique do you use to line up your form objects? (See "Tutorial: Building a Basic Form.")

4. Can you select more than one object in radio buttons? (See "Tutorial: Inserting Radio Buttons.")

5. What makes check boxes different from radio buttons? (See "Tutorial: Inserting Check Boxes.")

6. Name a few values you can specify for a textarea. (See "Tutorial: Inserting a Textarea and a List.")

7. How does a list work? (See "Tutorial: Inserting a Textarea and a List.")

8. Can you change the event that triggers a behavior? (See "Tutorial: Using Jump Menus.")

9. What is the difference between a list and a jump menu? (See "Tutorial: Using Jump Menus.")

10. Do you need to add a behavior when you add a jump menu form using the jump menu icon in the Forms Bar? (See "Tutorial: Using Jump Menus.")

In this session, you learned how to add a variety of forms from a simple textfield to a jump menu. You made these forms on separate pages so that you can add them to any document where you can customize the backgrounds and the text.

» Additional Projects

If you want to practice making a jump menu, you can add one to the default.asp page of the DataBase intranet site. Session 18 has you repeat step 1 if you choose not to use it.

1. Copy the DataBase folder from the CD-ROM to your hard drive (not in the CompleteCourse folder). Define the site in Dreamweaver and name it PDGdynamic.

2. Open the default.asp page. You notice the jump menu is already there but there is plenty of space below it to practice on.

3. Add the form field.

4. Add the jump menu.

5. Add the following List Values (you can add the links now or in the Jump Menu behavior):

    Intranet Home: Link of: ../Library/default.asp

    Contacts List: Link of: contacts_list.asp

    View Contacts: Link of: ../Library/view_contacts.asp

    Add Contact: Link of: ../Library/add_contact.asp

    Modify Contact: Link of: ../Library/mod_contact.asp

    Delete Contact: Link of: ../Library/delete_contact.asp

6. Add the Jump Menu behavior. Don't select the Select First Item After URL Change option.

7. In the Behaviors panel be sure the Event of the behavior is `onChange`.

8. Close the document and don't save the changes.

Last Name	
First Name	
Address 1	
Address 2	
City	
State	
Zip or Regional Code	
Country	
Home Phone	
Work Phone	
Fax Number	
Email Address	

Send Info   Clear Form

Session 13

Building a Frame-Based Site

Love/Hate Relationship of Frames

Using frames to design a site is an extremely controversial topic. Designers usually either love them or hate them. I'll list some of the pros and cons later in this session. But you'll be thrilled to discover that most of the cons will be addressed and converted into pros in this session.

The best argument and solutions I've seen for developing frame-based Web pages comes from Al Sparber and Gerry Jacobsen of Project VII (www.projectseven.com). They developed an extension for a special jump menu that works wonderfully with frames.

In this session, you will make an alternative Web site design. It isn't linked to the main project in any way except that you'll use some of the image resources. I felt it would be an injustice to you not to show you how to develop a frame-based site. Of course all the issues surrounding frame-based sites can't be covered, but the major issues and the basics will get you started if you want or need to build a frame-based site.

TOOLS YOU'LL USE
Property inspector, Behaviors panel, Jump menu extension, Frames panel

MATERIALS NEEDED
The PDGFrames folder on the CD-ROM

TIME REQUIRED
90–120 minutes

Tutorial
» Building the Frameset

In this tutorial you will build the frameset structure. I have supplied a few new images for a new design, added some pages for the site, and attached the pdg.css style sheet.

1. **Copy the PDGFrames folder from the CD-ROM to your hard drive.**
   You can copy it anywhere but in the CompleteCourse folder.

2. **In Dreamweaver, define a new site (Site→New Site) and name it PDGFrames.**
   This new site contains images, a style sheet, and enough files to learn how to put together and link a frame-based Web page. I didn't make a new home page or fill in all the content, but it'll be a great start for you.

3. **Use the untitled document that opens when you open Dreamweaver. Do not save it yet.**

4. **Choose View→Visual Aids and click Frame Borders.**
   Frame Borders is not on by default. While designing the frameset, you'll need to see the borders.

5. **Click the expander arrow in the Advanced Layout panel and click the Frames tab.**
   The Advanced Layout panel group opened when you opened the Layers panel in the previous session. If you don't have it docked anymore, then open the Advanced Layout panel group and make the Frames panel active by clicking its tab.

6. **Click the Frames category in the Insert Bar.**
   You'll be inserting a simple frame, and then I'll show you how to make the frameset more complex.

<NOTE>

The icons that show three frames with both horizontal and vertical areas are actually nested frames. Instead of using one of these, I will show you how to nest the frames yourself visually. Doing so will equip you with more knowledge of how to customize a frameset to meet your needs.

7. **Click the Left Frame icon in the Frames Bar.**
   You can now see the frame in the document. Also look at the Frames panel. The accessibility box will open if you are using this option. The default names entered are fine, so just click OK.

8. **Look in the Property inspector.**
   Notice that this is a frameset; you can set the borders for the frameset, which will affect all the frames. You can also set a specific column width. There is also a visual representation of the two frames. This frameset consists of three documents: the frameset document and the two individual frame documents.

9. **Click inside the left frame.**
   Look in the Tag Selector; see the <body> tag? This shows you it is a separate page with its own <body> tag. You can access each frame from the Frames panel as well. Notice the tag change.

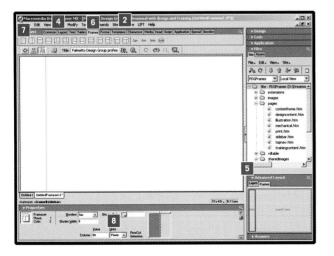

Tutorial
» Naming the Frames

In this tutorial you will set the properties of each frame and name them with meaningful names.

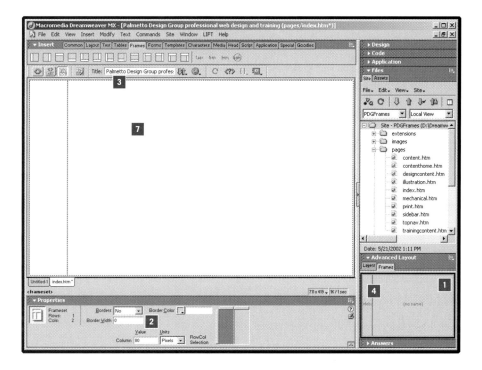

1. **Click the outer border in the Frames panel.**
   When you click the outer border of the frameset, you'll be working with the frameset document, which is actually three pages right now.

2. **In the Property inspector, set Borders to No and the Border Width to** 0.
   Remember, you have to type in zero; blank is not zero.

3. **In the Title area of the document, type** Palmetto Design Group professional web design and training.
   You don't need to title the individual frame pages because only the title from the frameset will appear in the user's browser.

4. **Select the left frame by clicking its border in the Frames panel.**

5. **In the Property inspector, name it** sidebar.
   Always give your individual frames meaningful names that describes their function.

6. **Leave No Resize checked and Scroll to No.**
   This option if unchecked would allow the user to resize the frame. Be extremely careful when you select No for scroll. Because this navigation area is small, I know it will fit in any browser without scrolling.

7. **Select the right frame and name it** content.

8. **Set the Scroll to Auto and click No Resize.**
   This frame will have an undetermined amount of content so the scroll is set to scroll if needed.

Tutorial
» Adding a Nested Frame and Saving the Frameset

In this tutorial, you will be adding a frame to the top of the content frame to act as the top navigation and logo frame. This is called a nested frame. You will then save the frameset and the three individual frames.

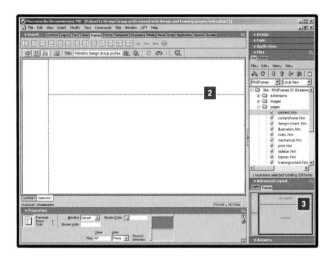

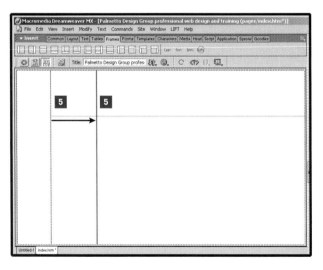

1. **Click the content frames border.**
   Notice in the Property inspector you now see this frame only, not both of the frames. This is important because now you are going to add a nested frame in this frame.

2. **In the document window, drag the top border of the content frame down to about 1/4 of the space.**

3. **Select the new frame and name it** topnav.

4. **Set the Scroll to No and click No Resize to select it.**

5. **Click the inside sidebar border in the document window and drag a bit larger, about 1/4 of the document window.**
   When you place the cursor over the inside border you will see a double arrow; click and drag to the new position.

6. **Click the outer border of all the frames to select the frameset.**
   Look in the Tag Inspector; the `<frameset>` tag will be bold.

7. **Click File→Save Frameset As.**

8. **Name it** index.htm **and save it in the Pages folder.**

9. **Click inside the sidebar frame.**

10. **Click File→Save Frame As and name it** sidebar.htm**. Save it in the Pages folder.**

11. **Click inside the topnav frame.**

12. **Click File→Save Frame As and name it** topnav.htm**. Save it in the Pages folder.**

13. **Click inside the content frame.**

14. **Click File→Save Frame As and name it** content.htm**. Save it in the Pages folder.**

Tutorial
» Adding Content to the Frames

In this tutorial you will insert the .HTM files that will load into the index.htm file whenever it opens. I have supplied the pages you can use for this practice.

1. **Click the sidebar border in the Frames panel.**
   Be sure you can see the name sidebar in the Property inspector. Another way to tell if you've got the frame selected is to check the Tag Selector. `<frame#sidebar>` will be bold.

2. **Open the Site panel and open the Pages folder.**

3. **In the Property inspector, click and drag the Point to File icon and drag to the sidebarcontent.htm page in the Pages folder.**
   The frame may be too small or too large for the content. You can click and drag the border to fit but you can be more precise in the Property inspector.

4. **Change the Column size to** 200 **and press Enter/Return.**
   If you don't see the Column size option, click the frameset border to access it.

5. **Select the topnav frame (**`<frame#topnav>` **will be bold).**

6. **Use the Point to File icon and drag it to the Pages folder and release the mouse on topnavcontent.htm.**

7. **Select the topnav frame border and change its Row width to** 69.

8. **Select the content frame.**

9. **Use the Point to File icon and drag it to the Pages folder and release the mouse on contenthome.htm.**

10. **In the Property inspector in the Column area, click the right frame in the little image.**

11. **Set the Units to Relative and save.**
    This setting will expand this column based on the browser window size.

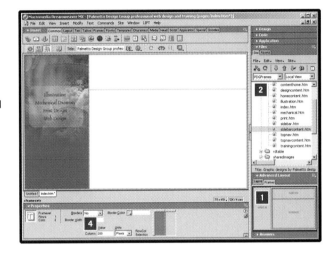

Tutorial
» Linking the Navigation

In this tutorial you'll add links to the sidebar navigation, which will open pages in the content area. Then you'll click a link in the content area, which will open a document in the same area.

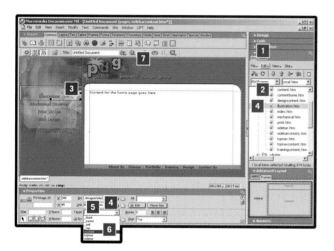

1. **Open the Site panel.**

2. **Open the Pages folder.**

3. **Click the Illustration image in the document sidebar.**

4. **In the Property inspector, drag the Point to File icon to the illustration.htm file and release the mouse.**

5. **Click the down arrow for Target.**

6. **Click content.**

7. **Preview your work in the appropriate browsers.**

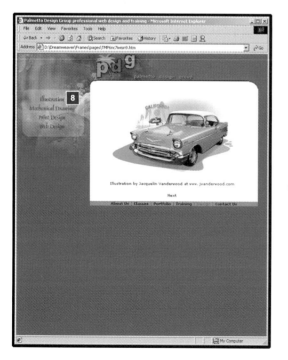

8. **Click the Illustration button.**
   The image of the Bel Air loads in the content area.

9. **Repeat for Mechanical Drawing and Print Design.**
   There is no file for Web Design, so you can use a null link or just skip it.

< N O T E >

I had you replace the sidebar with the links because it's going to be loaded with the design page. You developed the links while preparing the frameset for teaching purposes. You will learn a technique that will load the sidebar frame and the content frame both with one click.

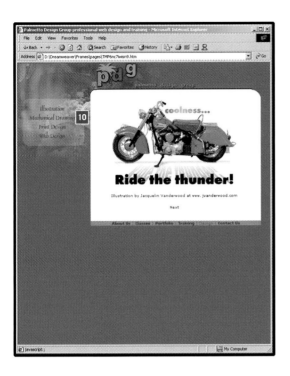

10. **Check the Mechanical Drawing and Print Design links in a browser.**
    Notice how the content area expands to fit the different sized images.

11. **Double-click the illustration.htm file to open it and highlight the word Next.**

12. **Drag the Point to File icon for the link to the mechanical.htm file and release the mouse.**
    If this were a real site, you'd probably have more samples under the illustration link. Because we don't, you are simply using the next category for the next link.

13. **Click the arrow for the Target.**

14. **Click _self.**
    This will open the link on top of the current page. It will therefore replace the current page.

15. **Preview your work in the appropriate browsers. Click the Illustration link, and then click the Next link.**

16. **Repeat for mechanical.htm and print.htm. Link Print Design to illustration.htm to make a loop.**

17. **Save your file.**

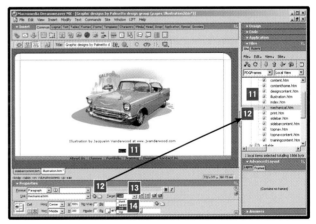

<NOTE>

The drawings were provided by Jacquelin Vanderwood of
www.jvanderwood.com.

Tutorial
» Adding Multiple Links

Because you've already learned how to insert images and make an image map, I've added these parts for you to begin this tutorial.

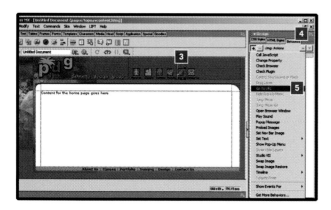

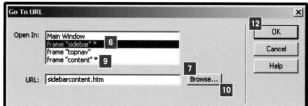

1. **Copy the index.htm file from the Session13 folder on the CD-ROM (not from the final folder) and paste it into your Pages folder inside the Frames folder.**
   It will overwrite the current index page.

2. **Double-click the index.htm file in the Pages folder to open it.**
   You'll see the icons across the top with blue boxes around them.

3. **Click the Design icon (second from the right).**

4. **Open the Behaviors panel, which is in the Design panel group.**

5. **Click the plus sign and click Go to URL.**
   The Go to URL dialog box opens. This is a pretty neat feature.

6. **Click frame "sidebar"*.**

7. **Click the Browse button and navigate to the Pages folder.**

8. **Click sidebarcontent.htm and click OK.**
   If you recall, this is the page we linked the Illustration, Mechanical Drawing, Print Design, and Web Design links to.

9. **Click frame "content"*.**

10. **Click the Browse button.**

11. **Navigate to the Pages folder, click designcontent.htm, and click OK.**

12. **Click OK.**
    You'd simply repeat these steps for other links. Wasn't that easy?

13. **In the Behaviors panel, click the down arrow for the Go To URL behavior.**

14. **Click** onClick.
    Of course you can use any one of the options you see listed in the menu. You can even have the sidebar and content both load onLoad if you'd like.

15. **Preview your work in the appropriate browsers.**

16. **Click the Design icon.**
    Notice how the sidebar and the content window change; isn't that cool?

17. **Click File→Save All.**

Tutorial
» Coding for Search Engines

One of the greatest arguments for not using frames is the fact that they are difficult to index in a search engine. If you code your page properly, you can overcome this drawback. Of course I'll show you how to do that now.

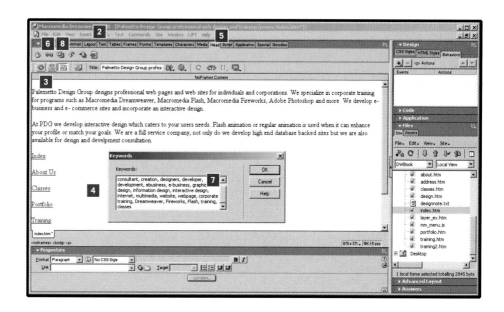

1. **Open the index.htm file if it isn't open.**

2. **Click Modify→Frameset→Edit NoFrames Content.**

3. **In the blank window that opens, type a description of your site.**

<NOTE>

This is the window that browsers that don't support frames will see. It is also the information that the search engine will use to index your site, so use keywords and phrases in your description. I filled in this one using as many keywords as I could. I'm not a copywriter though. For these kinds of things I'd consult with some- one who is really good at writing these sort of descriptions. This and your Meta tags are some of the most important things you can do to be found in search engines.

4. **Add links to every page that you'd like a search engine to index.**
Type the text names for the links. When you add the actual link in the Property inspector, use an absolute URL. I used http://www.palmettodesigngroup.com and then added each file name to the end.

5. **Click the Head tab in the Insert Bar.**

6. **Click the Add Keywords icon.**

7. **Enter the keywords you'd like and click OK.**
I just copied the ones used in the PDG site that we've already done.

8. **Click the Description icon.**

9. **Type a description and click OK.**

Tutorial
» Adding a Specialized Jump Menu

This is an enhanced jump menu that is great for using with frames. It doesn't fit with the sample design because you can't have multiple links, so you will build it in a new page.

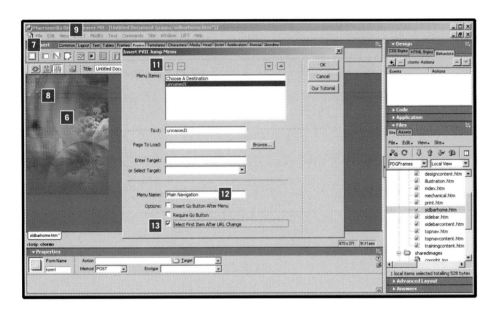

1. **Open the Goodies folder in the Session13 folder on the CD-ROM.**

2. **Copy the extensions in it and paste them into the Downloaded Extensions folder in the Dreamweaver MX program files.**

3. **Double-click each extension to install it.**

4. **After you accept the licensing agreement, the extension will be installed and will display a message saying that it has successfully installed.**

5. **Double-click the sidebarhomejump.htm page to open it.**

6. **Click the layer named jumpmenu.**
   It's below the logo. You can select this layer in the Layers panel if you'd like.

7. **Place your cursor inside the layer and, in the Forms Bar of the Insert Bar, click the Forms icon.**
   This field is required for this menu to work in Netscape 4X.

<NOTE>
You may wonder how you were able to add a form to the sidebar with an image. It's because this image is set as a background image. I attached the pdg.css style sheet to the sidebarhome.htm file. I then edited the body style and used the image for the background. To attach a style sheet you simply click Text→CSS Styles→Attach Style Sheet and click the Link option.

8. **Click inside the form field in the sidebar frame.**

9. **Click Insert→StudioVII→Jump Menu.**

10. **In the text field, type Choose A Destination.**

11. **Click the plus sign (+) to enter the menu item.**

12. **Type Main Navigation in the Menu Name field.**

13. **Click the Select First Item After URL Change field.**
    This option will return the Choose A Destination item to the menu. You don't need to add any links yet because this is just the beginning item the users see.

14. **In the Text field, highlight the current entry and type** About Us.

15. **Click the plus sign.**

16. **Type** javascript:; **in the Page to Load field.**
Normally, you would click the Browse button and select the about.htm file but we don't have that page done.

17. **Type** content **for the Enter Target field.**
If you were working within the frameset, you'd be able to click the down arrow for Select Target and click Content.

18. **Click the plus sign.**

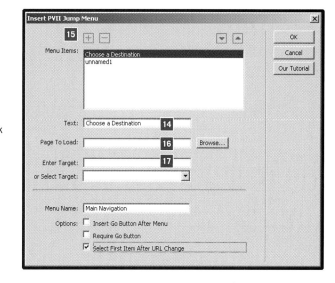

19. **Repeat steps 14–18 for Classes and Portfolio.**

20. **Type** Training **in the Text field.**

21. **Click the Browse button and navigate to the Pages folder. Click trainingcontent.htm.**

22. **Type** content **for the Enter Target field.**

23. **Click the plus sign.**

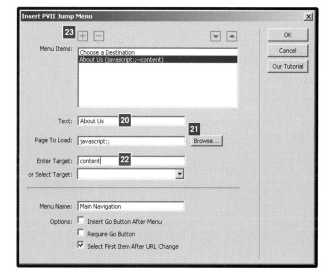

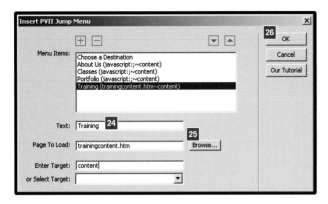

24. **Type** Design **in the Text field.**

25. **Click the Browse button and select the designcontent.htm file as the page to load.**

26. **Type** content **in the Enter Target filed and click OK.**

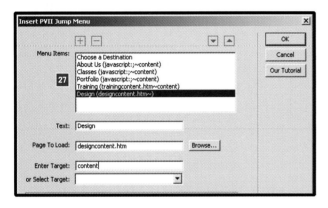

27. **Save the file.**

    You can preview the menu in a browser now, but if you want to preview in the frameset you'll need to perform the following steps.

28. **Open the index.htm page.**

29. **Select the sidebar frame in the Frames panel.**

30. **Drag the Point to File icon for Src to the sidebarhomeJump.htm file and release the mouse.**

31. **Preview your work in the appropriate browsers. Click Training and then click Design.**

32. **Select the sidebar frame again and return the Scr link back to sidebarhome.htm.**

33. **Click File→Save All.**

» Session Review

It's time to test yourself again to see how much of the frames information you've retained. You may have to work with frames a bit more to have it really sink in. You may want to repeat this session if you find you can't answer the majority of these questions.

1. Name one way to insert a frame. (See "Tutorial: Building the Frameset.")

2. What is a frameset? (See "Tutorial: Building the Frameset.")

3. How do you select a frameset? (See "Tutorial: Naming the Frames.")

4. How do you add a nested frame? (See "Tutorial: Adding a Nested Frame and Saving the Frameset.")

5. How do you add content to the individual frames? (See "Tutorial: Adding Content to the Frames.")

6. When adding links, what is different about linking in a frame to open in another frame? What is this type of frame called? (See "Tutorial: Linking the Navigation.")

7. What method is used that enables you to link multiple frames to one link? (See "Tutorial: Adding Multiple Links.")

8. How do you save all the frameset files at one time? (See "Tutorial: Adding Multiple Links.")

9. Name two important features that allow search engines to index your site even if it's framed. (See "Tutorial: Coding for Search Engines.")

10. Do you have to have a Go button with a jump menu? (See "Tutorial: Adding a Specialized Jump Menu.")

» Additional Projects

If you'd like to practice some more, you could add some content to one of the other categories.

1. Open the sidebarhome.htm file on the CD-ROM (not the one you just saved).

2. Save the file in your Pages folder as portfolio.htm.

3. Add a jump menu (Dreamweaver or PVII one).

4. Use any names you'd like for the menu items.

5. Add a portfolio content page with identifying text in it (such as a content page for portfolio). This will help you identify whether it works property when you test it.

6. Link the Portfolio icon to open the new sidebar and content `onClick`.

7. Add a content page or two to correspond to your menu item links.

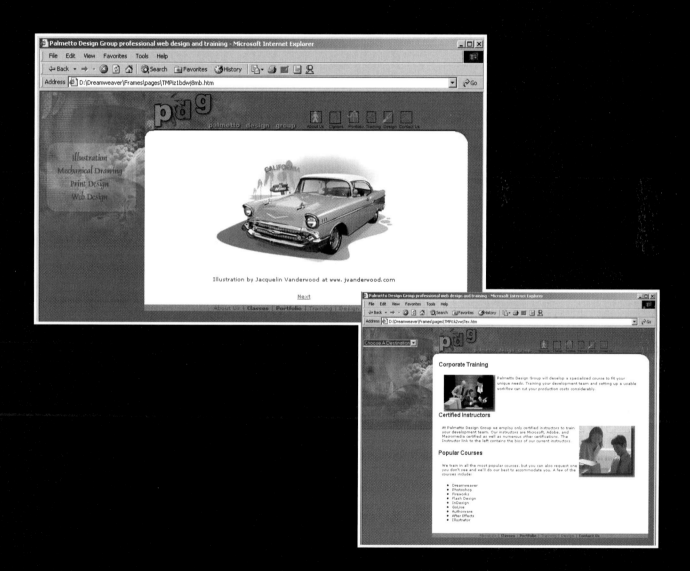

Part V:
Site Management

Performing Site Checks

```
<html>
<head>
<meta http-equiv=Content-Type content="text/html; charset=windows-1252">
<title>Our Commitment</title>
<style><!--
.Section1
  {page:Section1;}
-->
</style>
</head>
<body bgcolor="#FFFFFF" class="Normal" lang=EN-US>
<div class=Section1>
 <p>Our Commitment</p>
 <p>Palmetto Design Group is committed to working with you to </p>
 <p>develop your on line presence. An PDG website is an effective </p>
 <p>communicator which incorporates your market plans and </p>
 <p>strategies. At Palmetto Design Group we are dedicated to </p>
 <p>meeting your business objectives </p>
 <p>Our Process</p>
 <p>Palmetto Design Group starts the developing process of your </p>
 <p>Website by getting involved with you to better understand </p>
 <p>your business and your marketing plan. We work with you by </p>
 <p>using our extensive Survey Form. We do this to better </p>
 <p>understand your goals and expectations for your Website. When </p>
```

Tutorial: **Running a Site Report for Links**

Tutorial: **Checking Site Reports**

Tutorial: **Using Find and Replace**

Tutorial: **Finding and Replacing Code**

Checking Your Work

There isn't really anything you need to replace in the site you are developing but the Find and Replace function is a powerful tool that you'll find is indispensable when you have to edit a site. It's inevitable — a client changes his/her mind. You may need to change the name of something or you discover a word that has been misspelled — or worse, someone's name is incorrect. These kinds of things are extremely easy to fix, whether it's one page or an entire site. But you can also search for tags or for text inside tags; you can use wildcards and develop some pretty complex searches. In this session, you learn how to add a style sheet link to an entire site, which currently has no style sheets.

You discover some of the site reports that are available in Dreamweaver. You can check for Accessibility, Alt tags, broken links, and much more.

TOOLS YOU'LL USE
Results panel group, Find and Replace function

MATERIALS NEEDED
None

TIME REQUIRED
45 minutes

Tutorial
» Running a Site Report for Links

In this tutorial, you run a site report for checking broken links in the PDG template as well as checking the external links site wide.

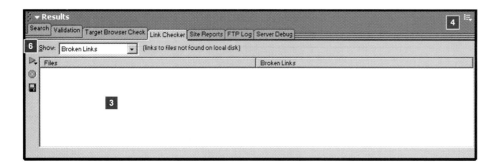

1. **Open the CompleteCourse site in the Site panel. Double-click the PDG.dwt file in the Templates folder.**
   Because all the site's pages are based on the template, you must run several site reports on this page.

2. **Click Window➔Results➔Link Checker.**
   Notice that below the Property inspector a new panel group docks itself. This is the Results panel group with seven categories. Each category has additional options.

3. **Look in the white field for the report results.**
   In this case, the area is blank because none of the links are broken on this particular page. Now you can check the entire site.

4. **Click the arrow to access the options for the Show drop-down list.**

5. **Click External Links.**

6. **Click the arrow near the green arrow icon.**

7. **Click Check links for entire site.**
   You can now see three items. The first two are mm_menu.js items. This is the JavaScript menu of the sample pop-up menu you made links to. Because all we have is a template in the template folder, the path doesn't show that it links to the JavaScript file.

8. **Double-click the icon near the Text/aboutus_text.htm file.**

   The problem area is highlighted in the code (be sure you are using Split view or Code view). The site file that is affected is the aboutus_text document, which was originally produced in Microsoft Word.

9. **Click Commands→Cleanup Word HTML.**

10. **Click OK in the Clean Up Word HTML dialog box, using the default settings.**

    The results appear. This command cleaned up four Meta tags, 67 instances of the word XML (which was the problem you encountered in the link check), 47 Word [if...]s removed, 45 instances of unneeded inline CSS removed, nine Word-only mso styles removed, and one instance of unused CSS style definitions removed. This demonstration should help you appreciate the good code that Dreamweaver generates.

11. **Click OK to close the results dialog box.**

12. **Click OK to Save the HTML file.**

    All that shows now is the JavaScript menu, which is just fine.

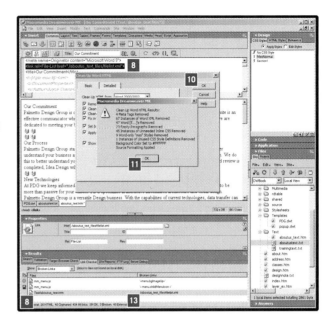

< N O T E >

If you have other broken links that you happened to miss, click the yellow folder and locate the correct image or document and select it. When it is fixed it disappears from the list.

13. **Look along the bottom of the Results panel group.**

    You can see the statistics of the site. Notice there are 40 orphaned links. This means that these 40 items are not linked to anything.

14. **Click the arrow for the Show field and click Orphaned Files.**

    You can double-click any of the icons for the files and see what they are. For the most part, the orphaned links are for the text files I provided for you to copy and paste. The extra background images I included in the background folder show up as orphans as well as the forms we made. The two broken links are the JavaScript menu links.

15. **Save the file.**

Tutorial
» Checking Site Reports

In this tutorial, you run a few site reports for the Palmetto Design Group.

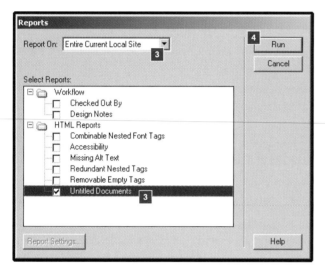

1. **Click the Site Reports category tab in the Results panel group.**

2. **Click the Green arrow.**
   The Reports dialog box opens.

3. **Click the Report On field arrow and select Entire Current Local Site. Click Untitled Documents to select it.**
   There is nothing worse than seeing Untitled Documents in a browser's title bar. Run this check to assure that you didn't miss any.

4. **Click Run.**
   If you get any returns, double-click the icon and give the page/s a title.

5. **Click the green arrow again to run a new report.**

6. **This time click Missing Alt Text.**

7. **Click Run.**
   The report field should be empty, but if it isn't, double-click the missing item and add alternative text.

8. **Continue running different checks if you desire.**
   Most of the options, such as Redundant Nested Tags and Removable Empty Tags, all return no errors since we have let Dreamweaver do the coding. These options come in handy when checking your own coding.

9. **Click the Panel Options menu and click Close Panel Group.**

Accessibility Tests

I didn't have you run the Accessibility test because all kinds of things are shown. Although we added blank Alt text values for the spacer images, the Dreamweaver accessibility test results show them all. Another issue that appears in the Dreamweaver report is all the tables. A more effective way to test for accessibility is to use the full version of the program named Lift (www.usable net.com). This program gives you all kinds of options to customize the checks such as how to handle your tables and other nonvital images. With Lift, you can also fix each error as it is discovered. If you need to make a totally accessible site, you should definitely read up on the issues involved. The Alt text we've been using is one major part of the accessibility guidelines, but there are a lot of other issues as well.

Tutorial
» Using Find and Replace

In this tutorial, you learn how to use the Find and Replace function. You don't really have anything to replace, but this is a tool you may need to use, and it's important to understand how powerful it really is.

1. **Double-click the training.htm page to open it.**

2. **Highlight the words Palmetto Design Group in the first paragraph.**
   When you highlight words prior to searching for them, they appear in the Search field. This is not required, however.

3. **Click Edit→Find and Replace.**
   The Find and Replace dialog box opens. The highlighted text appears in the text field. If you were going to make a change to the company name, you would type it in the Replace With area.

4. **Click the arrow for the Find In field.**
   Notice that you can search the current document, the entire site, a specified folder, and specified files.

5. **Look at the Options field.**
   If you are looking for specific words with capitalization, check the Match Case option. It's a good idea to leave the Ignore Whitespace Differences checked. This option looks for a phrase without regard to spacing differences.

6. **Click the Find All button.**
   The Results panel group now displays the results of the search. You can double-click each entry to check them if you'd like.

7. **Click the green arrow to open the Find and Replace dialog box again.**

8. **You would now click Replace or Replace All if you were actually changing this text.**
   You can either close the dialog box now or leave it open for the next tutorial.

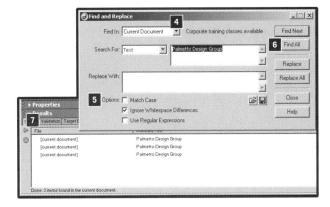

<NOTE>
This dialog box is different from most of the Dreamweaver windows because it stays open while you continue working. Most dialog boxes have to be closed to continue working.

<NOTE>
Regular expressions (a list can be found in the Dreamweaver Help) are useful in performing wildcard searches and are more flexible than searching for exact strings.

Saving Queries

You can develop some pretty complex queries using wildcards with the Find and Replace function and using regular expressions. If you find yourself reusing functions consistently, you can save them by clicking the disk icon in the Find and Replace dialog box.

The settings are saved with a .DWR file extension. You can reuse a saved query by clicking the yellow folder to the left of the disk icon. Just navigate to the location and open the file.

Tutorial
» Finding and Replacing Code

In this tutorial, you learn how to search code as well as text. A common task you might find yourself doing is attaching a style sheet to Web pages that didn't formerly use them. This tutorial shows you how to do that quite easily.

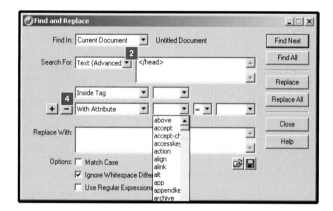

1. Change to the PDG frames site that you defined. Open Find and Replace if it isn't already (Edit→Find and Replace).

2. In the Search For field, click the arrow and click Text (Advanced). Notice that there are now additional options. You can search specific tags or search for text outside of a tag.

3. Click the plus sign to see additional options.
   As you can see, you can come up with some pretty complex queries with all these options. Click the different arrows to see the lists you can choose from.

4. Click the minus sign to close the attribute row, and then click the minus sign again to close the tag row. You won't need these to add the code for the style sheet that you are going to add.

5. Click the arrow of the Find In field and click Entire Current Local Site.

6. Click the arrow of the Search For field and click Source Code.

7. In the search field type `</head>`.
   You are going to find all instances of the ending `</head>` tag. The link to a style sheet is placed inside the `<head>` tags.

8. In the Replace With field, you type the link information for the style sheet you want to attach.
   For the frames pages, it would be this information: `<link href="../Stylesheet/pdg.css" rel="stylesheet" type="text/css"> </head>`.

9. Click Find All.
   The results show all of the main pages of this site. If you were really adding the style sheet link you would now click Replace All. Don't click it now! The style sheets are already linked to for this site. What would happen with the Replace All is that the link would be added and the closing `</head>` tag would be replaced. You used the `</head>` tag to search, but you need to be sure that it isn't removed.

10. Click Close.

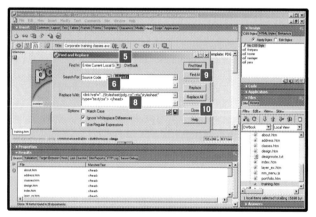

<N O T E>

In the following steps, you see how you can attach a style sheet to multiple Web pages. In the frames site you developed, I attached style sheets to the individual pages by clicking Text→CSS Styles→Attach Style Sheet. You can accomplish the same thing for an entire site by using the Find and Replace function.

<N O T E>

If you are adding a CSS style sheet to a site that didn't have one, you'll want to clean up and remove the `<font>` tags. You can use a previously made style sheet and edit the attributes if you'd like. You'll have to manually apply any custom classes.

» Session Review

I know that there were not many things to fix in this site, but hopefully some of the site reports available to you make more sense now. Test yourself now to see how much you can recall.

1. How do you access the various reports you can run? (See "Tutorial: Running a Site Report for Links.")

2. How do you view the results of various reports? (See "Tutorial: Running a Site Report for Links.")

3. What is the full-featured program called that is recommended for those who are serious about accessibility issues? (See "Tutorial: Checking Site Reports.")

4. What is unique about the Find and Replace dialog box? (See "Tutorial: Using Find and Replace.")

5. Name two things you can search for. (See "Tutorial: Using Find and Replace.")

6. Can you reuse queries you have developed? (See "Tutorial: Using Find and Replace.")

7. What part of the document would you add a link to a style sheet to? (See "Tutorial: Finding and Replacing Code.")

Session 15

Round-Trip Between Dreamweaver and Fireworks

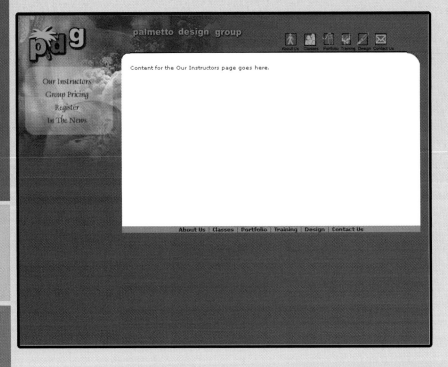

Editing in Fireworks

In this session, you learn to edit images in several ways. Dreamweaver makes it possible to edit in Fireworks and, with a click of the button, allows you to automatically apply changes in Dreamweaver. But you may find circumstances when this option is not the best way to go. You also learn how to edit directly in Fireworks.

As a bonus, you get an accelerated look at many of basic functions in the various tutorials of this session. You learn how to slice, optimize, and export images with complete HTML code and tables from Fireworks. You can then insert a fully functional and linked navigational graphic from Fireworks into Dreamweaver.

You need to install Fireworks for this session. If you don't have it, a trial version is available on the CD-ROM. If you are new to using graphics editors, you may find this session challenging. There is a lot packed in to give you the most exposure to Fireworks as possible in one session.

TOOLS YOU'LL USE
Fireworks MX, Preferences panel, Slice tool, View tools, Optimize panel, Export panel, Preview panels

MATERIALS NEEDED
Session 14 files from the CD-ROM added to your CompleteCourse root folder if you didn't complete the previous tutorial

Source folder from the CD-ROM; place it outside the CompleteCourse folder.

TIME REQUIRED
120 minutes

Tutorial
» Setting the Graphics Editor Preferences

In this tutorial, you set up the graphics editor of your choice (Fireworks MX I hope) to open and edit images from within Dreamweaver. The tutorials in this session do assume you've installed Fireworks MX (there's a trial version on the CD-ROM). If you installed the Macromedia Studio MX, this will already be done and you can skip to the next tutorial.

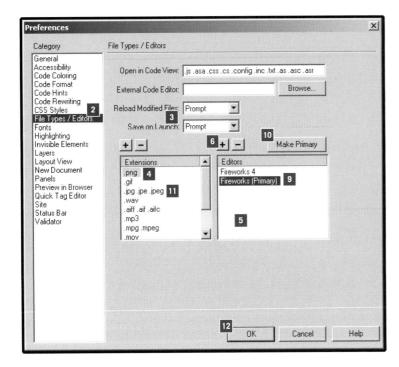

1. **Click Edit→Preferences.**

2. **Click the File Types/Editors category.**

3. **Reset the Reload Modified Files if you'd like to. I prefer to be prompted, so I leave the default. Do the same for Save on Launch.**

4. **Click the .PNG extension.**

5. **If any editors are specified for this file type, they appear in the Editors section.**

6. **Click the plus sign if no editor is present or if you want to add one.**

7. **Navigate to the application folder for Fireworks MX (or editor of choice) and select the executable file.**

8. **Click Open.**

9. **Select Fireworks MX in the Editors section.**

10. **Click the Make Primary button.**

11. **Repeat for the GIF and JPEG extensions.**

12. **Click OK to close the Preferences dialog box.**

Tutorial
» Editing and Slicing in Fireworks

In this tutorial, you edit the two logo images directly in Fireworks and not through Dreamweaver. You'll see why later in this session. You also learn how to use the Slice tool.

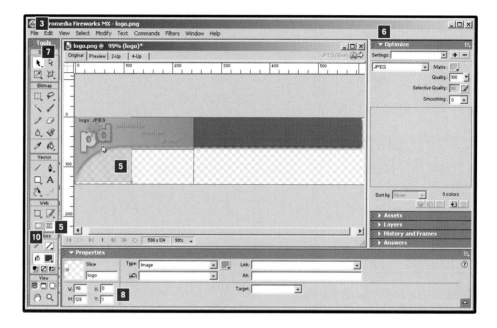

1. **If you don't have Fireworks MX installed (or another version), you can install the trial version from this book's CD-ROM.**

< N O T E >

You should also have copied the Source folder from the CD-ROM and placed it outside of the CompleteCourse folder.

2. **Open Fireworks.**

3. **Click File→Open and navigate to your Source folder.**

4. **Click logo.png and click Open.**

5. **You should see two green slice overlays. If you don't see them, click the Show Slices and Hotspots icon.**

6. **Click the expander arrow of the Optimize panel to open it.**

7. **Click the Pointer tool and select the slice that has the large PD and tree in it.**

8. **Look in the Property inspector and write down the height and width of the slice. Also write down the x and y coordinates. Repeat for the second one as well.**

< N O T E >

I'm having you write down the dimensions because I am going to show you how to make your own slices, but they will need to be the same size so nothing is messed up later in the Web site design in Dreamweaver.

9. **Delete both slices now by selecting each slice and pressing the Delete key.**

10. **Click the Hide Slices and Hotspots icon.**
    Before you make slices or optimize or export the images, you will change the color of the text.

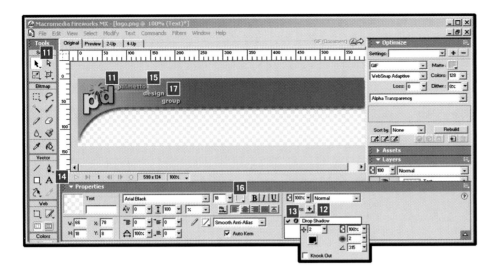

<NOTE>

It is beyond the scope of this book to go into great detail about optimizing and exporting. If you follow the directions carefully, you can see how easy it is to prepare images for the Web in Fireworks.

11. **With the Pointer tool, click the word palmetto.**

    In the Property inspector you will see the text properties since this is text. Although it has an effect applied to it, it is still fully editable.

12. **Look in the Effects area of the Property inspector.**

    In the Effects list, you will see any effects applied to the selected object.

13. **Click the little icon next to Drop Shadow.**

    Notice the different settings. The shadow Distance is 2 pixels with a Softness of 2. You can set the angle and opacity as well.

<NOTE>

We aren't making any changes, I just wanted to show you how you can edit and/or see what effects are applied to an object. If you wanted to make a change, such as Knockout, you would click the option to select it, and then press Enter/Return to accept the change. This applies to any of the settings. If you try a setting, be sure to go back and uncheck it before proceeding to the next step.

14. **Click the Text tool.**

15. **Highlight just the "almetto" part of the word palmetto.**

    You can use the Zoom tool or Ctrl+spacebar+click (⌘+spacebar+click) to zoom in on the text.

16. **Click the color box in the Property inspector. Using the Eyedropper, pass it over the green tree and click to use that color.**

17. **Using the Text tool, highlight just the "esign" part of the word design and change its color to green as well. Repeat for the word group.**

18. **Click the Slice tool and drag a selection around the first logo piece.**
    You can't optimize individual parts of an image until you have defined a slice. You can have different image formats for each slice, if desired. Don't worry about the exact size; you'll take care of that in a moment.

19. **In the Property inspector, highlight the current width and type** 116.

20. **Highlight the current height and type** 128.

21. **Be sure the x coordinate is 0 and the y coordinate is 1.**

22. **Highlight the current slice name and type** logo.

23. **Press Enter/Return for the changes to take effect.**

<NOTE>
Before making another slice, click View→Guides→Snap to Guides if there is no check mark by Snap to Guides. This will help your slices line up without overlapping.

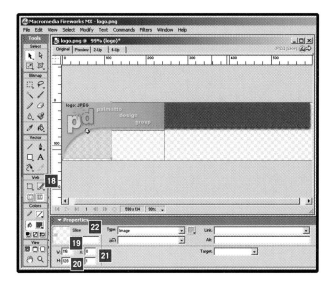

24. **Using the Slice tool, draw the second slice and enter these properties:**

    » W: **128**

    » H: **64**

    » x: **116**

    » y: **1**

    » Name: **logo_2**

25. **Press Enter/Return.**
    Don't close the image yet; you need it for the next tutorial.

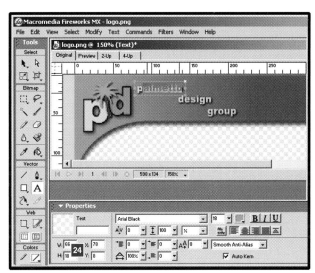

Tutorial
» Optimizing in Fireworks

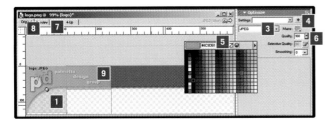

<NOTE>
For this JPEG image, if you didn't select a Matte color it exports with a white background. The Matte color on GIF images is the color that the edges of the image mix with when they are anti-aliased. This is why you see fringes around images at times. This means that the image was exported using a different matte or background color than the color it is placed upon.

1. **Using the Pointer tool, click the first slice (PD) to select it.**

2. **In the Optimize panel, click the arrow for the File Format.**
   Notice the list of options.

3. **Click JPEG.**

4. **Click the color box for the Matte color.**

5. **Type #ACB7C5.**
   The Matte color is the color used for the background when exporting. To find the color of the background, you can check the files in Dreamweaver. Easier yet, look in the Color category of the Dreamweaver Assets panel to get the Hex number.

6. **Move the Quality slider up to 100.**
   These are the only settings you'll work with for this image. You don't need to add Selective Quality or Smoothing.

7. **In the document window, click the Preview tab.**
   You see what the selected slice looks like using the current settings you made in the Optimize panel. If you'd like to see what a lower quality setting would look like, move the slider down. I opted to use 100% for the sake of the shadow and to improve the text.

8. **Click the Original tab again.**

9. **Click the second slice.**

10. **Because this slice (100% JPEG and the blue matte) has a gradient fill, use the same settings as you did for the previous slice. Preview it.**

11. **Click File→Save.**
    This overwrites your logo.png file. The Save command saves as a Fireworks PNG file.

12. **Don't close the logo.png file just yet; you will export these two slices next.**

Tutorial
» Exporting from Fireworks

In this tutorial, you export the two slices you've made. You also learn how you can export the entire image as a table, including the HTML code.

1. **Notice in your logo image that there are red lines.**

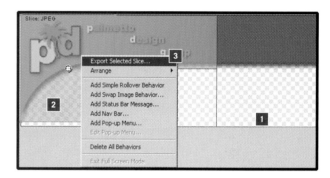

< N O T E >
These lines indicate slice areas that Fireworks will slice for you automatically if you so choose. These types of slices can't receive behaviors such as rollovers in Fireworks but can receive Dreamweaver behaviors if exported and inserted into Dreamweaver.

2. **Right-click the first logo image.**

3. **Click Export Selected Slice.**
   You can also select the slice and click File→Export. But this method does not automatically have the Selected Slices Only option checked. If you forget to click the Selected Slices Only, all the slices, including the non-defined slices in the red areas, are also exported.

4. **Navigate to the shared folder in the CompleteCourse folder and click logo.jpg. Click OK to overwrite with the edited image.**

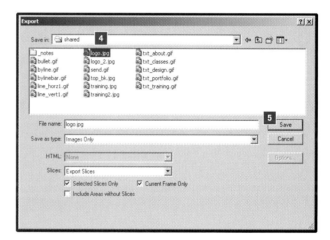

< N O T E >
If you want to include all the slices, including the undefined ones, you click the Include Areas Without Slices option. If you want to export this entire image with HTML code, you click the arrow for the Save as Type field and click HTML and Images.

5. **Click Save.**

6. **Repeat the steps for the second slice, except overwrite the logo2.jpg image file.**

7. **Save your image, close Fireworks, and open Dreamweaver.**

8. **Open the training.htm file.**

9. **Notice that the new images are shown.**
   You didn't have to do anything in Dreamweaver for the edits to take effect because you overwrote the image files that these images point to.

10. **You can close the training.htm file now.**

Tutorial
» Editing a Source Image in Fireworks from Dreamweaver

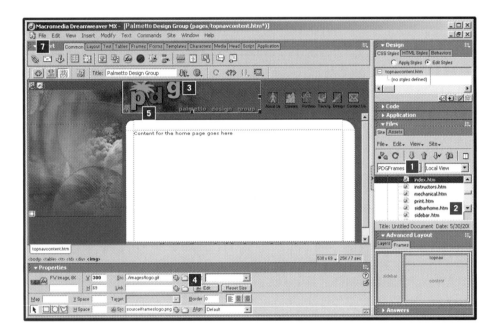

1. Open the site you defined for frames. Mine is called **PDGFrames.**

2. **Double-click the index.htm file (in the Pages folder) to open the frameset.**

3. **Click the PDG logo image to select it.**
   I don't care for the logo in this image; I think it would look better in the left top corner. Plus the transition from the sidebar background image into this image isn't very smooth so you will edit it now.

4. **Click the Edit button in Dreamweaver.**
   Fireworks will open with the image displayed; notice how this document window is different. There is a Done button and a Dreamweaver icon with an arrow to a Fireworks icon, indicating you came from Dreamweaver to Fireworks.

<NOTE>
The source image automatically opened in Fireworks because I supplied the source file for you in the proper folder. If the source can't be found (you've moved it since exporting), a dialog box will open so you can locate it. Or at the bottom of the Property inspector you will see a small Fireworks icon. You can click the folder to locate the frameslogo.png file that will open in Fireworks.

5. **If you see a green overlay, it's the slice. Click on the Hide Slices and Hotspots icon (Web area) in the Tools panel. In the logo, click the p. Shift-click the tree, d, and g.**

6. **Press Ctrl/⌘-C (Edit→Copy).**

7. **Click File→New. Be sure the background is transparent and click OK.**
   The canvas is the correct size for the image you have copied in memory.

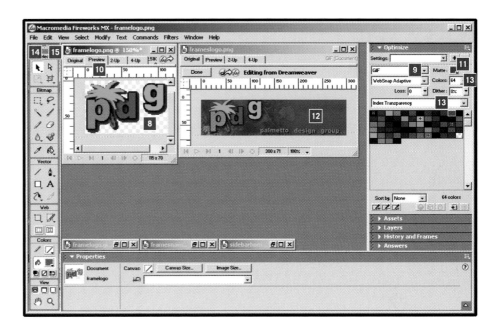

8. Press Ctrl/⌘-V (Edit→Paste) to paste the logo into its own document.

9. In the Optimize panel, choose the GIF format.

10. Click the Preview tab for the new logo image.

11. Click the color box for Matte.

12. Use the Eyedropper to sample the dark blue from the logo image composite.

13. In the Optimize panel, change the colors to 64 and the Transparency to Index Transparency.

    Notice that in the preview the background is transparent but there is a blue border around the text. This is the shadow blended in with the blue of the background color.

14. Click File→Save As and navigate to the Source folder in the Frames folder. Save the image as framelogo.png.

15. Click File→Export. Navigate to the Images folder in the Frames folder and name the image framelogo.gif. Click Save.

16. You can close this image now (the logo); you will use it later in Dreamweaver.

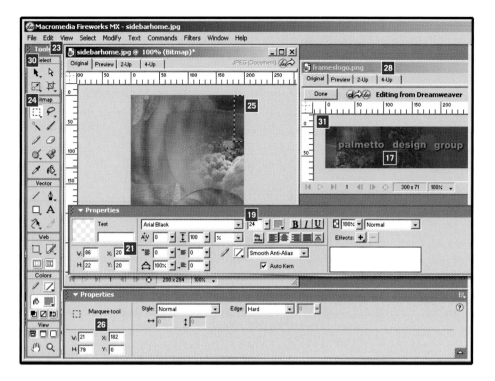

17. **Delete the p, d, g, and tree now from the composite image.**
Some of the steps to come may be a bit difficult for you if you've never used an image-editing program before. But if you follow the steps you'll be able to do it even if you don't understand it all. In the Source folder inside the Session15final folder is the new framelogo.png file. This is the one you are working on in this tutorial if you need it.

18. **Shift-select all three words, palmetto design group.**

19. **In the Property inspector, change the font size to 24.**

20. **Click anywhere so the text isn't selected.**

21. **Select the word "palmetto". In the Property inspector, type 20 for the x and y coordinates. Press Enter/Return.**

22. **Position the words "design" and "group", checking that the y coordinate is at 20.**
The next thing you will do is fix the left edge of the image so it blends better with the sidebar background image.

23. **Click File→Open and navigate to the Images folder in the Frames folder. Click sidebarhome.jpg and open it.**

24. **Click the Rectangular Marquee tool.**

25. **Drag to make a selection in the top-right corner of the sidebarhome image.**

26. **In the Property inspector, type a width of 21 and a height of 79. Press Enter/Return.**

27. **Copy the selection (Ctrl/⌘-C).**

28. **Select the masked image in the Layers panel (the image with a black-and-white gradient to the right of it) and paste the selection (Ctrl/⌘+V)**

29. **Click Don't Resample.**

30. **Click the Pointer tool.**

31. **Drag the pasted selection to the left edge of the logo image.**

32. **Don't close the image yet.**

Tutorial
» Blending the Logo Image in Fireworks

In this tutorial, you use a mask to blend the right edge of the pasted portion of the logo into the rest of the image. A mask involves two graphic objects — one on top of the other. The object on top affects what you can see of the one below. The object on top is the mask.

1. **Click the expander arrow for the Layers panel to open it.**

2. **Click the image that shows the pasted portion. It's labeled "Bitmap".**

3. **Click Modify→Merge Down.**

4. **Click OK in the dialog box that warns you that the mask will be flattened into the bitmap.**

5. **Click the Rubber Stamp tool.**

6. **In the Property inspector, change the size to 15 and the edge to 26.**

7. **Click the Source Aligned field.**

8. **Change the opacity to 50%.**

9. **Press the Alt/Option key and click in an area just below the word "palmetto".**
   This sets the sampling point. When you click another part of the image, the pattern below the sampling point will be copied. As you move your cursor, the sampling point stays aligned to the cursor because you selected Source Aligned.

10. **Click the edge of the pasted portion adjacent to the source area you just defined.**
    Because the opacity is set to 50%, you are painting the source image to the edge at 50% so it blends better.

11. **Click again on the bottom-right edge of the pasted portion and then again at the top-right edge.**

12. **Change the Rubber Stamp Size to 10.**

13. **Press Alt/Option and click just above the p to the right of the pasted portion.**

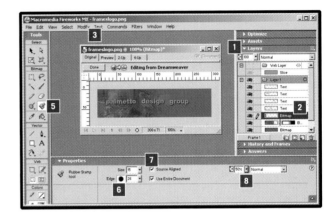

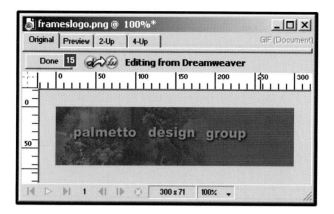

14. **Click the edge of the pasted portion near the p.**

    The pasted portion now blends nicely into the image. Getting good with the Rubber Stamp tool takes some practice. Just remember, press the Alt/Option key and choose the area you want to sample from. Then simply click where you want to paint or rubber stamp.

15. **Click the Done button.**

16. **In Dreamweaver, the repaired and changed image has replaced the former image.**

    Don't worry about how it looks in Dreamweaver. The images don't line up visually when you have the view set to show the invisible elements (yellow icons).

17. **Preview your efforts in the appropriate browsers.**

Quick Masking in Fireworks

It's beyond the scope of this book to go into great detail, but there is a simple way to mask in Fireworks MX. Masking blends one image into another. Select the image you want to blend. Click Commands→Creative→Fade Image. Click the icon, which represents the way you want the fade to happen, and then click OK. To edit the fade, click the Bitmap Mask icon in the Layers panel using the Pointer tool, and then drag the gradient handles to adjust the areas that fade.

The Fade Image command adds a rectangle above the image, which is filled with a linear gradient of white to black. Wherever there is white you will see the image show through; black is totally transparent. To better understand how masking works in Fireworks, check out the tutorial at my Web site (www. JoyceJEvans.com).

18. Click the Draw Layer icon.

19. Draw a layer in the top-left corner for the logo initials.

20. Click inside the new layer.

21. Click the Insert Image icon.

22. Navigate to the Images folder in the Frames folder and click framelogo.gif. Click Open.

23. Enter the alternate text of Palmetto Design Group logo.

24. Select the layer by clicking the white box or by clicking the name in the Layers panel.

25. In the Property inspector, change the left position to 20px and the top position to 20px.

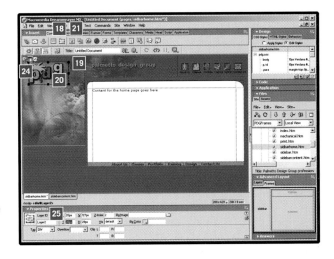

26. View your work in the appropriate browsers.

27. Click OK to save the files.

Tutorial

» Making Navigational Graphics in a Fireworks Table

This tutorial is totally Fireworks but I want to show you how to add Fireworks images and HTML into Dreamweaver. You will make the navigation for the training page of the framed site.

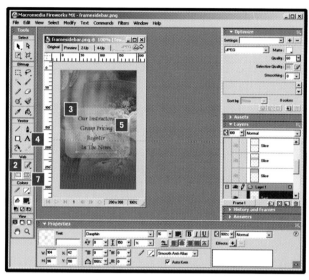

1. **In Fireworks, open the framesidebar.png file from the Source folder of the Frames folder.**

2. **Click the Hide Slices and Hotspots icon to remove the visibility of the slices.**

3. **Using the Pointer tool, click the text area to select it.**
   You will see a blue rectangle around the text, plus the Property inspector will display font properties.

4. **Click the Text tool.**

5. **Highlight the word "Illustration" and type** Our Instructors.

6. **Replace the rest of the text with** Group Pricing, Register, **and** In The News.

7. **Click the View Slices and Hotspots icon.**

<NOTE>

Notice how this image is already sliced. Each text area is a slice that can have a behavior or a link or both added to it. You can do that in Dreamweaver or it can be done in Fireworks. It's easier to do in Dreamweaver because all you have to do is drag the Point to File icon to the filename you want to link to. But you will add the first link here in Fireworks so you can see that the code will import into Dreamweaver and still work.

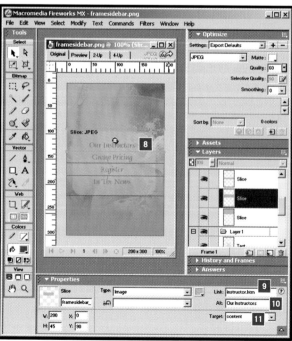

8. **Using the Pointer tool, click the Our Instructors image to select it.**

9. **In the Property inspector type** instructor.htm **for the link.**

10. **Type** Our Instructors **in the Alt field.**

11. **Type** content **in the Target field.**

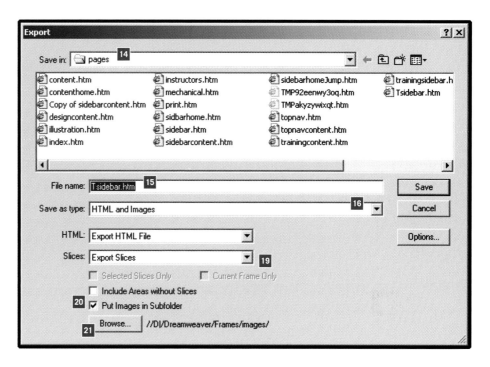

12. **Click File→Export.**

13. **Click OK on the warning that slices will be ignored.**
    You will select the option in the Export panel.

14. **Navigate to the Pages folder in the Frames folder.**

15. **Type** Tsidebar **for the file name.**

16. **Click the arrow for the Save as Type field.**

17. **Click HTML and Images.**

18. **Click OK for the warning again.**

19. **Click the arrow for Slices and click Export Slices.**

20. **Click the Put Images in Subfolder option.**
    The other two, Selected Slices Only and Include Areas without Slices, should not be selected since I have sliced up the entire image. The Current Frame Only option relates to frames in Fireworks, not Dreamweaver.

21. **Click the Browse button.**

22. **Navigate to the Images folder of the Frames folder. Double-click the Images folder to open it, and then click Open.**

23. **Click Save.**
    The HTML file is now in the Pages folder and the images have been added to the Images folder.

24. **Click File→Save As, and name the source file Tsidebar.png. Click OK.**
    Your Source folder should have opened, but in the event that it didn't, navigate to it and save the new source file in it.

Tutorial
» Inserting Fireworks HTML into Dreamweaver

In this tutorial, you insert the Fireworks HTML with the images and the table into Dreamweaver and check the link you added.

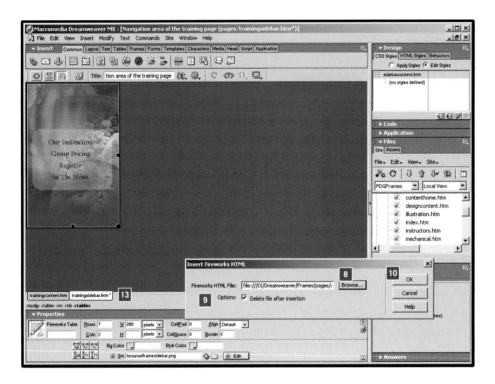

1. **Open Dreamweaver.**

2. **Open your defined frames site if it isn't already open.**

3. **Double-click the sidebarcontent.htm page to open it.**

4. **Click each image in the navigational area and delete it.**
   You will be deleting all the images in the table.

5. **Click File→Save As and name the page** trainingsidebar.htm.

6. **Click inside the now-empty table.**

7. **Click Insert→Interactive Images→Fireworks HTML.**

8. **Click the Browse button and navigate to the Pages folder. Click Tsidebar.htm.**

9. **Click the Delete File After Insertion option to select it.**
   You won't always want to select this option. If you choose it, the file you exported will be deleted. That's OK for this page since it will be incorporated into the pages code.

10. **Click OK.**

\<NOTE\>
Notice that the images are in a table. Click the images and check them out. It looks just as it did in Fireworks. Click the Our Instructors image and notice the link information is shown in the Property inspector. You can add the other links to the other images if you'd like, right here in Dreamweaver. The inserted code is fully editable in Dreamweaver.

11. **Open index.htm, the frameset, and click the logo layer (white box) you added earlier.**

12. **Copy the layer (Edit→Copy).**

13. **Click the tab at the bottom of the document window that says trainingsidebar.htm and paste the layer (Edit→Paste).**
    If your images disappear after pasting, choose Edit→Undo. Deselect the image and then paste the layer.

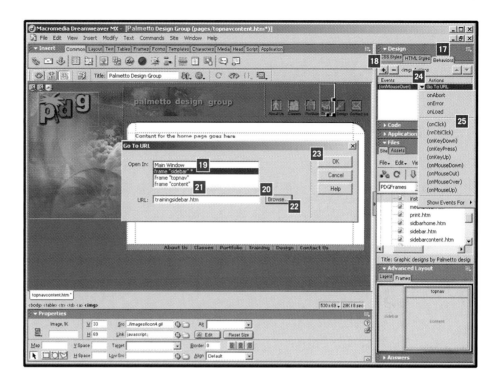

14. **Click File→Save and close the file.**

15. **Click the index.htm tab to make it active.**

16. **Click the training icon to select it.**

17. **Open the Behaviors panel.**

18. **Click the plus sign and click Go to URL.**

19. **Click frame "sidebar"*.**

20. **Click the Browse button. Find trainingsidebar.htm and click OK.**

21. **Click frame "content"*.**

22. **Click the Browse button. Find trainingcontent.htm.**

23. **Click OK.**

24. **Click the little arrow in the Behaviors panel next to the Go To URL.**

25. **Click** OnClick **if you see it; if not, click Show Events For and click 4 and later browsers.**
Now when you click the arrow, you can click (OnClick).

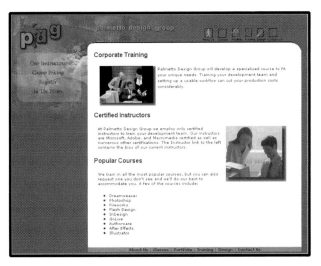

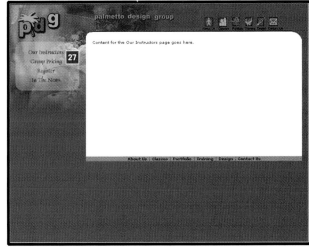

26. **Preview your work in the appropriate browsers and click the training icon.**

The sidebar will load as well as the training content.

27. **Click the Our Instructors link.**

Notice that the instructor's page loaded. The logo wasn't added to the sidebar but you could add it if you like.

28. **Now is a good time to make a duplicate copy of the entire CompleteCourse folder.**

< N O T E >
In the next session, you will be uploading your site. In case of a mistake, it's a good idea to have a backup. You'll be making some changes to the format that could mess up the site if done improperly.

Editing from Dreamweaver

You'll see more on this in upcoming tutorials in this session, but I wanted to explain a bit why you couldn't make this edit from within Dreamweaver. When you click the Edit button in Dreamweaver you have the option of editing the source file (the PNG) or the GIF or JPEG image. Because you wanted to change the color of the text, which is fully editable in the PNG file, you would need to use the source image. But if you did that this entire image would open, you'd edit the text and click Done. The entire header would be added to Dreamweaver, which is certainly not what you want. The only way around this is to make the PNG image of just the two slices. But that wouldn't work in this instance because of

the drop shadow. If you shortened the header, the shadow would be added to the edge of the image (unless you changed the angle of the shadow). Remember that a slice of the header with the drop shadow is used for the background; this is why there is no shadow on the side of the flexible column.

If you had edited the GIF or the JPEG images, which are bitmaps, you'd have had to use the Magic Wand tool to make a selection of the text and then change the color. The results would be extremely iffy and not nearly as sharp as editing the source.

» Session Review

If you've never used Fireworks before, I'm sure you found this session a bit challenging. Time to see how you fared in the retention area.

1. Is Fireworks the only editor you can edit your images in? (See "Tutorial: Setting the Graphics Editor Preferences.")

2. Why couldn't we edit the large logo image directly from Dreamweaver? (See "Tutorial: Editing and Slicing in Fireworks.")

3. Was the text in the logo.png file editable? (See "Tutorial: Editing and Slicing in Fireworks.")

4. Which file format should you use to optimize an image that contains a gradient? (See "Tutorial: Optimizing in Fireworks.")

5. Which file format is best suited for flat areas of color, such as text or vector drawings? (See "Tutorial: Optimizing in Fireworks.")

6. What is the best way to export only one image? (See "Tutorial: Exporting from Fireworks.")

7. In Dreamweaver, if you want to edit an image, how do you do it? (See "Tutorial: Editing a Source Image in Fireworks from Dreamweaver.")

8. Which tool was used in Fireworks to blend the pasted image into the logo? (See "Tutorial: Blending the Logo Image in Fireworks.")

9. What is the technique used to blend one image into another in Fireworks? (See "Tutorial: Blending the Logo Image in Fireworks.")

10. Do links you add in Fireworks still work in Dreamweaver? (See "Tutorial: Making Navigational Graphics in a Fireworks Table.")

11. How do you use Fireworks HTML in Dreamweaver? (See "Tutorial: Inserting Fireworks HTML into Dreamweaver.")

» Additional Projects

The same images used for this site were altered some for the database sessions. In the DatabaseChapter folder, you can open the default.asp page to see the icons used if you'd like. I included the icon source file in the Source folder on the CD-ROM for your practice.

1. Open about.png from the Source folder.

2. Click Modify→Canvas Color. Click the color well in custom and type #556721. Click OK.

3. Select the icon, and then click Modify→Ungroup.

4. Select the inside image of the man and click the fill color box in the Property inspector (be sure the option is Solid). Click the white swatch.

5. Select the outline and click the stroke (pencil) color box in the Property inspector. Click a gold color swatch.

6. With the outline still selected, click the fill color box and type #7E9DB1.

7. In the Optimize panel, choose a GIF setting and 32 colors.

8. Click File→Export.

9. Name and export the image.

Our Instructors
Group Pricing
Register
In The News

Content for the Our Instructors page goes here.

Getting Your
Web Site Online

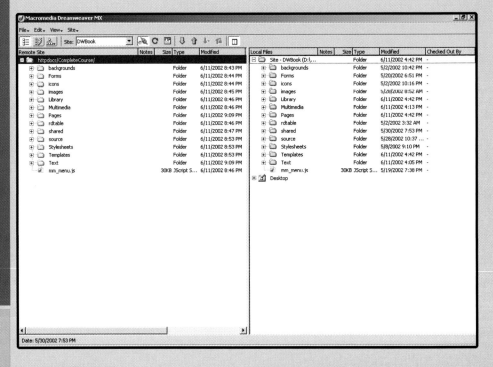

Tutorial: **Finding a Host**

Tutorial: **Setting FTP Preferences**

Tutorial: **FTPing Files to Your Host**

Tutorial: **Synchronizing the Local and Root Folders**

Uploading to a Remote Site

In this session, you upload your site to a Web server using FTP, which stands for File Transfer Protocol. This is how you get your completed site from your computer to the Internet. Prior to uploading your files, you need to get a domain name if you want one and a hosting service or an ISP (Internet Service Provider), which rents space on a computer.

In order to complete this session, you need space on a Web server, or you can use a free service to practice with until you are ready to secure your own domain name and server space.

TOOLS YOU'LL USE
Fireworks MX, Preferences panel, View tools, Optimize panel, Export panel, Preview panels, Site panel

MATERIALS NEEDED
Session 15 files from the CD-ROM added to your PDG Frames root folder if you didn't complete the previous tutorial

TIME REQUIRED
60 minutes

Discussion
» Finding a Host

This tutorial is a bit different. I can't really take you through all the steps of setting up a hosting account, but I can list some of the things you should think about before purchasing space on a Web server.

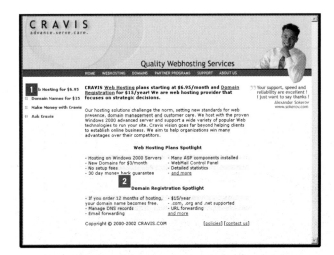

1. **Do you need or want a domain name?**
   Do you want a unique Web address? If so, you have to register a domain name.

2. **Register the name you want (or the closest that is available).**

3. **Do you need a database?**
   If so, what type? If you use ASP, ColdFusion, PHP, or other technologies, you need to be sure that the hosting service you are considering supports that technology.

4. **What kind of support is available?**
   If you are experienced, online help may be enough. If you are new to the game, a live person makes it much easier to set up your first site, especially when there is a database involved.

5. **Is support free? Is there an 800 number?**
   I'd recommend asking a few questions and then sitting back and waiting to see how long it takes for a response. If it takes too long prior to ordering a service to get a response, imagine how long it may take after they get your money. Also, by checking up on service ahead of time, you can discover if they communicate in a way that you understand.

6. **How much bandwidth is included with the service?**
   Some servers have no limitations on *bandwidth*—the amount of data transfer—others do. Quite often you get a limit on band-width and then pay an additional fee for extra usage.

7. **How much space are you allowed on the server: 10, 20, 50MB? More or less?**

   Often times this is a very large determining factor when choosing a hosting service. If you have very little space requirements then your options at a reasonable price are vast. If you require a great deal of space, the price of hosting usually increases dramatically.

8. **Carefully compare the different service plans of several hosting services.**

   There is a list of links for hosting services that have been recommended by other Web designers. I collected these links from different Web design lists I participate in. I have listed my server and my second choice first.

9. **Are Web statistics included?**

   Sometimes the site stats are available at no additional charge and sometimes there is an additional fee. The statistics can help you determine which browsers people use to view your site, which pages are mostly frequently visited, which entry pages are being used the most (how people are accessing your site), and many other statistics. Armed with this information, you can tweak your site to best serve your audience.

10. **Do you need a shopping cart (for a site that sells merchandise and needs to be secure)? Does the server provide one? What is the cost?**

11. **How many e-mail accounts are included?**

12. **How do you manage your site?**

    Is it easy to upload and make changes? How do you set up your e-mail, forwarding, auto responders, and the like? I have two domains with Plesk (www.plesk.com) on the same account with an easy-to-use interface that I use to manage both of the domains.

13. **Do you have access to a CGI-BIN folder for online forms?**

Domain Registration

There are many places you can register a domain name. It used to be you had to register through Network Solutions only, but now many other companies offer the same service for less money. The hosting services that offer domain registration would like you to also use their hosting services, but many don't require that you do so. In fact, the ones I've used have very reasonable registration fees and allow you to park (let the name be registered and not used without actually paying a hosting company) the domain for free until you are ready to move the domain to a Web server of your choice. For example, I registered my domain through Cravis (www.cravis.com) for $15 a year. You can also register through Tucows (www.tucows.com) and many more places. I've used Tucows, Cravis, and others (see the CD-ROM for links). I liked the domain-forwarding package that Tucows provides but I like Cravis' customer support better. With both of these there is free parking available. Once you decide on your hosting service, it's pretty easy to transfer your domain name to them. Often times the hosting service does it for you. If not, they supply you with the information you need to make the transfer. If this part is scary to you or causes you some trepidation, ask your potential host if they provide this service to you.

Tutorial
» Setting FTP Preferences

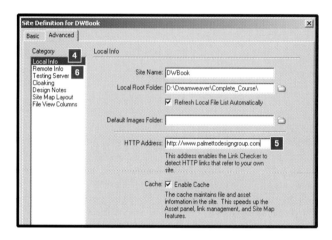

1. **Click the Site panel to make it active.**

2. **Click Site→Edit Sites.**

3. **Click the site you defined for this course and click the Edit button.**

4. **Click the Local Info category.**

5. **Type your domain name or Web address in the HTTP Address field.**
   I typed **http://www.palmettodesigngroup.com**.

6. **Click the Remote Info category.**

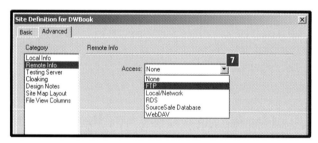

7. **Click the down arrow in the Access field and click FTP if you are using a dialup connection.**
   If you are using a network cable, choose Local/Network Server Access. When you click the Access drop-down menu you can see that there are various other options for transferring your files. You may need to ask your Network Administrator how to upload to a network server.

8. **Type the FTP Host information.**

   It may be the IP address numbers or it may be the host name. Check with your host to determine what is required.

9. **If you are FTPing to a specific directory, type that directory into the Host Directory field as well.**

   Once again, your hosting service should give you this information. For example, for one host I have to put my site inside of a directory called Public; for another host I put my files into a directory called httpdocs.

10. **Enter your login name.**

    This is the user name your hosting service gives you.

11. **Enter your password.**

    Whether you need to check the Use Passive FTP, Use Firewall, or Use SSH encrypted options depends on your server and or your personal security settings. These are unchecked by default.

12. **Click Automatically upload files to server on save if you'd like to utilize this feature.**

    If you are making a lot of changes or save frequently, you may not want to use this feature.

13. **Click Enable File Check In and Check Out if you are using this feature.**

14. **Click the Test button to see whether you can connect to the server.**

15. **Click OK and then click Done to close the Edit Sites dialog box.**

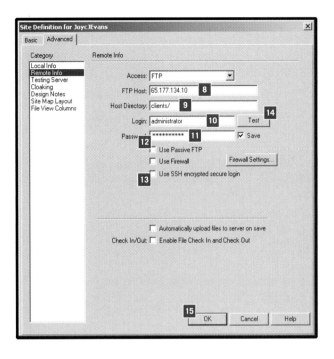

Choosing a Hosting Service

There are many determining factors to consider when purchasing server space. For example, the server I chose cost me a bit more, but it is someone I worked with previously and I'm comfortable with the customer service. Not only can I speak with a real person, but there is also a 1-800 number. I think these two things alone more than justify the extra $50 a year I spend compared to my second choice. I highly recommend Cravis as well; they answered any of my questions in an extremely fast time (via e-mail) and I have another friend who does use them and rates them highly. You can host multiple domains on the same account at Cravis. When I have a problem I like to know that I can get quick answers and results. I also required more bandwidth and the service I chose provided it. The bottom line is: You need to take the time to determine what your needs are and what your budget is, and then start looking around for a service that meets your needs.

There are also free hosting services available. These are great for personal sites or for beginners to use as a testing platform. You can't normally have your own domain name with a free service and you usually have to put up with banner ads. You have to determine what you are willing to sacrifice in order to get free space. Please be aware that if you plan on using a free service to host a business site, you may lose a great deal of credibility with potential clients.

Your ISP (the service you use for dialup accounts) often times gives you a small amount of space for a small Web site. You won't be able to use a domain name, but it is a great way to practice or to host a personal site.

Tutorial

» FTPing Files to Your Host

Now you upload your files to a server. You must have either a Web host or have acquired one of the free services to continue with this session. I've used my host for the illustrations in this tutorial (of course I don't use my real FTP information). You, on the other hand, must FTP right from within Dreamweaver. You will be FTPing the entire site.

1. **In the Site panel, be sure the site you want to upload is selected and you have an Internet connection.**
   Notice that the field next to the site name says Local view. These are the files as seen on your computer.

2. **Click the Connects to Remote Host button.**

3. **Click the site root folder.**

4. **Click Put File/s.**

5. **Click OK in the dialog box that opens asking you if you are sure you want to put the entire site.**
   Now you just wait for the transfer of files to finish.

6. **Click the Expand/Collapse icon to see the remote and local sites.**
   You have just made an exact mirror of your local site to the remote server. By having a mirror you can easily manage your site and any changes to it. Although the files on the remote server are the same, they are not in the same order. If you see this, you may want to do the next few steps.

7. **Click Site→Synchronize Files.**

8. **Click the CompleteCourse (or whatever you named the folder) from the Synchronize drop-down menu.**
   Notice the options in the Direction field. See how you can choose to just upload newer files. You can also choose to delete files from the remote server if they aren't present in the local folder.

9. **Click Preview.**
   A dialog box says no synchronization is necessary. No files have been replaced but the folders and files now are in the same order as your local view. The remote server is now laid out the same as the local site. What happens if you make changes to the local folder? Let's move some things around and see.

Tutorial
» Synchronizing the Local and Root Folders

In this tutorial, you see how you can make changes to your local site and then automatically make the same changes to the remote server.

1. **Click the Expand/Collapse icon if the Site panel isn't open to view the Remote and Local views.**

2. **Right-click the root folder and click New Folder (Local View).**

3. **Name the folder** Pages.

4. **Click and drag all the .HTM files and drop them into the Pages folder. Don't move the mm_menu.js file.**

5. **Click Update to update all the files and their links.**

6. **Click the Reconnect button if you've lost your connection.**

7. **Click Site→Synchronize and click the entire site.**

8. **Click the Delete remote files not on local drive option to select it.** This deletes the .HTM files after they are placed in the Pages folder.

9. **Check the report that opens. Leave everything checked.** You could uncheck anything you didn't want to upload, but in this case, you want to upload everything that changed as a result of moving pages into a folder.

10. **When it's done synchronizing, you can choose to save a log and/or click Close when you are done.** Notice that the Remote site folder now looks just like the Local view folder with the Pages folder and all the .HTM pages inside.

11. **Click the Disconnects from Remote Host icon.**

12. **Click the Expand/Collapse icon to return to the workspace.**

13. **Double-click training.htm to open it.** Notice that all the images are still intact, even though the file moved. That's because Dreamweaver updated all the links to images when you moved them. If you did this outside of your root folder all the image links would be broken.

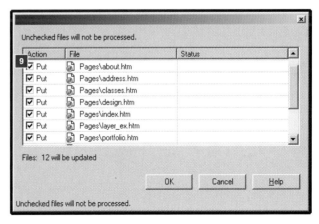

» Session Review

If you had an Internet connection and a hosting service, this session should have been a breeze for you. Test yourself to see how many of the powerful FTP features of Dreamweaver you can recall.

1. What must you do if you want a unique Web address? (See "Tutorial: Finding a Host.")

2. Name three important things to consider when looking for a hosting service. (See "Tutorial: Finding a Host.")

3. What is one drawback to a free hosting service? (See "Tutorial: Finding a Host.")

4. Can you transfer files from your computer to a remote server by any means other than FTP? (See "Setting FTP Preferences.")

5. How do you get the information you need (such as FTP host, directory, and so on) when setting up FTP access? (See "Tutorial: Setting FTP Preferences.")

6. Can you automatically upload any new files you've added to the local directory? (See "Tutorial: Setting FTP Preferences.")

7. Do you need a separate FTP program to transfer your site files to a remote host? (See "Tutorial: Setting FTP Preferences.")

8. Can you make changes to the local directory and have those changes reflected in the remote directory? (See "Tutorial: Synchronizing the Local and Root Folders.")

9. If you can do so above, how is it done? (See "Tutorial: Synchronizing the Local and Root Folders.")

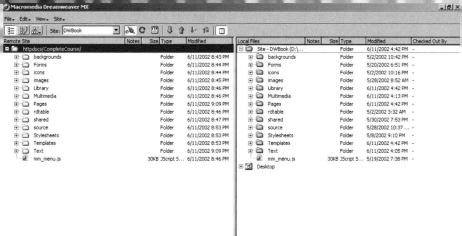

Part VI:
Working with
a Data Source

Setting Up a Database Connection

Working with a Data Source

A good Web site is one that provides meaningful and current content with a minimum of effort. However, updating a site on a daily basis just isn't feasible. In this project, you learn to build a small Web application with pages that support a database designed to collect and store contact information from the Palmetto Design Group Web site.

A Web application is a collection of static and dynamic pages. Static pages contain fixed content and are served up without change when requested by the visitors. A dynamic page contains partly or entirely undefined content. When the page is requested from the Web server, final content based on the visitor's actions is added.

Web applications can be used to collect, save, and analyze data, provide search functionality for page or site content, and/or dynamically update the content of a page.

This session walks you through the process of setting up your site and creating a connection to the contact database.

TOOLS YOU'LL USE
Site panel, Application panel group, Databases panel

MATERIALS NEEDED
Session 16 files from the CD-ROM added to your CompleteCourse root folder if you didn't complete the previous tutorial

The DatabaseChapter folder from the CD-ROM

Web server software (PC with PWS or IIS or a Web hosting service with database and ASP 2.0 support)

If you use an online service, you need an active Web connection.

TIME REQUIRED
90 minutes

Tutorial
» Installing a Personal Web Server (Windows 98)

In this tutorial, Windows 98 users install Microsoft PWS (a scaled-down version of IIS) that runs on Windows 98 and NT Workstation, if you don't have it already. This is not the same as the Personal Web Server that ships with FrontPage.

To make dynamic pages, you must have a Web server and some sort of application server. To develop ASP pages, you need an application server that supports Microsoft Active Server Pages 2.0. Microsoft Personal Web Server (PWS — a scaled-down version of IIS) runs on Windows 98 and NT Workstation and IIS runs on Windows 2000 and Windows XP.

Sun Chili!Soft ASP may be used on Windows, Linux, and Solaris platforms. Macintosh users should use a Web hosting service with ASP 2.0 support or install IIS or PWS on a remote (Windows) computer. Macintosh users must (and Windows users may) use a Web hosting solution. Look for a company that supports ASP 2.0 and Access database.

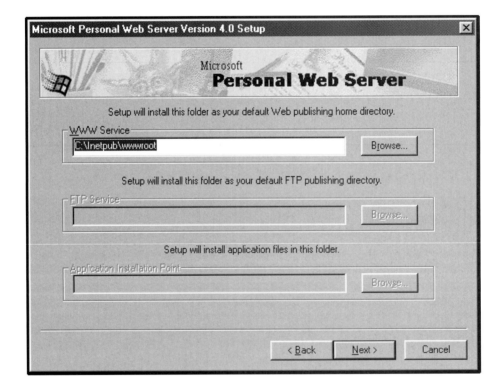

1. **Check your C or D drives to see if you can find an Inetpub folder.**
   If not, you need to install PWS or IIS, or opt to use a hosting service.

2. **Double-click the PWS installation file on the Windows 98 CD.**
   Or double-click the file downloaded from the Microsoft Web site.

3. **Follow the installation wizard directions.**

4. **When asked for the default Web publishing home directory, accept the default** C:\Inetpub\wwwroot.

5. **Click Finish to end the installation.**

Tutorial
» Installing IIS

In this tutorial, Windows 2000 and Windows XP users install Microsoft IIS, which comes with Windows NT Server, Windows 2000, and Windows XP Professional.

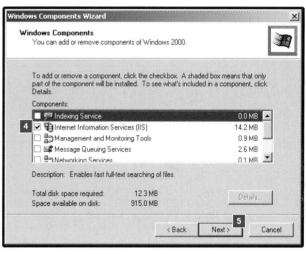

1. **Check your C or D drives to see if you can find an Inetpub folder.** If not, you need to install PWS or IIS, or opt to use a hosting service.

2. **In Windows 2000 and Windows XP, choose Start→Settings→Control Panel→Add/Remove Programs.**

3. **Choose Add/Remove Windows Components.**

4. **Select the IIS box.**

5. **Click Next.**

6. **Follow the installation steps.**

Dynamic Pages

Dynamic pages require a connection to a Web server and a data source. There are many data source types; which one you use depends upon the nature of the pages you plan to build — the type of Web server used to host your pages. The Web server contains special application software that is used to process the scripts contained in a Web page. The software reads the code, and then removes it from the page and passes the page on with the processed results. When the users receive the page, all they see is the resulting HTML.

For all of this to work, you must first set up the correct information in your Site Definition. Until now, you have only worked with the

local information when defining a site. Dynamic pages require a live connection; this means that you must set up the proper access to a Web server with support for your application technology. Because this project uses ASP and an Access database, your local Web server or your provider's Web server must have the latest Microsoft Access Drivers (4.0) and allow a connection to a database.

You need the latest MDAC drivers from Microsoft. You can download MDAC 2.5 and 2.6 for free. Be sure to install 2.5 first, and then 2.6. Windows 2000 with service pack 2 and Windows XP contain the latest drivers.

Tutorial
» Defining a Dynamic Web Site

This step-by-step exercise should have you ready to build a dynamic site in no time! You define a new site for the data-driven portion of the Palmetto Design Group intranet site. To build a Web application, you generally start with HTML, and then write server-side scripts or tags to make the page dynamic. The users (visitors) never see the scripts because the Web server processes the code to provide the requested content, which is then sent to the users. The scripting or tags used are based upon your choice of server technologies; you have many options. Dreamweaver can work with CFM (ColdFusion), ASP (Active Server Pages), ASP.NET (next generation ASP .NET pages), JSP (Java Server Pages), and PHP (Hypertext Preprocessor) pages. The scope of this chapter does not allow for in-depth discussion of all these solutions.

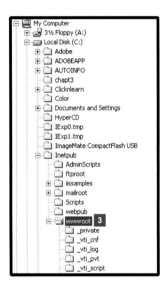
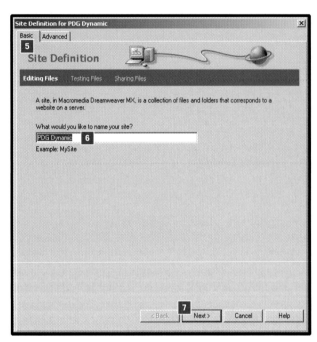

1. **Right-click/Option-drag to copy the DatabaseChapter folder on the CD-ROM.**
   You can save it to your hard drive or to the desktop.

2. **PC users can paste the DatabaseChapter folder to their hard drive.** Option-dragging copies and pastes the folder on the Macintosh.

3. **PC users should also copy the same set of files to** C:\Inetpub\wwwroot.

4. **Open Dreamweaver MX and click Site→New Site.**

5. **Click the Basic tab.**

6. **Type** PDG Dynamic **for the site name.**

7. **Click the Next button.**
   The Editing Files, Part 2, dialog box opens.

8. **Select the Yes I want to use a server technology option in Editing files, Part 2.**

9. **Choose ASP VBScript as the server technology.**

10. **Click the Next button.**
    The Editing Files, Part 3 dialog box opens.

    For Mac users and PC users testing on a remote machine, skip to step 22 now.

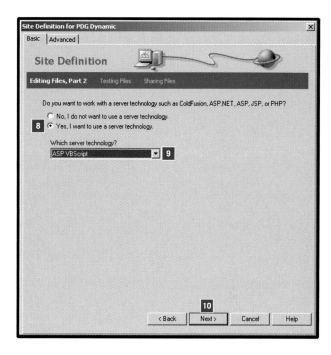

11. **Users with PWS or IIS should choose Edit and Test Locally.**

< N O T E >
This is your development environment. For those using PWS or IIS, this is a temporary testing location. For Mac users or PC users who prefer to work with a hosted server, this may be either the final location of your files or a special testing folder set up just for development purposes.

12. **Click the folder icon to tell Dreamweaver where you want to store the files on the testing (or application) server.**

13. **Navigate to the location where you saved your DatabaseChapter folder and select it.**

14. **Click the Next button.**
    The Testing files dialog box opens.

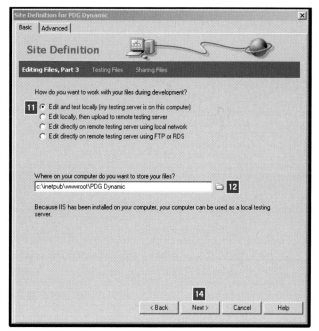

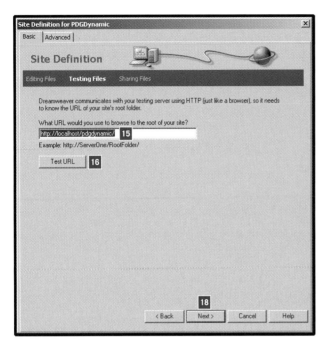

15. **For PC users testing locally, the URL shown in the Testing Files panel should read** `http://localhost/pdgdynamic/.`

< N O T E >

For those using a hosted solution, the URL prefix may be set incorrectly by Dreamweaver, as the program takes the host name and appends any directory paths after it. In some cases, this may include a folder like `wwwroot`, which wouldn't be correct for the URL prefix but is correct for FTP. If in doubt, try to think of what the URL would be to get to this site folder using your browser. You may upload to `yourdomain.com/wwwroot`, but you surf to the site at `www.yourdomain.com`.

16. **Click the Test URL button to test your connection.**

17. **Click OK on the URL Prefix Test was successful pop-up.**

18. **Click Next.**

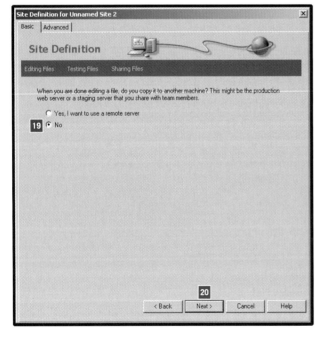

19. **Click the No radio button because you are going to test locally only.**

< N O T E >

If you are going to be using a remote server, you see how to do the remote settings using the Advanced tab in the "Setting Up a Remote DSN Connection" tutorial.

20. **Click the Next button.**
    A Summary dialog box opens showing you the settings you chose.

< N O T E >

You can access the choices in the Summary dialog box at any time through the Advanced Setup. You should take a look at the various Local, Remote, and Testing categories in the Advanced Setup to familiarize yourself with where all the information you supplied is placed. The Advanced Setup is much faster to use, but more complex, requiring you to understand what goes where.

21. **Click Done.**

    With your Web and application server setup complete, you are ready to begin working with the pages inside the DatabaseChapter sample folder. Because this session is all about working with a database, you need to set up a connection to that database. There are several types of connections possible and which you use depends upon your setup.

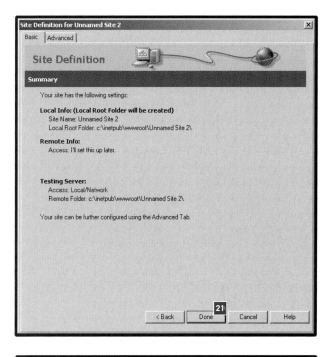

22. **This step continues from step 10 for Mac and PC users using a Remote server and FTP to connect. Click "Edit directly on remote testing server using FTP or RDS".**

23. **Enter the path to a local file on your computer to save to.**

24. **Uncheck "Automatically upload files to my server every time I save". Click Next.**

    You don't have to uncheck this option. I prefer to upload when I'm done working, but you may prefer to upload automatically.

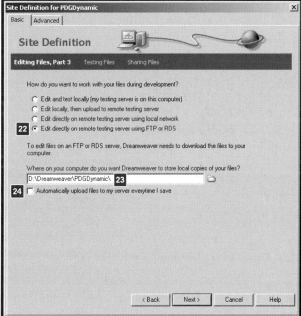

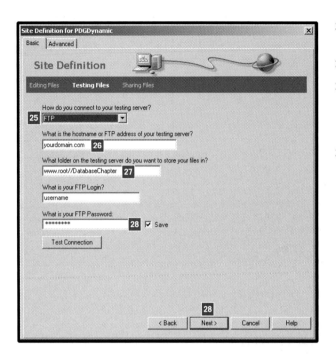

25. **Click FTP for the "How do you connect to your testing server?" question.**

26. **Enter your domain address.**

27. **Enter the folder your database is being uploaded to.**
    You might need to get that information from your hosting service. A database is usually kept in a secure location away from the main site.

28. **Enter your username and password. Click the Test Connection button and then click Next.**
    If you have everything set up properly, the test will be successful. If not, check the path to the database.

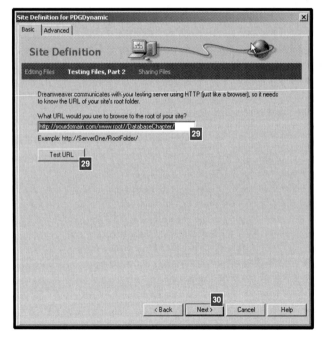

29. **Enter the path to the root of your site and then click the Test URL button.**

30. **Click Next.**

31. **This option depends on how you work, but I'd suggest checking the "No, do not enable check in and check out" option unless you need it.**

32. **Click Next.**
    You are now presented with a summary of your options.

33. **Click Done.**

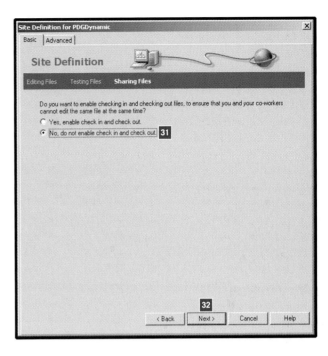

A Note Before You Proceed . . .

Each of the next four tutorials are methods that set connections named connPDG. USE ONLY ONE of the methods or use different names. Each method uses the same name in the tutorials because that is the connection used by the project. The choices are in order:

» Setting up a local DSN connection — PC only. This tutorial should be done by Windows users who want to test on their local machine using PWS or IIS.

» Setting up a remote DSN connection — PC or Mac, with a remote server that has the DSN set by the Web host.

» Setting up a connection string (DSN-less) — PC or Mac; this tutorial should be done by users who have a remote hosting

service and cannot or prefer not to use a DSN connection. With this method, you don't have to rely on the host to set up the DSN for you (but permissions for the folder do need to be set).

» Using the MapPath method — PC or Mac with a remote hosting service. MapPath determines the full path of your database if, for some reason, your hosting service didn't provide it for you.

Perform the Setting up a DSN Name tutorial only if you choose to test locally or remotely using a DSN connection. The Setting Up a Connection String (DSN-less) and the MapPath Method don't need a DSN name defined.

Tutorial
» Setting Up a DSN Name

Do this tutorial *only* if you choose to test locally or remotely using a DSN connection. With Dreamweaver, you can use a data source name (DSN) or a connection string to connect to the database. You learn how to do both, but first you have to set up the DSN name to test locally using a DSN.

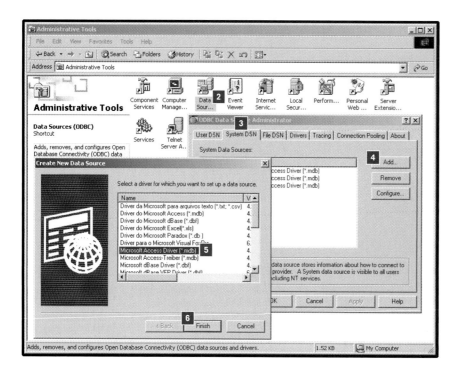

1. **Open Dreamweaver and be sure your PDG Dynamic folder is the active defined site.**

2. **Choose one of the following options (the figures show Windows 2000):**

   » Windows 98 — Click Start→Settings→Control Panel. Then select ODBC Data Source (32 bit).

   » Windows NT — Click Start→Settings→Control Panel. Select the ODBC icon.

   » Windows 2000 — Click Start→Settings→Control Panel. Open Administrative tools and click the Data Sources (ODBC) icon.

   » Windows XP — Click Start→Settings→Control Panel. Open Administrative tools and click the Data Sources (ODBC) icon.

3. **Click the System DSN tab.**

4. **Click the Add button.**
   An ASP application must connect to a database through an open database connectivity (ODBC) driver or an object linking and embedding database (OLE DB) provider. You use an ODBC Microsoft Access Driver.

5. **Click the Microsoft Access Driver.**

6. **Click Finish.**

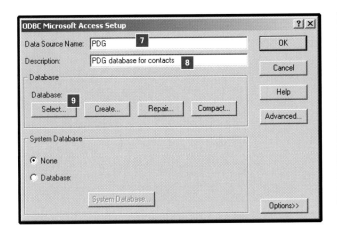

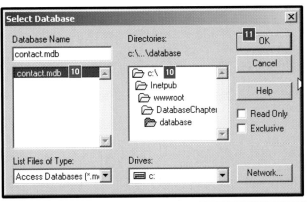

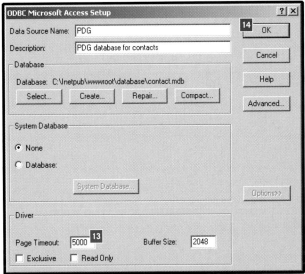

7. **Type** PDG **in the Data Source Name field.**

8. **Type** PDG database for contacts **in the Description field.**

9. **Click the Select button in the Database section of the ODBC Microsoft Access Setup dialog box.**

10. **Navigate to the** C:\InetPub\wwwroot\Database Chapter\database **folder and click contact.mdb.**

11. **Click OK.**

12. **Click the Options button.**

13. **Type** 5000 **in the Page Timeout field.**

14. **Click OK.**
    The ODBC Data Source Administrator dialog box now shows the contact database you added.

15. **Click PDG.**

16. **Click OK to complete the setup.**

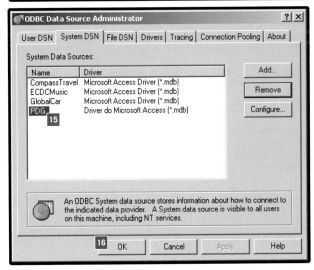

Tutorial
» Setting Up a Local DSN Connection

In this tutorial, you set up a connection to connect to your local Web server (PWS or IIS). It assumes you have already set up a DSN for the database named PDG.

A DSN works like an alias—it is a one-word identifier that points to the database and contains information needed to connect to it, such as driver information and path structures and, in some cases, an ID and password.

To use a DSN Connection, the proper ODBC driver must be installed on your machine. PC users will have created a local DSN in their system's registry.

Mac and PC users opting for a hosted Web server may need to request their provider to create a DSN at the remote system using a specific name. Or, if that is not allowed, they must substitute the name the provider gives when working through this tutorial. If that all seems too complicated, you may opt to use a connection string instead (DSN-less connection).

1. **Open your defined site for PDG Dynamic in the Site panel.**

2. **Double-click contact.asp to open it.**

3. **Click the expander arrow of the Application panel group to open it.**

4. **Click the Databases tab to make it the active panel.**

5. **Click the Add (+) button.**

6. **Click Data Source Name (DSN).**

7. **Type connPDG in the Connection Name field.**

8. **Click the down arrow for Data Source Name (DSN) and click PDG.**
   If that is not an available option, you may need to click the DSN button and determine whether your DSN name appears.

9. **Click the Using Local DSN radio button to select it.**

10. **Click the Test button.**

11. **Click OK to close the dialog box.**
    The connection provides access to the tables, views, and/or stored procedures of the data source. For this project, you will work only with a data table. Click the plus sign next to connPDG in the Databases panel to see what is available.

Tutorial
» Setting Up a Remote DSN Connection

If you have a Web server and want to test on the remote site, you want to do this tutorial. This is the most complex part of setting up a dynamic site, because the information needed varies in structure from service to service. The examples shown here presume that PDG owns a domain and hosts it with a provider.

1. **Open your defined site for PDG Dynamic in the Site panel.**

2. **Click the site definition down arrow and click Edit Sites.**
   You now set up the Remote and Testing servers.

3. **Click PDG Dynamic.**

4. **Click Edit.**

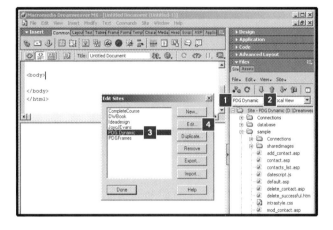

5. **Click the Advanced tab.**

6. **Click the Remote Info category.**

7. **Click the arrow for Access and click FTP.**

8. **Type your FTP Host connection information in the FTP Host field.**

9. **Type the directory of your database files.**
   Where your files are stored may depend on your server. Most virtual domain NT servers serve the public Web from the wwwroot directory.

10. **Enter your login and password information.**

11. **Do not check the Check In/Out option.**
   This is an option generally used when working in a team environment and is designed to lock files in use by other developers.

12. **Click the Test button.**

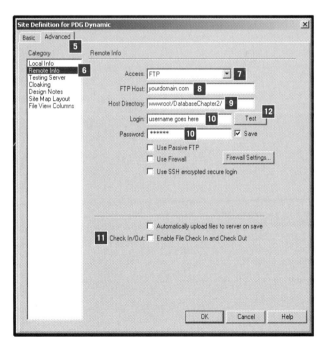

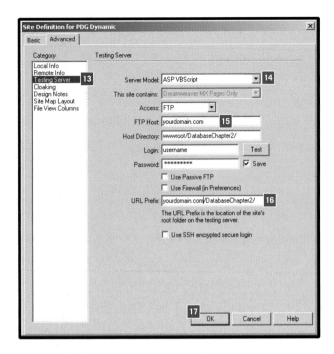

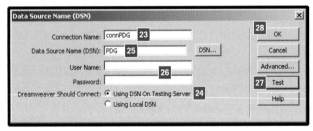

13. **Click the Testing Server category.**

14. **Click the down arrow for the Server Model field and click ASP VBScript.**
    This is the server technology that is being used to communicate with the database. Notice the other server models available to you.

15. **The FTP Host information is generated by what you added in the Remote Info category.**

16. **The URL prefix should be the path to your DatabaseChapter folder.**
    Think of it as the path that a browser would use to find your folder. In other words, if your site uses a `wwwroot` or some other administrator type of folder, that part would not go into the URL prefix, just the domain name and the path to the folder.

17. **Click OK and Done.**
    You are now ready to make the remote connection.

18. **Double-click contact.asp to open it.**

19. **Click the expander arrow of the Application panel group to open it.**

20. **Click the Databases tab to make it the active panel.**

21. **Click the Add (+) button.**

22. **Click Data Source Name (DSN)**

23. **Type connPDG in the Connection Name field.**

24. **Click the Using DSN on Testing Server option.**
    Mac users will not see this option.

25. **Type PDG into the Data Source Name (DSN) field.**

26. **You do not need to fill in the User Name and Password fields.**

27. **Click the Test button.**
    Be sure you are online prior to pressing the Test button.

28. **Click OK to close the dialog box.**
    The connection provides access to the tables, views, and/or stored procedures of the data source. For this project, you work only with a data table.

Tutorial
» Setting Up a Connection String (DSN-less)

Using a DSN-less connection, your hosting server doesn't have to set up a DSN name for you but you should ask for the full path to your database. This tutorial uses a connection string to connect, but you may easily substitute a DSN if you are able to set it up. If you do not or cannot use a DSN connection, you have to set up a custom connection string to provide the database driver and path structure information to Dreamweaver and the browser. The easiest way to determine the path to your database once you upload the site folder is to ask your service provider's technical support person. An alternative option is to use the MapPath method (explained in the next tutorial).

Your provider must also set the correct permissions for the DatabaseChapter\database folder to allow Dreamweaver and browser pages to access your database. Because you specifically have the contact.mdb database in a different folder, you have to ask your provider to set the proper permissions for your folder.

1. **Open contact.asp from the sample folder using the Site panel.**

2. **Click the expander arrow to open the Application panel group. Click the Databases tab to make it the active panel.**

3. **Click the Add (+) button.**

4. **Click Custom Connection String.**

5. **Name your connection** connpdg.

6. **In the Connection String field, add the following (all in one line!):**

   `"DBQ=d:\mydomain.com\wwwroot\Database Chapter\database\contact.mdb;DRIVER= {Microsoft Access Driver (*.mdb)}"`

   This is the path to your database and the driver to be used. This next string is the same but in reverse. You may find that one works better for you than the other. With database connections it may take some practice and lots of testing.

   `"DRIVER={Microsoft Access Driver (*.mdb)}; DBQ=d:\mydomain.com\wwwroot\DatabaseChapter\ database\contact.mdb"`

7. **Select the Using Driver On Testing Server option.**
   Mac users do not see this option.

8. **Click the Test button.**

9. **Click OK.**

<NOTE>
A *connection string* is a hand-coded line of text that does the same thing as a DSN connection, but is often faster and uses fewer system resources. When you use a DSN, you are looking up the alias to find out the same information contained in a connection string. Connection strings are sometimes called DSN-less connections.

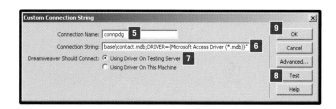

<NOTE>
If your domain name is www.mydomain.com, your host server is mydomain.com, and your provider tells you that you must place your Web pages in a directory at wwwroot. Therefore, your structure may look something like: D:\mydomain.com\wwwroot\ DatabaseChapter\database\contact.mdb. When you have the proper path structure, you add it to the driver information to create a custom connection string.

<NOTE>
You would replace mydomain.com with your domain name. You might also have to replace other parts of this structure to match the path given to you by your service provider.

<NOTE>
Be sure you are connected to the remote server first. Dreamweaver should return a success message. If not, you need to check your string for errors and/or verify with your service provider that they have the latest Microsoft Access Drivers (4.0). If your connection is successful, you are ready to begin developing dynamic pages.

Tutorial
» Using the MapPath Method

If you know the virtual path to your database folder (supplied by the hosting service), you can determine the physical path using the MapPath method. When you have uploaded your DatabaseChapter files to the remote server, your files end up in a folder structure for that server. For example, on a server running MS IIS, the path or folder structure to the database could be:

`C:\Inetpub\wwwroot\accounts\users\yourfolder\DatabaseChapter\database\contact.mdb`

This is a physical path to your file. But the URL to access a file doesn't use the physical path. Most, if not all, service providers are set up to use the name of the server or domain, followed by a virtual path, such as:

`http://www.mydomain.com/yourfolder/DatabaseChapter/database/contact.mdb`

A virtual path is a "shortcut" for the physical path. Host providers use this method for security and convenience, as it hides the true path and eliminates writing the longer URL. Your provider typically gives you a URL to view your pages on the Internet using the virtual path.

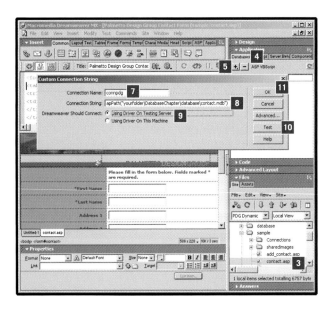

\<NOTE\>

This code is entered all on one line! The format of this book doesn't provide space to show it to you that way.

\<NOTE\>

Using MapPath is less desirable than a DSN or connection string that uses the physical path, as it requires an extra step to the process each time the database is requested. Most host providers give you the proper path to your database.

1. Upload your files to the remote server and make a note of the virtual path.

2. Be sure that you are connected to the remote server and you know the virtual path.

3. Open the contact.asp page from the local site root folder using the Site panel.

4. Click the Databases panel in the Application panel group.

5. Click the Add (+) button.

6. Click Custom Connection String.

7. **Name this connection** connpdg.

8. **In the Connection String field, add the following:**
`"DRIVER={Microsoft Access Driver (*.mdb)};DBQ=" & Server.MapPath("yourfolder\Database Chapter\database\contact.mdb")`

9. **Select the Using Driver On Testing Server option.** Mac users do not see this option.

10. **Click the Test button.**

11. **If the connection is successful, close the dialog box by pressing OK.** If not, check the virtual path and the rest of your string to be sure that all quotes, ampersands, and such are in place.

» Session Review

You may not be able to answer all these questions depending on which option you chose for testing—local or remote—but go ahead and see how you do.

1. How can you tell if PWS has been installed on your machine? (See "Tutorial: Installing Personal Web Server (Windows 98).")

2. Where do you place your database files on a PC for testing locally? (See "Tutorial: Defining a Dynamic Web Site.")

3. What does DSN stand for? (See "Tutorial: Setting up a DSN Name.")

4. Which panel do you access to add connection information? (See "Setting up a Local DSN Connection.")

5. How does the URL prefix differ from the host directory? (See "Tutorial: Setting Up a Remote DSN Connection.")

6. Why would you want or need to use a DSN-less connection? (See "Tutorial: Setting Up a Connection String (DSN-less).")

7. Do you need a separate FTP program to transfer your site files to a remote host? (See "Tutorial: Setting FTP Preferences.")

8. What does a custom connection string do? (See "Tutorial: Setting Up a Connection String (DSN-less).")

9. Do you enter the custom string containing the driver information and the path information on two lines? (See "Tutorial: Setting Up a Connection String (DSN-less).")

10. When would you use the MapPath method? (See "Tutorial: Using the MapPath Method.")

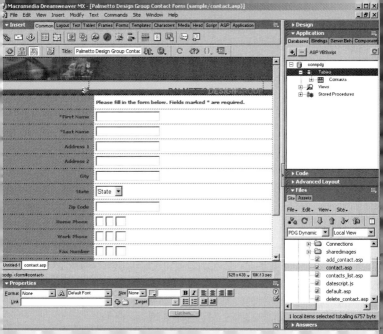

Session 18

Building a Web Application

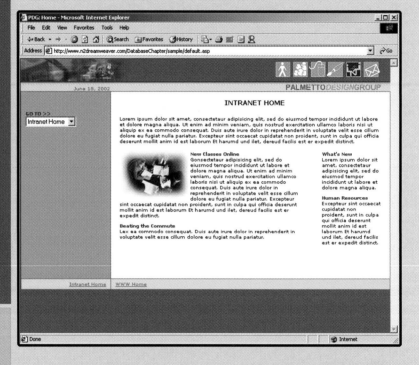

Building Dynamic Pages

Now that your connection is in place and you can successfully connect to your database, you are ready to begin using Dreamweaver to build dynamic pages. In this session, you explore the basics of manipulating a data source (the database) to provide dynamic Web content.

Dreamweaver contains many useful tools and functions to set up, connect, and script your pages. In this chapter, you learn to bind data and add server-side logic to the site pages to collect, view, and modify information obtained from a contact form and database.

The building block of your Web application is the record. In a database, records are stored in related blocks of information, formatted in tables. Each piece of information in a record is called a *field*. A collection of records that share the same fields is called a *table* because the information is easily presented in table format; each column represents a field and each row a separate record. In fact, you can substitute the words column for field and vice versa. The same is true for row and record. Throughout this session, you use column/field information and display rows/records dynamically.

TOOLS YOU'LL USE
Site panel; Application panel group; Databases, Bindings, and Server Behaviors panels; Live Data view; Property inspector; Insert Bar; and the StatePostaLABR extension available from the Macromedia Dreamweaver Exchange

MATERIALS NEEDED
Chapter 17 must be completed before attempting this session.

Web Server software (PC with PWS or IIS or a Web hosting service with database and ASP 2.0 support)

If you use an online service, you need an active Web connection.

TIME REQUIRED
120 minutes

Tutorial
» Adding a Recordset

Your first dynamic page takes the information from a contact database and displays it on a list of contacts page. This project uses Active Server Page (ASP) technology so the name of each page uses the extension .ASP. The .ASP extension tells the Web server to process the page prior to serving it via the Web browser. In this tutorial, you run a database query. A query consists of search criteria relating to the requested subset (table) of the database. The result of the query is a recordset. A *recordset* consists of data returned by a database query that is temporarily stored in the application server's memory for faster data retrieval.

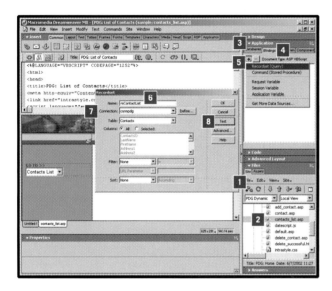

1. **Be sure you are online and connected to your server if you're using a remote service provider.**

2. **Double-click contacts_list.asp in the Site panel for the PDG Dynamic site.**

3. **Click the expander arrow of the Application panel group.**

4. **Click the Bindings panel tab to make it active.**

5. **Click the Add (+) button to add a Recordset (Query).**

6. **Set the recordset name to** rsContactList.

<NOTE>
Most developers use a naming convention when working with recordsets. By using rs for a recordset, when you see rs(name of set) in your code, you may be certain that it is a reference to your recordset.

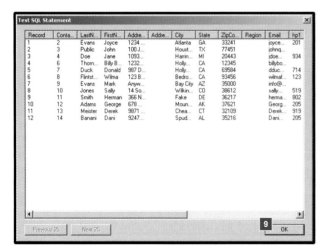

7. **From the Connection menu, choose connpdg.**
Selecting the connection populates the Table menu and gives you access to a table in your database. This database contains one table, so the menu lists only the Contacts table. The columns (data fields) in the table populate the columns list.

8. **Click the Test button.**
You should see all the present contacts in this table.

9. **Click OK to close the Testing dialog box and click the OK button on the Recordset dialog box to close it as well.**
Now you build a table to hold the dynamic data.

10. **Place your cursor into the main (white) area of the page.**

11. **Click the Insert Table icon and add a new table with the following settings:**
    Rows: **2**
    Columns: **2**
    Width: **90%**
    Border: **0**
    Padding: **5px**
    Spacing: **0**

    Click OK.

12. **Type** Last Name, First Name **into the first cell.**

13. **In the second cell, type** Email Address.

14. **Set each row height to 20.**
    Click inside each row and set the height in the Property inspector.

15. **Place your cursor into the first cell of the top row.**

16. **Right-click/Ctrl-click the** <td> **tag in the Tag Selector to apply the class tabletop. Repeat for the remaining cells (2 in top row, 2 in bottom).**

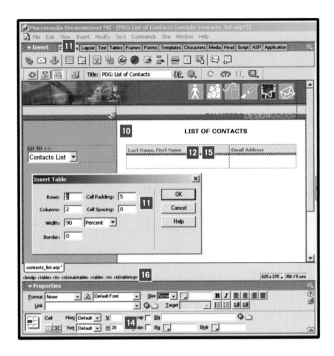

<NOTE>
To create a dynamic page, you place dynamic fields that refer to specific columns or data fields in the rsContactList recordset. Dreamweaver provides several methods for placing the code. You can drag and drop from the Bindings panel or select a data field and use the Insert button at the bottom of the panel.

17. **From the Bindings panel, open (click the + button)** rsContactList **to reveal the data fields within.**

18. **Locate LastName in the** rsContactList **recordset.**

19. **Select and drag LastName to the first column of the second table row and release the mouse.**

20. **Place your cursor after the LastName dynamic field and add a comma, followed by a space.**

21. **Insert the FirstName data field the same way (drag and drop or select and insert).**

22. **Drag Email from the Bindings panel and drop it into the second cell of the second row.**

23. **Save your page.**

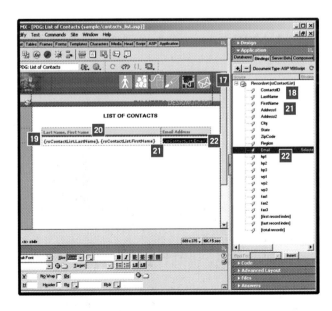

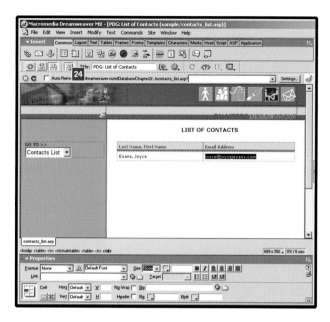

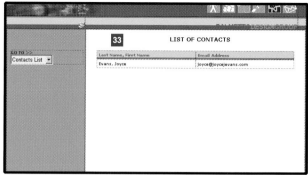

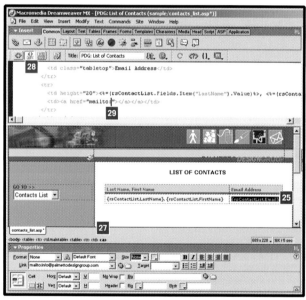

<NOTE>

Depending upon your computer setup and your Web server settings, previewing may require a save or auto-save. In all cases, it's a good idea to add the saved page to the remote server. You can press the Live Data View button to see how your page looks with one set of data, but you are not able to test the functionality of the dynamic link and subject line unless you preview in the appropriate browsers.

24. **Click the Live Data View button in the Document bar.**
You must be online if you're using a remote application server (but not if you are using PWS or IIS). Live Data View displays the first record of the Contacts table in the database. The e-mail address is displayed, but it is not active. Next you add a `mailto:` link, and then add a dynamic data field in the `href` of the `mailto:` link.

25. **Select the Email dynamic field.**

26. **In the Link field of the Property inspector, type** mailto.

27. **Select the** `<a>` **tag (use the Tag Selector).**

28. **Click the Code and Design View icon and locate the opening anchor tag (**`<a href="mailto:"`**).**

29. **Insert your cursor just after the colon in the tag.**

30. **Go to the Bindings panel and drag and drop the Email data field just after the colon. The code is now:**
```
<a href="mailto:<%=(rsContactList.Fields.Item
("Email").Value)%>"></a>
```

31. **Place your cursor just after the dynamic data field to provide a subject line to the e-mail sent by this link.**

32. **Add** `?subject=From Palmetto Design Group` **before the ending quote. Now the code for the cell is:**
```
<td><a href="mailto:<%=(rsContactList.Fields.
Item("Email").Value)%>?subject=From Palmetto
Design Group "><%=(rsContactList.Fields.Item
("Email").Value)%></a></td>
```

33. **Save and preview your work (click Live View).**

Tutorial
» Using Repeating Regions

To display all records of the data table in this page, you use the Repeat Region server behavior. A server behavior is predefined server-side logic that adds specific functionality and interaction through application logic. The application server processes server-side logic before it is sent to the browser. Dreamweaver server behaviors give you powerful logic without having to write any ASP code.

1. Open contacts_list.asp if you've closed it and select the second row by clicking its <tr> tag.

2. Click the Server Behaviors tab (Application panel group).

3. Click the Add (+) button and choose Repeat Region from the menu.

4. Enter these settings:
   Recordset: rsContactList
   Show: All Records

5. Click OK.

6. Press the Live Data View button to view all records in your page. Repeat Region code adds a new row for each record in the data source. The dynamic fields display the last and first names and the e-mail addresses, and create a live e-mail link for each, complete with subject line.

7. Click the Live Data View button again to turn off the view.

8. Save your page (File→Save).

9. In the Site panel, click contacts_list.asp.

10. Click the Put button (you have to be online with a remote server). Alternatively, you can click the File Management icon and select Put from that menu.

11. In the browser, click one of the e-mail links. The user's e-mail client opens with the subject line added and the e-mail field filled in.

<NOTE>
When using Repeat Region to display dynamic data, carefully set up the HTML structure to make it easily repeated. Paragraphs and table rows are very easy to repeat. Individual columns are not.

12. Close the page; you won't need it for the next tutorial.

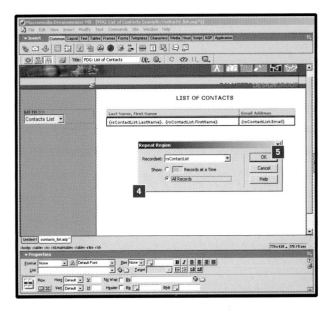

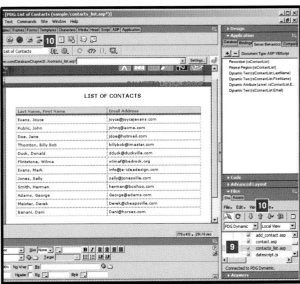

Tutorial
» Using Insert Record on Forms

The Palmetto Design Group Contact Form collects information to add to the Contacts database. In this tutorial, you use the Insert Record server behavior to bind the form fields to the data columns.

The Palmetto Design Group contact form is accessed by the Web site and is used by PDG's clients. The PDG Intranet site maintains a link to the form for adding contact information that is received by mail.

Forms work by creating name-value pairs. A named form object collects a value, supplied either by the author of the page or by the user in a Web browser session. Submitting the form adds a record to the database, matching named form fields to data fields (columns.)

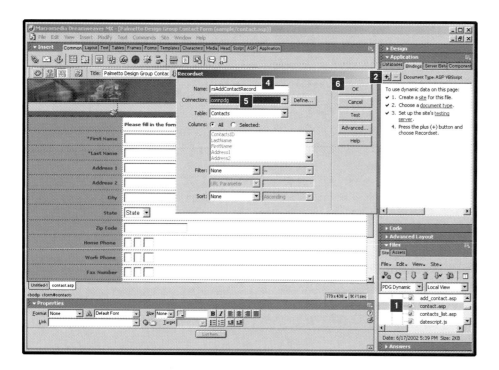

1. **Double-click the contact.asp page to open it.**
   This page contains a prepared form that needs application logic to make it useful.

2. **Click the Add (+) button in the Bindings panel.**

3. **Click Recordset (Query).**

4. **Type** rsAddContactRecord **in the Name field.**

5. **Use these settings for the rest of the Query fields:**
   Connection: connpdg
   Table: Contacts

Columns: All
Filter: None
Sort: None

You might need to be patient while the connection loads the database table(s). If your database contained multiple tables, you would need to select the correct table from the Tables menu. In this case, it does not.

6. **Click OK to close the dialog box.**

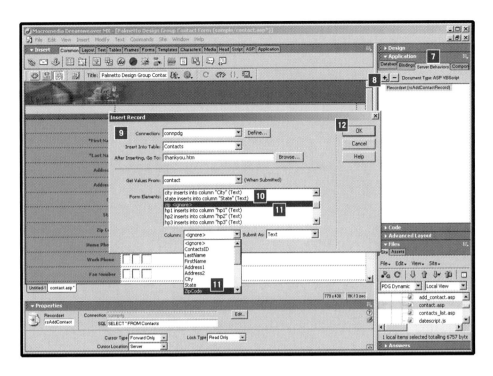

7. **Click the Server Behaviors panel to make it active.**

8. **Click Add (+) Insert Record.**

9. **In the dialog box, use these settings:**
   Connection: connpdg
   Insert into Table: Contacts
   After Inserting, Go To: thankyou.htm

   Look in the list at the bottom of the dialog box. After the table information loads, the first few fields find a matching column, but some fields don't. When a form field's name and a column's name match, the Insert Record server behavior is smart enough to see the relationship. The Column menu is used to match form fields to data columns.

10. **To set the appropriate state to State, simply highlight it in the list, and then use the Column menu to select the correct column.**

11. **Select and set the zip element to ZipCode.**
    The rest of the form objects match database columns and are already set.

12. **Click OK to close the dialog box.**

13. **Save the page.**

14. **Upload this page to test in the appropriate browsers.**

15. **Fill in the form and add a record to the database.**

16. **Keep the page open because you will use it in the next tutorial.**

< N O T E >
Upon submitting the form, you are redirected to the thank you page.

Tutorial
» Validating Your Forms

In this tutorial you learn how to validate your forms, checking to be sure that the required information has the proper format on specific areas of a form.

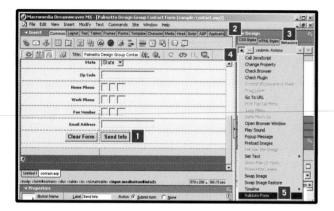

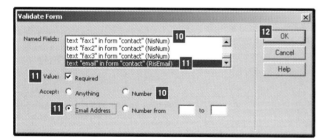

1. **Select the Send Info button.**
   You should have the contact.asp page open.

2. **Click the expander arrow for the Design group panels.**

3. **Click the Behaviors panel to make it active.**

4. **Click the Add (+) button.**

5. **Click the Validate Form behavior.**

6. **In the Validate Form dialog box, highlight or select text "firstname" in form "contact".**

7. **Set this value as required.**

8. **Leave the default Anything radio button selected.**

9. **Repeat for text "lastname" in form "contact".**

10. **Go through the phone and fax number fields and set each to Number.**

11. **Set the Email field as Required and choose the Email Address option.**

12. **Click OK to close the dialog box.**

13. Save and test your page.

14. Close the file.

Validation

The process of adding information to a database should have some sort of validation process to be sure that the required information has the proper format. Some fields are required (by the database and the form) and others are not. To be sure that the page does not return errors from the database, a form validation script runs to catch any empty required fields prior to sending the page to the application server. The validation script is written in JavaScript, and is processed client-side, as opposed to the server-side logic of ASP. Client-side scripts are processed by the user's Web browser.

Tutorial
» Building Update Pages

Occasionally, it's necessary to update the information in the contact database. Rather than add a new contact, it's better to modify the original entry to change information. The Update Record server behavior adds this complex application logic with a minimum of effort!

1. **Double-click the mod_contact.asp page to open it.**

2. **Open the Bindings panel in the Application panel group.**

3. **Click the Add (+) button.**

4. **Click Recordset (Query).**

5. **Type** rsUpdateContacts **in the Name field.**

6. **Select the connpdg connection.**

7. **Click OK to close the dialog box.**

8. **Place your cursor below the page heading (Modify Contact).**
   This actually places the cursor just to the right of the heading.

9. **Add a paragraph return (press Enter/Return).**

10. **Select Insert→Application Objects→Record Update Form.**
    Because this page does not contain a form with fields, you are inserting one to collect a value for every field in the database.

11. **Match these settings:**
    Connection: connpdg
    Table to Update: Contacts
    Select Record From: rsUpdateContacts
    Unique Key Column: ContactsID [uncheck Numeric if it's checked]

<NOTE>
A Unique Key Column is a special field in the database that is auto-generated by Access (or any other database) to control the data records. Although it is possible to have two records with identical information, it is not possible for each of them to have the same unique key. A primary key is set up when the database is created. This database auto-generates a number value when an entry is added.

12. **Remove the ContactsID column by selecting it and pressing the Remove (–) button.**
    You removed the ContactsID column because Access takes care of the key. You don't want anyone to be able to modify this field and corrupt the database.

13. **Click OK to set this form.**

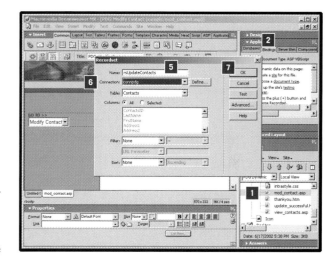

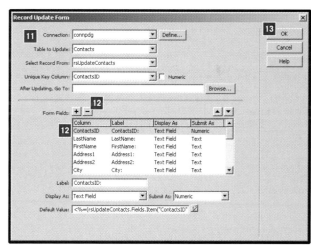

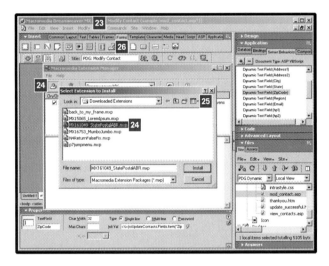

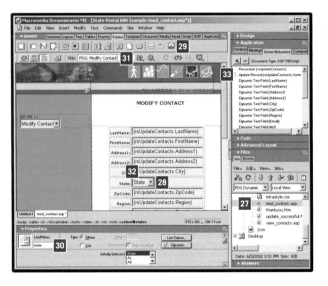

14. **Select the state form object.**
    This is a text field.

15. **Look at the Server Behaviors panel.**
    You should see Dynamic Text Field (State).

16. **Double-click the entry to take a look at the details of this behavior.**

17. **Close the entry when you're done.**

18. **Because it is possible to set the specifics of the Update behavior, select the field from the form and delete it.**
    Don't worry about deleting this field; you add a list of states here instead.

19. **Save this file.**
    You need to download and install the StatePostalABR extension now if you haven't done so already. If you've already installed the extension, skip to step 26.

20. **Click Help→Dreamweaver Exchange.**

21. **Type** StatePostalABR **into the Search Extensions field.**

22. **Download the extension into your Downloaded Extensions folder (inside the Dreamweaver MX application folder).**

23. **Click Commands→Manage Extensions.**

24. **Click the Install New extension icon and select the StatePostalABR from the list.**

25. **When the installation is complete, close the Extensions Manager. Close Dreamweaver and restart it.**

26. **Click the Forms tab in the Insert Bar.**
    Notice that an icon for ABR has been added. The icon looks like an envelope.

27. **Double-click the mod_contact.asp page to open it.**

28. **Be sure your cursor is in the cell of the recently deleted text field.**

29. **Click the State Postal ABR icon in the forms panel to add the menu to the space.**

30. **In the Property inspector, rename the object** state.

31. **Give the page a new title of** PDG: Modify Contact.

32. **Select the new State object.**

33. **In the Server Behaviors panel, your Update Record behavior should now have a red exclamation mark next to it.**
    It's there because you deleted an item used by this behavior.

34. **Double-click the server behavior and you will get a message stating the form object cannot be found.**

35. **Use the Form Elements menu to select state and choose state from the Columns menu.**

36. **Click OK to close the dialog box.**

37. **Save your page. Upload it, if needed, and preview it to test.**
    The tables generated by Application Objects contain undesirable HTML markup. In the next set of steps, you'll make some adjustments to the layout of the table and form objects, to make the layout match the rest of the site and to improve the readability of the form.

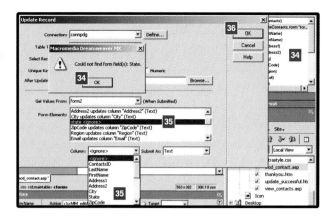

38. **Click into the form and select its table in the Tag Selector.**

39. **Set the width of the table to 90%.**

40. **Select all the cells in the left column of the table.**

41. **Click the CSS Styles panel (in the Design panel group) to make it active.**

42. **Click Apply Styles and set the class of the left column to tabletopNobg.**

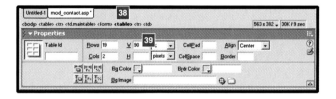

43. **In this step, adjust the various labels in the left column of the table, adding spaces where necessary to match this list. Where a label is not listed, leave it as the default. Most of the names need a space.**
    Last Name:
    First Name:
    Address 1:
    Address 2:
    City:
    State:
    Zip Code:
    Region:
    Email:
    Home Phone: [this replaces hp1. ignore hp2 & hp3]
    Work Phone: [this replaces wp1. ignore wp2 & wp3]
    Fax: [this replaces fax1. ignore fax2 & fax3]

< N O T E >

Unfortunately, this extension has this small quirk, but it is a tiny price to pay to prevent the need to create your own states menu! The extension author is aware of the problem, so if you find that it doesn't occur, he may have fixed the issue.

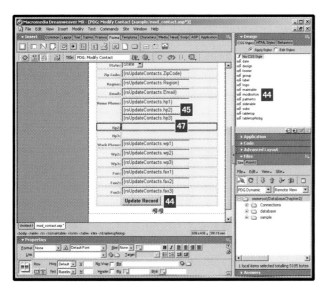

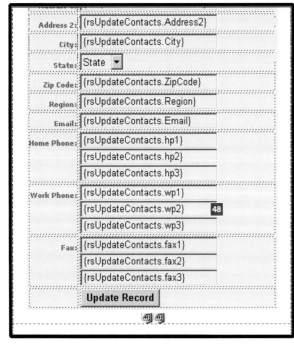

44. Select the Form button and apply the `modbutton` class and then repeat for the Update Record button.

45. Click and drag the hp2 and hp3 form objects to the right of the hp1 form object.
You now have 3 fields for the phone number, one for the area code, one for the prefix and one for the suffix.

46. Select each of the phone number fields, and in the Property inspector change the Char Width and Max Chars. The first one needs to be set at 3, the second field needs to be 3, and the third needs to be 4.

47. Select and delete the empty hp2 and hp3 rows.
Click the `<tr>` tag to select the row.

48. Use the same method to adjust the `wp` and `fax` fields, moving the form objects and deleting the extra rows.

49. Save and upload your page, and then test it in the appropriate browsers.
Your page should list only the first record in the database. Make a small change to see if your page updates the record and sends you to the success page. Of course, to be useful, you would need to be able to update all the records. In the next tutorial, you learn to add a Recordset Navigation Bar to gain access to each record.

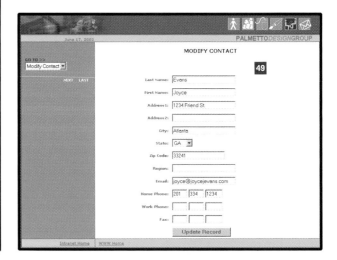

Tutorial
» Inserting a Recordset Navigation Bar

Updating the contact database requires access to all records. In this tutorial you insert a Recordset Navigation Bar to allow access to all records.

1. Double-click the mod_contact.asp page to open it.

2. Click the jump menu in the left side of the page to select it.

3. Select the form tag using the Tag Selector and then press your right arrow key to move just outside and after the form code.

4. Choose Insert→Application Objects→Recordset Navigation Bar.

5. Match the following settings:
   Recordset: rsUpdateContacts
   Display Using: Text

6. Click OK in the dialog box to close it.

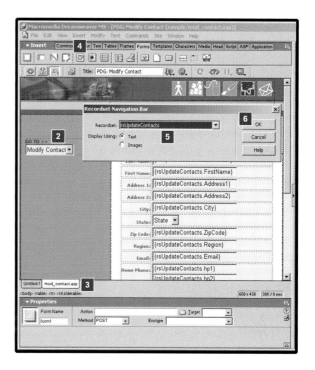

Recordset Navigation Bar Object

The table and link elements may be modified in layout or labeling. Be careful, though, when doing so, because scripting has been applied to the links to cycle through all records in the database. If you look in your Server Behaviors panel, you see that new behaviors have been added to each of the links. As you select each new behavior, Dreamweaver shows you where, on the page, it is applied.

There are two behaviors to each link. The first behavior, Show If Not First Record, and the second behavior, Move to First Record, are applied to the first link. When live, this link does not display when the record being viewed is the first in the database. Of course, if the link doesn't display, you are on the first record and would not need to move there!

The Recordset Navigation Bar object really saves you time! You could build your own navigation bar and add the logic to each of your links. The behaviors needed are accessed from the Add (+) button in the Server Behaviors panel. The individual behaviors are found under Recordset Paging and Show Region.

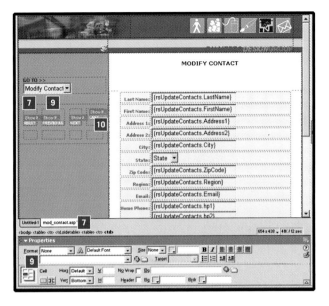

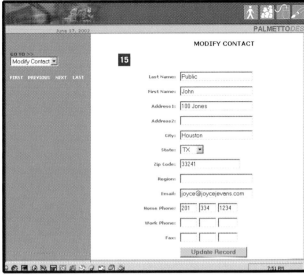

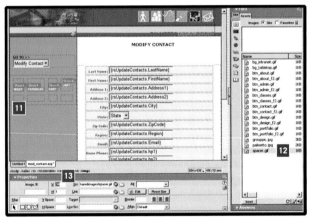

7. **Select the new navigation table.**

8. **Use the Property inspector to match these settings:**
   Table Width: **180px**
   Cell Spacing: **10px**
   Cell Padding: **0**
   Border: **0**
   Align menu: **Default**

9. **Click inside the cells in the row (one at a time) and match these settings:**
   Width: **30, 50, 30, 30** [there are four cells, from left to right]
   Horz Align: **Default [all]**
   Vert Align: **Bottom [all]**

10. **Place your cursor into the last cell and tab to add a new row.**

11. **Click inside the left cell of the new row.**

12. **In the Assets panel, click spacer.gif and the Insert button.**

13. **Set the size of the spacer to 30px wide (the same size as the cell); set the height to 1px.**

14. **Repeat steps 11–13 for all the cells except make the second spacer 50px wide.**

15. **Save, upload, and test the page.**
    When you test in the browser, click the Next link. You see the First and Previous links appear.

16. **When you have tested the page, close it.**
    In the next tutorial, you work in a different page.

Tutorial
» Building Delete Pages

Chances are that you will want to delete a contact from time to time. With another of Dreamweaver's incredibly useful application objects, you can set this up in a few clicks.

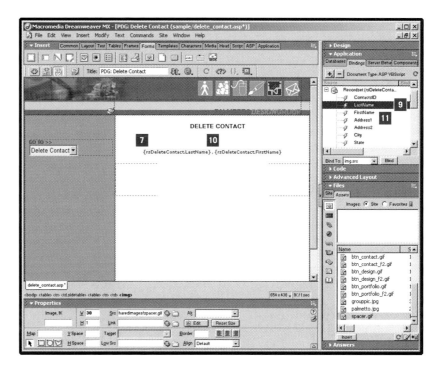

1. Double-click the delete_contact.asp page to open it.

2. Open the Bindings panel.

3. Click the Add (+) button.

4. Click Recordset (Query).

5. Name it rsDeleteContact and choose pdgconn for the Connection field.

6. Click OK in the dialog box.

7. Place your cursor just below the page heading and add a paragraph return.

8. Click the plus sign for the rsDeleteContact recordset in the Bindings panel to see its Columns.

9. Select LastName and click the Insert button at the bottom of the panel.
   You can also drag and drop LastName to the cursor location.

10. To the right, add a comma followed by a space.

11. Click FirstName in the Bindings panel and insert it.

12. Add a paragraph return.

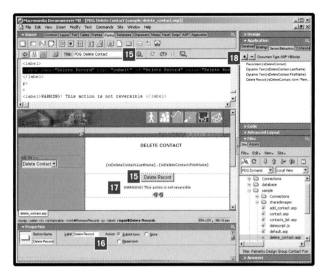

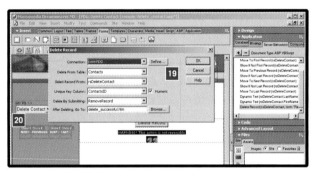

13. **Choose Insert→Form.**

14. **Name the form RemoveRecord.**

15. **Place your cursor inside the form and click the Button icon in the Forms category of the Insert Bar.**

16. **Label the button** Delete Record **(if you are using Accessibility options, name that label as well).**

    Deleting a record is a serious proposition, as there is no confirmation dialog box on clicking the button. To ensure that the user understands this, you add a warning notice below to the button.

17. **After the button, add a paragraph return and type the following:**
    WARNING! This action is not reversible.

18. **While still inside the form, use the Server Behaviors panel to Add (+) the behavior Delete Record.**

19. **In the dialog box, match these settings:**
    Connection: connpdg
    Delete From Table: Contacts
    Select Record From: rsDeleteContact
    Unique Key Column: ContactsID
    Delete by Submitting: RemoveRecord
    After Deleting, Go To: delete_successful.htm

    Be sure to check the Numeric check box as well.

20. **Now position your cursor just below the jump menu in the left side of the page.**

21. **To navigate through all the records, choose Insert→Application Objects→Recordset Navigation Bar, just as you did for the previous page.**

    Refer to the previous tutorial (steps 9-14) to format the navigational table. You want to maintain a consistent look for similar page elements.

22. **Save your page.**

23. **Upload this page and test.**

24. **Close the page.**

Tutorial
» Making Master Detail Pages

The Contacts List page limits the information you can see about each record. It would be more useful to view a list of names, and then select a single contact to view all its details. You could use the existing list page, and apply separate bits of logic, but instead, you create two new pages and let Dreamweaver do the work! In this tutorial, you use a Master Detail Page Set to do just that.

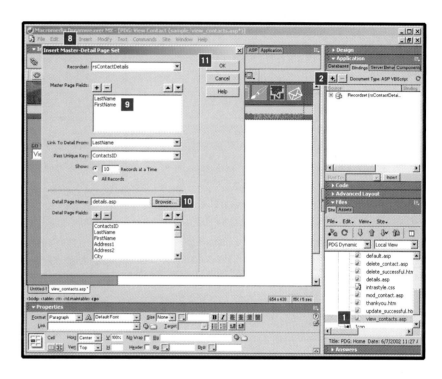

1. **Double-click the view_contacts.asp page to open it.**

2. **In the Bindings panel of the Application panel group, click the Add (+) button.**

3. **Click Recordset (Query).**

4. **Name the recordset** rsContactDetails.

5. **Choose the connpdg connection and the table and columns will load. This should be a familiar routine by now.**

6. **Click OK and close the dialog box.**

7. **Place your cursor in the main content area after the heading and add a paragraph return.**

8. **Choose Insert→Application Objects→Master Detail Page Set.**

9. **The Recordset menu should list** rsContactDetails.
   Master Page Fields: LastName, FirstName [select and remove (–) others]
   Link to Detail From: LastName
   Pass Unique Key: ContactsID
   Show: 10 Records at a time

10. **Click the Browse button to find details.asp in the sample folder.**

11. **Leave everything else at the default and click OK.**

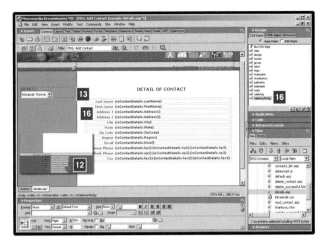

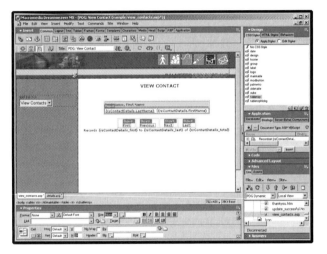

12. **In details.asp, select the newly inserted table and press Ctrl-X/Cmd-X to cut it.**

13. **Place your cursor in the main cell after the heading and Ctrl-V/Cmd-V to paste it.**

14. **Save the page.**
The layout of the table needs some work because the phone numbers are displayed inconveniently.

15. **Select the table and match these settings:**
Table Width: 90%
Cell Spacing: 0px
Cell Padding: 5px
Border: 0
Align menu: Default

16. **Shift-select all of the cells in the left column and apply tabletopNobg using the CSS Styles panel in Apply Styles Mode.**

17. **Set the cell Horz Align to Right.**

18. **Relabel and rearrange the form objects as you did in the earlier exercise to put the phone and fax numbers together in single cells.**

19. **Delete empty rows where necessary.**

20. **Save and upload this page.**

21. **Click the view_contacts.asp page to open it.**
This page could use a little formatting as well.

22. **Select the first row of the table and merge both cells.**
Click and drag across the cells to select. Right-click/Control-click, and then select Table→Merge Cells.

23. **Place a comma and space between LastName and FirstName and add spaces between the words as well.**
The Repeat label obstructs the view of the word, LastName. You can use your arrow key to position the cursor and press the spacebar to add a space, or do it in the Code view.

24. **Select the merged cell and apply the tabletop class.**

25. **Set the cell's height to 20px.**

26. **Select the table and make the border 0 and 400px wide.**

27. **Save and upload the page.**

28. **Preview and click a link to view the details.**

Where to Go from Here

The future of Web sites is data-driven. With the frantic, content-now pace of today, there's just no time to maintain static Web pages with content that changes from day to day. Dreamweaver provides an easy introduction to the world of Web application development with built-in server behaviors and auto-generated forms, but you've barely begun to scratch the surface in this chapter!

Unlike HTML, you cannot simply view the source to see how your favorite site accomplished that very cool new feature. If you are drawn to the development end of Web design, you need to explore different technologies, such as ColdFusion and ASP.NET. There are some great free and inexpensive options as well, such as MySQL, PostgreSQL, and PHP. Increase your knowledge of how a database functions. There are many good books on all these subjects.

As well, Dreamweaver Help includes information for readers from a variety of backgrounds, from novice to expert. Be sure to read *Absolute Beginner's Guide to Databases* or *Database Design for Mere Mortals* if you are new to using a database or need to develop your own.

» Session Review

You just made your site dynamic! It's amazing how much power Dreamweaver gives you even with little knowledge of coding. Test out your newly learned knowledge.

1. What type of server technology did you use for this session? (See "Tutorial: Adding a Recordset.")

2. What is a recordset? (See "Tutorial: Adding a Recordset.")

3. Which panel do you use to add a recordset? (See "Tutorial: Adding a Recordset.")

4. What does a repeating region do? (See "Tutorial: Using Repeating Regions.")

5. How do you make sure that parts of a form are filled in correctly? (See "Tutorial: Validating Your Forms.")

6. What is Unique Key Column? (See "Tutorial: Building Update Pages.")

7. How do you install an extension? (See "Tutorial: Building Update Pages.")

8. After you added the recordset navigation and tested it, you only saw two of the four links. Why? (See "Tutorial: Inserting Recordset Navigation Bar.")

9. Once a record is deleted, can you change your mind and undo it? (See "Tutorial: Building Delete Pages.")

10. When you added the table to the details page, what happened to it? (See "Tutorial: Making Master Detail Pages.")

Appendix A:

Resources

Resources List

In this appendix are recommendations for tools that you may find useful. When designing, you often need other resources to enhance the design or to help you be more productive with your development time. None of these products is required; I just wanted to give a little input and help in finding things you may need or want. I've also included a couple of bios of people that helped out in the development of this book. I have not included a list of links to Dreamweaver resources because they are included on the CD-ROM.

The Other Ladies Behind this Book

There are three ladies I'd like to acknowledge at this time.

Japi Honoo (www.escogitando.it)

Japi did the layout, logo, and icon design for the index page of this book. I was pressed for time and needed a great-looking index page — fast! Making the images for a Web site is a breeze for me, but I don't conceptualize very quickly. Japi came to the rescue and using the palmetto tree and composite images I sent her, put aside her work and pulled together what you see on the index page of the Palmetto Design Group Web site.

Japi is a resident of Venice, Italy, and designs Web sites and organizes the Italian Fireworks Web site, www.escogitando.it. Before taking the plunge into Web design, Japi worked as a bookkeeper. A job in a software house, however, allowed Japi to free her creativity and turn her energies toward digital art. Japi has since dedicated her life to encouraging the appreciation of Fireworks (that's a slight exaggeration — but not much!). Her diversions include intense music, oriental culture, films, and a love of emoticons. :-)

Donna Casey (www.n2dreamweaver.com)

Donna designed the Palmetto Design Group intranet site and wrote the two database sessions. She was also my unofficial tech editor, which I appreciated greatly. Whenever I ran into a problem, she was quick to help find the solution (or problem). There are a lot of extra notes that are the result of her pointing out how code doesn't always select or insert properly. One of the reasons I have you look at the code now and then is so you can get a feel for how it's supposed to look.

Donna Casey is a designer, developer, and instructor with over eight years of experience working on Web- and CD-ROM-based projects for corporations such as AirTouch Cellular, Macromedia, Palm Computing, Verizon Wireless, and Aeris.net. She is a painter/sculptor with a Fine Arts degree and brings real-world design and production expertise to teaching Web design and development. Her Web site (www.n8vision.com) was featured in the *Fireworks 3 Bible.* She has been a featured designer on Macromedia's Web site as well as a speaker at Macromedia's EUCON (Paris) and WebBoston and CNETBuilder (New Orleans). As an experienced instructor she has also authored the *Intermediate Dreamweaver 4* and *Fireworks 4 Training* CDs for Lynda.com, and contributed to the *Fireworks F/X & Design* book as well as the *Dreamweaver MX Magic* book.

Angela C. Buraglia (www.dreamweaverfaq.com)

Angela runs the Dreamweaver FAQ. She graciously let me use her extensive list of links to a lot of Dreamweaver resources. You'll find them categorized on the CD-ROM. (All of the links were working at the time of this writing, but you know how links are, they become inactive pretty quickly sometimes.)

After six years as an independent film makeup artist, Angela realized she wanted a career that would allow her to start a family and stay home with her husband and child. In an effort to give back to the Macromedia Dreamweaver newsgroup community that helped and encouraged her in her new career, she founded DreamweaverFAQ.com. Although she only intended to be a Web developer, life's path has led her to become that and more.

Angela is the Lead Technical Editor for the *Dreamweaver MX Bible* (Wiley Publishing, formerly Hungry Minds), contributing author to *Dreamweaver MX Magic* (New Riders) and contributing author to *ColdFusion MX Web Application Construction Kit* (Macromedia Press). Currently, she is also a Team Macromedia volunteer for Dreamweaver. Angela's future plans are to continue developing DreamweaverFAQ.com, to build and sell Dreamweaver extensions, to give presentations at conferences, and perhaps to become involved in new book projects. Long gone are the days of applying makeup; now Angela applies behaviors and CSS to Web sites, and — most importantly — is home with her little boy.

Products

The products listed here are only the ones I've used and found useful. I thought perhaps you might be interested in some of them. I won't be including links to Dreamweaver resources because there is a large list of them on the CD-ROM.

TopStyle Pro (www.bradsoft.com)

You can get a trial version at the Web site listed here. Dreamweaver has wonderful new support for CSS, but if you want all the power and flexibility you can get, try the TopStyle editor. It's reasonably priced at $49 and is Dreamweaver MX compatible.

CSS is actually quite simple, but getting it to work in multiple browsers is a challenge. This is where TopStyle is unique in that it checks your style sheets against multiple browser implementations, letting you know about bugs and incompatibilities that may affect your design. It also provides site management from a CSS perspective, providing you detailed style information about your entire site.

LIFT (www.usablenet.com)

The accessibility validation feature in Dreamweaver MX uses technology from UsableNet. UsableNet develops easy-to-use software to automate usability and accessibility testing and repair. For additional assistance with accessibility testing, try the UsableNet LIFT for Macromedia Dreamweaver MX, a complete solution for developing usable and accessible Web sites. UsableNet LIFT for Macromedia Dreamweaver MX includes fix wizards for complex tables, forms, and images; a global ALT editor; customizable reporting; and an active monitoring mode that ensures content is accessible as pages are being built. Request a demo of LIFT for Macromedia Dreamweaver MX at www.usablenet.com.

Project VII (www.projectseven.com)

Project Seven (PVII) is a leader in Dreamweaver development. The company was founded in 1997 by Al Sparber and Gerry Jacobsen. Its Web site (www.projectseven.com) attracts over 50,000 Dreamweaver visitors each week. I checked with Al and Gerry and as of June 2002, there have been over 600,000 PVII Dreamweaver extensions downloaded worldwide. PVII Dreamweaver Extensions, Extension Kits, Design Packs, and Tutorials are in a class by themselves — and they all work in Dreamweaver MX.

Dreamweaver Extension Kits, like Menu Magic and Geewizz, automate the creation of DHTML menus and scrollers from the comfort of the Dreamweaver interface. PVII Design Packs are not just templates, but learning tools that come with comprehensive user guides that lead you by the hand. I frequent the site's forum and a lot of users get the packs to practice and learn different techniques. While visiting PVII, check out MXVISION — an experimental site (`www.project seven.com/mxvision`).

Eyeland Studio (`www.eyelandstudio.com`)

I found these CDs to be wonderful starting points. I use the Photoshop Foundry files as a starting point. I redraw the bitmap images in Fireworks and make them vectors instead, using many of the same effects that were applied in Photoshop. The Flash Foundry is excellent as well.

Flash Foundry

Flash Foundry includes over 100 layered Flash interface files, over 200 animations, over 100 audio loops, SmartClips/Components, and much more. You get access to the monthly-updated member area, which contains all of the contents of the CD plus any updates. The Flash Foundry provides resources that you can customize for use in your own Web projects or use to learn more about making interfaces and animations with Flash. Each interface and animation is provided in layered Macromedia Flash format (.FLA), making it easy to combine a layer from one interface with a layer from another. You can also easily change the colors, alpha, tint, or brightness of the various components in the interfaces as well as add audio loops or background animations and much more. The interfaces and animation can be used as a learning tool for people who are just getting started with Flash because you can dissect the files and see how they work.

Photoshop Foundry

Photoshop Foundry is a membership area that contains a large variety of Web interfaces and buttons that you are free to customize for use in your own Web projects. These "Web interfaces" are stylized navigation systems for your Web site, with buttons, graphical widgets, space for your logo, an area reserved for a banner ad, and so on.

Alien Skin Software (www.alienskin.com)

Eye Candy 4000

Eye Candy 4000 includes 23 prescription-strength special effects. This major upgrade to Alien Skin's award-winning Eye Candy includes five new filters — Marble, Wood, Drip, Melt, and Corona — and many powerful improvements. Eye Candy 4000 combines practical filters you'll use every day like Bevel Boss, Shadowlab, and Gradient Glow with effects like Chrome, Smoke, and Fire. New features include bevel profile and color gradient editors, a preview that allows you to see underlying layers, seamless tiling, unlimited "undo," and more. You can even trade your favorite settings with others.

Splat!

I love this one; you can make some pretty great edges with it. What I especially like is the expandability of it. You can edit or make your own effects. This section shows a couple I made in just minutes.

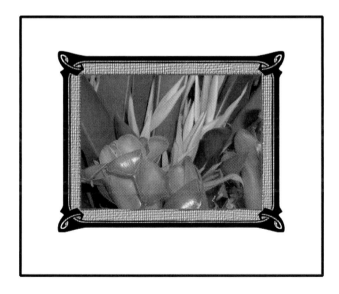

» **Frame**: Adds realistic frames and mattes to any photo or other rectangle. Choose from 100 frames, including traditional wood frames, Dover, and geometric borders.

» **Resurface**: Adds any of 100 high-resolution surface textures to an object or selection. Adds natural media with only a few clicks, distorting your image to match the surface. Textures include paper, concrete, leather, brick, stone, metal, wood, and more.

» **Edges**: Adds versatile, decorative edge effects such as halftone dots, torn paper, and pixelated edges. This effect works with any selection and looks great applied to text.

» **Fill Stamp**: Fills any selection with familiar objects. Choose from over 100 stamp files, and then scale the objects to fit. Fill Stamp adapts to any shape and works well on text. This effect can seamlessly tile and be colorized to match your image.

» **Border Stamp**: Applies the power of Fill Stamp to borders, creating borders from everyday objects such as pebbles, pills, and tickets. Great for themed borders, Border Stamp includes realistic drop shadows and adapts to any shape.

» **Patchwork**: Re-creates images as mosaics such as light pegs, ASCII art, ceramic tile, and cross-stitch. Simply browse the Patchwork libraries, scale your tiles, and apply.

Image Doctor

This one is new and is in public beta as of this writing. I'm sure it will be available by the time this book is. It has some really cool editing effects. I've tried some of the effects, such as repairing blockie JPEGs, and it did a wonderful job.

It is an all-new set of powerful image-correction filters for Photoshop, Fireworks, Paint Shop Pro, and other image editors. Image Doctor removes blemishes and defects, repairs over-compressed JPEGs, and replaces unwanted details and objects. Professional and amateur photographers, photo editors, archivists, graphic designers, and Web designers can more quickly fix their images with Image Doctor.

Image Doctor delivers these effects in a clean, easy-to-use interface. Users can tweak their effects in a huge preview that includes a before/after toggle, command menus, keyboard shortcuts, and unlimited undo capability.

Image Doctor is the only filter set to offer selection-based image repair. Use the familiar selection tools of your image editor, and then correct large as well as small areas in one pass. The intelligent pattern matching of Image Doctor makes it the perfect complement to existing photo-editing tools.

Auto FX (www.autofx.com)

I don't use plug-ins very often, but when I do, I use these sets (and Alien Skin) most often. I'm giving you information only about the few that I like the best, but you can check the vendor's Web site for additional offerings.

DreamSuite Series One

This includes 18 unique and effective visual design solutions for type, graphics, and photographs. With Series One, designers are given artistic freedom with thousands of possible visual results. These effects are easy-to-use and are designed so anyone, not just the pros, can achieve stunning results. This section shows a few I made.

Series One effects include: 35mm Frame, Chisel, Crackle, Crease, Cubism, Deckle Dimension X, Focus, Hot Stamp, Instamatic, Liquid Metal Metal Mixer, PhotoBorder, PhotoDepth, PhotoTone, Putty Ripple, and Tape.

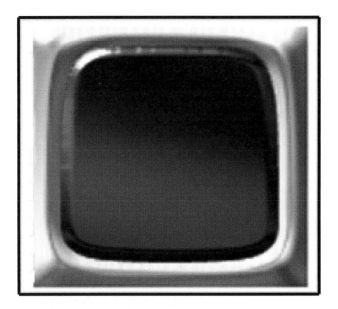

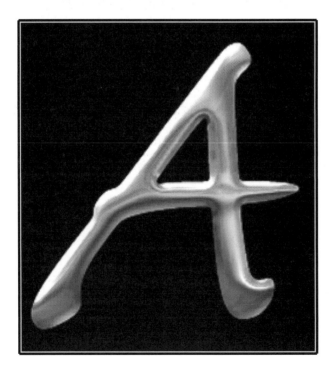

DreamSuite Series Two

The series is loaded with innovative options that can turn your photos into works of art and enhance your designs with ease. DreamSuite Series Two features 12 new looks. Turn your photos into puzzles or develop your photo inside a translucent film frame.

DreamSuite Series Two effects include: 2 1/4 Frame, 4 x 5 Frame, FilmGrain, FilmStrip, Film Frame Art, Mesh, PhotoPress, PhotoStrips, PlasticWrap, Puzzle Pieces, Tile, and Wrinkle.

DreamSuite Gel Series

This series is a fun visual arts tool that lets you create translucent colored artwork and images. DreamSuite Gel Series allows you to add reflective and refractive depth effects. Gel includes advanced brush-based tools to let you paint on depth and translucent reflections, colors, and textures.

Gel effects include: Gel, Gel Painter, Liquid Crystal, Crystal Painter, and Gel Mixer.

All products from Auto FX Software serve as either a stand-alone application or as a plug-in for image editing programs like Adobe Photoshop, Adobe Elements, Corel PhotoPaint, and Paint Shop Pro.

Hemera Technologies, Inc (www.hemera.com)

Hemera's Photo-Objects is my absolute favorite collection for quick photo images. They contain no backgrounds and have a fantastic browser. The images I used in the Confidence Builder (the birdhouse and birds) are from the collections.

Hemera Photo-Objects 50,000 Volumes I & II

Photo-Objects are photographic images of people, animals, and objects that have been isolated from their original background, and pre-masked so they can be quickly and easily dropped into any design. These images are great for business and design professionals. Photo-Objects can enhance everything from presentations and annual reports to marketing collateral such as advertisements and brochures. Each collection of 50,000 Photo-Objects is available for Windows and Macintosh.

The Big Box of Art

The Big Box of Art is a digital image collection of the great quality and variety that includes Hemera Photo-Objects, clip art, illustrations, professional stock photos, Web graphics, and more.

Photosphere (www.photosphere.com)

The images I used on the training page came from the Office Situations CD collection. PhotoSphere Images is a premiere supplier of professional, royalty-free stock images. It is fast and easy to access the library of more than 2,800. The keyword search engine will help you find specific images quickly. Each of the 30 collections of stock images includes 80-100 images.

All images are available online in JPEG format and on CD in Photo CD format. The pricing is very competitive.

Helpful Accessories

When you work with graphics, there are a few items that might make your job easier. I have tested a few pieces of hardware and accessories; only those worthy of mention (worth the money) will be listed here.

Matrox Millennium G450 32MB DualHead Graphics Card
(www.matrox.com/mga)

If you are tired of moving your panels and palettes around your screen all the time, you have to try dual monitors — it's great. I have Fireworks running on one monitor and the panels on another. Sometimes I keep Fireworks on one monitor and open Word on the other. It made writing this book much easier, because I could perform the tutorials on one monitor and write on the other.

Some of the highlights of the Matrox G450 are that you can use monitors with separate resolutions, or a monitor and a TV. The Matrox G450 is also compatible with LCD flat screens.

Wacom Graphire Tablet
(www.wacom.com/graphire/)

A pressure-sensitive tablet comes in handy with a program like Fireworks. Many of the strokes and the Brush tool take advantage of pressure sensitivity, speed, and the direction you draw with. What's nice about the Graphire tablet is that it takes up the same amount of desk space as a mouse pad does. The price of $99.95, which includes the pen tool and cordless mouse, makes it a great deal for novice users. You can trace images on the tablet, design your own innovations, or sign your name. If you make the occasional map, a tablet makes the job much easier.

Key features of this tablet include:

- » Tablet is connected to the computer via a cable to either the USB or serial port
- » Patented cordless and batteryless pen and mouse
- » Pen features pressure-sensitive tip, two side switches, and pressure-sensitive eraser
- » Mouse features three buttons and rubberized scrolling wheel
- » Ambidextrous mouse design
- » No-ball mouse design always tracks smoothly and never clogs up
- » All buttons and switches can be set to user's preference
- » Mouse scrolling wheel speed is customizable
- » Tablet features clear plastic overlay for tracing
- » Tablet pen stand is detachable
- » It comes with a great software bundle, including Photoshop LE, Corel Painter, and more

SnagIt (www.snagit.com)

If you need a powerful screen-capture utility, this is it for PC users. I began using SnagIt by TechSmith when I received it for writing a review for *Web Review*. I have used it ever since. It was used for all the figures captured for this book. You can capture video and text as well, and add sound, annotations, and watermarks. I like the AutoScroll feature, which captures a whole Web page, even the part you can't see. You get all these features and more for only $39.95. You can find a share-ware version, which is fully operational, at the SnagIt Web site. If you'd like to see the full review I did about the product, go to www.webreview.com/2000/12_22/designers/index03.shtml.

Camtasia (www.camtasia.com)

Camtasia, another product of TechSmith, is what I use when I want to make movie tutorials of my actions on the screen. Camtasia captures the action and sound from any part of the Windows desktop and saves it to a standard AVI movie file or streaming video. You can share your Camtasia screen recordings on a Web site, or distribute them via e-mail, intranet, or CD.

Appendix B:
What's on the CD-ROM

This appendix provides you with information on the contents of the CD-ROM that accompanies this book. For the latest and greatest information, please refer to the ReadMe file located at the root of the CD-ROM. Here is what you will find:

» System Requirements

» Using the CD-ROM with Windows and Macintosh

» What's on the CD-ROM

» Troubleshooting

System Requirements

Make sure that your computer meets the minimum system requirements listed in this section. If your computer does not match up to most of these requirements, you may have a problem using the contents of the CD-ROM.

System requirements for Microsoft Windows:

» An Intel Pentium processor or equivalent, 166 MHz or faster, running Windows 98, Windows 2000, Windows ME, Windows NT (with Service Pack 3), or Windows XP

» Version 4.0 or later of Netscape Navigator or Microsoft Internet Explorer

>> 32MB of RAM (random-access memory) plus 110MB of available disk space

>> A 256-color monitor capable of 800 x 600 pixel resolution or better

>> A CD-ROM drive

System requirements for Apple Macintosh:

>> A Power Macintosh running Mac OS 9.x or Mac OS X 10.x

>> 32MB of RAM (random-access memory) plus 135MB of available disk space

>> A 256-color monitor capable of 800 x 600 pixel resolution or better

>> A CD-ROM drive

Using the CD-ROM with Windows

To install the items from the CD-ROM to your hard drive, follow these steps:

1. Insert the CD-ROM into your computer's CD-ROM drive.

2. The interface will launch. If you have autorun disabled, click Start→Run. In the dialog box that appears, type **D:\setup.exe.** Replace *D* with the proper letter if your CD-ROM drive uses a different letter. (If you do not know the letter, see how your CD-ROM drive is listed under My Computer.) Click OK.

3. A license agreement appears. Read through the license agreement, and then click the Accept button if you want to use the CD. After you click Accept, you will never be bothered by the License Agreement window again.

   The CD interface Welcome screen appears. The interface coordinates installing the programs and running the demos. The interface basically enables you to click a button or two to make things happen.

4. Click anywhere on the Welcome screen to enter the interface. This next screen lists categories for the software on the CD.

5. For more information about a program, click the program's name. Be sure to read the information that appears. Sometimes a program has its own system requirements or requires you to do a few tricks on your computer before you can install or run the program, and this screen tells you what you might need to do, if necessary.

   If you do not want to install the program, click the Back button to return to the previous screen. You can always return to the previous screen by clicking the Back button. This feature allows you to browse the different categories and products and decide what you want to install.

6. To install a program, click the appropriate Install button. The CD interface drops to the background while the CD installs the program you chose.

7. To install other items, repeat steps 5 and 6.

8. When you have finished installing programs, click the Quit button to close the interface. You can eject the CD now. Carefully place it back in the plastic jacket of the book for safekeeping.

If you are using a Windows operating system other than Windows XP, you will have to change the read-only status of the copied tutorial files. Otherwise, you will not be able to write over the files as you work through the tutorials. To do so, select all the files in a folder that you have copied to your computer. Right-click one of the files and choose Properties. In the Properties dialog box, uncheck Read-only.

Also, you can instruct Windows to display the filename extensions of the copied tutorial files (if it is not already set up to show them) so that you can see the file formats (`.psd`, `.tif`, `.jpg`, and so on). Find your Folder Options dialog box. It is located in a slightly different place in different versions of Windows; in Windows XP, it is in the Appearance and Themes Control Panel; in Windows 2000 and ME, in the My Computer→Tools folder; in Windows 98, in the My Computer→View folder. Click the View tab. Uncheck Hide File Extensions for Known File Types, which is checked by default.

Using the CD-ROM with the Macintosh OS

To install the items from the CD-ROM to your hard drive, follow these steps:

1. Insert the CD-ROM into your CD-ROM drive.

2. Double-click the icon for the CD-ROM after it appears on the desktop.

3. Double-click the License Agreement icon. This is the license that you are agreeing to by using the CD. You can close this window after you have looked over the agreement.

4. Most programs come with installers; for those, simply open the program's folder on the CD-ROM and double-click the Install or Installer icon. *Note:* To install some programs, just drag the program's folder from the CD-ROM window and drop it on your hard drive icon.

What's on the CD-ROM

The following sections provide a summary of the software and other materials that you will find on the CD-ROM.

Tutorial Files

All the tutorial files that you will use when working through the tutorials in this book are on the CD-ROM in the folder named "Tutorial Files." Within the Tutorial Files folder are subfolders containing the tutorial files for each session. In each session subfolder, you will find all the files referenced in that session, including a file with the word `final` in the filename. The `final` file is an example of how the collage that you will work on in that session should look at the end of the session; this folder can be added to your defined site if you happen to have skipped a session. The beginning of each session will tell you which folder to add to your defined site if you missed the previous session.

Use the process described in the preceding section to copy the files to your hard drive. Windows users can access the Tutorial Files from the Start menu. Macintosh users can access the Tutorial Files from the Finder.

Applications

The following applications are on the CD-ROM:

> » **Dreamweaver MX** trial version — the best darn HTML editor and layout designer around.

> » **Fireworks MX** trial version — the premiere image editor what works hand in hand with Dreamweaver.

> » **Macromedia Flash MX** trial version — for all your motion graphic needs.

> » **TopStyle Pro** trial version — a CSS editor that is unique in that it checks your style sheets against multiple browser implementations, letting you know about bugs and incompatibilities that may affect your design. TopStyle also provides site management from a CSS perspective.

> » **WebSpice Objects** demo version — a nifty program that contains 3,000 high-quality buttons, labels, borders, and other art to give the professional look to your Web pages.

Trial, demo, or evaluation versions are usually limited either by time or functionality, such as being unable to save projects. Some trial versions are very sensitive to system date changes. If you alter your computer's date, the programs will "time out" and will no longer be functional.

Troubleshooting

If you have difficulty installing or using any of the materials on the companion CD-ROM, try the following solutions:

> » **Turn off any antivirus software that you may have running.** Installers sometimes mimic virus activity and can make your computer incorrectly believe that a virus is infecting it. Be sure to turn the antivirus software back on later.

>> **Close all running programs.** The more programs you are running, the less memory is available to other programs. Installers also typically update files and programs; if you keep other programs running, the installation may not work properly.

>> **Reference the ReadMe:** Please refer to the ReadMe file located at the root of the CD-ROM for the latest product information at the time of publication.

If you still have trouble with the CD-ROM, please call the Wiley Publishing Customer Care phone number: (800) 762-2974. Outside the United States, call 1(317) 572-3994. You can also contact Wiley Publishing Customer Service by e-mail at techsupdum@wiley.com. Wiley Publishing will provide technical support only for installation and other general quality control items; for technical support on the applications themselves, consult the program's vendor or author.

Index

Dynamic HTML. *See also* **HyperText Markup Language**

editing editable regions, 169

Dynamic HTML, animation

adding to Web pages, 166–168

creating, 166–168

editing, 175

first and last image, 167

frames per second, 167

keyframes, 167

play on opening, 167

playback speed, 167

timelines, 167

Dynamic HTML, extensions. *See also* **behaviors**

applying, 173–174

downloading, 170–171

Extensions Manager, definition, 170–171

Extensions Manager, opening, 172

file extension, 172

installing, 172

dynamic Web pages

defining, 268–273

definition, 266

»E«

editable regions, editing, 169

editing. *See also* **images, editing in Fireworks**

CSS, 309

DHTML animations, 175

documents with templates, 141

editable regions, 169

fonts, 97

library items, 146–147

style sheets, 120–122

templates, 141

editors

CSS, 309

graphics, 232

HTML, 128

Quick Tag Editor, 128

TopStyle Pro, 309

embedded style sheets, 119, 123

Evans, Joyce, 242

exclamation point (!), HTML reserved character, 14

Explorer. *See* **Internet Explorer**

exporting images, 237

extensions. *See* **Dynamic HTML, extensions**

Extensions Manager

definition, 170–171

opening, 172

external style sheets, 119

Eye Candy 4000, 311

Eyeland Studio, 310

»F«

Favorites list, 34

fields, definition, 286

file management, 32–33

File Management tool, 27

File Transfer Protocol (FTP)

setting preferences, 256–257

uploading files, 258

filenames, case sensitivity, 40

files

adding, 32–33

creating, 40

displaying a list of, 32–33

renaming, 32–33

saving, 40

temporary, automatic deletion, 42

uploading, 256–258

files, CD

accessing, 321–322

applications, 322

contents, 321–323

copying, 17–18, 322

installing on a Macintosh, 321

installing on Windows, 320–321

session final files, 18

tutorial files, 321–322

final files, 18

Find and Replace, 227–228

finding Web sites. *See* **keywords; <meta> (Meta) tags; search engines**

Fireworks. *See also* **images, editing in Fireworks**

Web site about, 306

***Fireworks 3 Bible*, 307**

***Fireworks 4 Training*, 307**

***Fireworks F/X & Design*, 307**

fixed tables

definition, 49

as home page, 57–62

Flash buttons, 113–114

Flash Foundry, 310

Flash movies

absolute URLs, 113

button animation, 113–114

managing, 34

relative paths, 113

SWF (Shockwave Flash) format, 73

text animation, 101–102

floating panels, 29

»G«

»H«

About Seybold Seminars and Publications

Seybold Seminars and Publications is your complete guide

to the publishing industry. For more than 30 years it

has been the most trusted source for technology events,

news, and insider intelligence.

Workflow
Media Te
Creation
Manageme
Digital As
Fonts ar
Digital M
Content
Managem
Workflow
Media Te
Creation
Manageme
Digital As
Fonts ar
Digital M
Content
Managem
Workflow
Media Te
Creation
Managem

Produced by

PUBLICATIONS

Today, Seybold Publications and Consulting continues to guide publishing professionals around the world in their purchasing decisions and business strategies through newsletters, online resources, consulting, and custom corporate services.

○ **The Seybold Report: Analyzing Publishing Technologies**
The Seybold Report analyzes the cross-media tools, technologies, and trends shaping professional publishing today. Each in-depth newsletter delves into the topics changing the marketplace. *The Seybold Report* covers critical analyses of the business issues and market conditions that determine the success of new products, technologies, and companies. Read about the latest developments in mission-critical topic areas, including content and asset management, color management and proofing, industry standards, and cross-media workflows. A subscription to *The Seybold Report* (24 issues per year) includes our weekly email news service, *The Bulletin,* and full access to the seyboldreports.com archives.

○ **The Bulletin: Seybold News & Views on Electronic Publishing**
The Bulletin: Seybold News & Views on Electronic Publishing is Seybold Publications' weekly email news service covering all aspects of electronic publishing. Every week *The Bulletin* brings you all the important news in a concise, easy-to-read format.

For more information on **NEWSLETTER SUBSCRIPTIONS,**
please visit **seyboldreports.com**.

CUSTOM SERVICES

In addition to newsletters and online information resources, Seybold Publications and Consulting offers a variety of custom corporate services designed to meet your organization's specific needs.

○ **Strategic Technology Advisory Research Service (STARS)**
The STARS program includes a group license to *The Seybold Report* and *The Bulletin,* phone access to our analysts, access to online archives at seyboldreports.com, an on-site visit by one of our analysts, and much more.

○ **Personalized Seminars**
Our team of skilled consultants and subject experts work with you to create a custom presentation that gets your employees up to speed on topics spanning the full spectrum of prepress and publishing technologies covered in our publications. Full-day and half-day seminars are available.

○ **Site Licenses**
Our electronic licensing program keeps everyone in your organization, sales force, or marketing department up to date at a fraction of the cost of buying individual subscriptions. One hard copy of *The Seybold Report* is included with each electronic license.

For more information on **CUSTOM CORPORATE SERVICES,**
please visit **seyboldreports.com**.

SEYBOLD
SEMINARS

ital Asse
Fonts an
ital Medi
Conten
Right
Proofin
On-Demand
Content
Tools Color
s Storage
rtals PDAs
echnology
Publishing
tal Rights
Proofing
On-Demand
Content
Tools Color

EVENTS

Seybold Seminars facilitates exchange and discussion within the high-tech publishing community several times a year. A hard-hitting lineup of conferences, an opportunity to meet leading media technology vendors, and special events bring innovators and leaders together to share ideas and experiences.

Conferences

Our diverse educational programs are designed to tackle the full range of the latest developments in publishing technology. Topics include:

- Print publishing
- Web publishing
- Design
- Creative tools and standards
- Best practices

- Multimedia
- Content management
- Technology standards
- Security
- Digital rights management

In addition to the conferences, you'll have the opportunity to meet representatives from companies that bring you the newest products and technologies in the publishing marketplace. Test tools, evaluate products, and take free classes from the experts.

For more information on **SEYBOLD SEMINARS EVENTS,**
please visit **seyboldseminars.com**.

Wiley Publishing, Inc.
End-User License Agreement

READ THIS. You should carefully read these terms and conditions before opening the software packet(s) included with this book "Book". This is a license agreement "Agreement" between you and Wiley Publishing, Inc."WPI". By opening the accompanying software packet(s), you acknowledge that you have read and accept the following terms and conditions. If you do not agree and do not want to be bound by such terms and conditions, promptly return the Book and the unopened software packet(s) to the place you obtained them for a full refund.

1. **License Grant.** WPI grants to you (either an individual or entity) a nonexclusive license to use one copy of the enclosed software program(s) (collectively, the "Software" solely for your own personal or business purposes on a single computer (whether a standard computer or a workstation component of a multi-user network). The Software is in use on a computer when it is loaded into temporary memory (RAM) or installed into permanent memory (hard disk, CD-ROM, or other storage device). WPI reserves all rights not expressly granted herein.

2. **Ownership.** WPI is the owner of all right, title, and interest, including copyright, in and to the compilation of the Software recorded on the disk(s) or CD-ROM "Software Media". Copyright to the individual programs recorded on the Software Media is owned by the author or other authorized copyright owner of each program. Ownership of the Software and all proprietary rights relating thereto remain with WPI and its licensers.

3. **Restrictions on Use and Transfer.**

   (a) You may only (i) make one copy of the Software for backup or archival purposes, or (ii) transfer the Software to a single hard disk, provided that you keep the original for backup or archival purposes. You may not (i) rent or lease the Software, (ii) copy or reproduce the Software through a LAN or other network system or through any computer subscriber system or bulletin- board system, or (iii) modify, adapt, or create derivative works based on the Software.

   (b) You may not reverse engineer, decompile, or disassemble the Software. You may transfer the Software and user documentation on a permanent basis, provided that the transferee agrees to accept the terms and conditions of this Agreement and you retain no copies. If the Software is an update or has been updated, any transfer must include the most recent update and all prior versions.

4. **Restrictions on Use of Individual Programs.** You must follow the individual requirements and restrictions detailed for each individual program in the About the CD-ROM appendix of this Book. These limitations are also contained in the individual license agreements recorded on the Software Media. These limitations may include a requirement that after using the program for a specified period of time, the user must pay a registration fee or discontinue use. By opening the Software packet(s), you will be agreeing to abide by the licenses and restrictions for these individual programs that are detailed in the About the CD-ROM appendix and on the Software Media. None of the material on this Software Media or listed in this Book may ever be redistributed, in original or modified form, for commercial purposes.

5. **Limited Warranty.**

   (a) WPI warrants that the Software and Software Media are free from defects in materials and workmanship under normal use for a period of sixty (60) days from the date of purchase of this Book. If WPI receives notification within the warranty period of defects in materials or workmanship, WPI will replace the defective Software Media.